**New Directions for
Community Colleges**

Arthur M. Cohen
EDITOR-IN-CHIEF

Richard L. Wagoner
ASSOCIATE EDITOR

Allison Kanny
MANAGING EDITOR

Leading for the Future: Alignment of AACC Competencies with Practice

Pamela L. Eddy
EDITOR

Number 159 • Fall 2012
Jossey-Bass
San Francisco

LEADING FOR THE FUTURE: ALIGNMENT OF AACC COMPETENCIES WITH PRACTICE
Pamela L. Eddy (ed.)
New Directions for Community Colleges, no. 159

Arthur M. Cohen, Editor-in-Chief
Richard L. Wagoner, Associate Editor
Allison Kanny, Managing Editor

NEW DIRECTIONS FOR COMMUNITY COLLEGES (ISSN 0194-3081, electronic ISSN 1536-0733) is part of The Jossey-Bass Higher and Adult Education Series and is published quarterly by Wiley Subscription Services, Inc., A Wiley Company, at Jossey-Bass, One Montgomery St., Ste. 1200, San Francisco, CA 94104. Periodicals Postage Paid at San Francisco, California, and at additional mailing offices. POSTMASTER: Send address changes to New Directions for Community Colleges, Jossey-Bass, One Montgomery St., Ste. 1200, San Francisco, CA 94104.

SUBSCRIPTIONS cost $89 for individuals in the U.S., Canada, and Mexico, and $113 in the rest of the world for print only; $89 in all regions for electronic only; $98 in the U.S., Canada, and Mexico for combined print and electronic; $122 for combined print and electronic in the rest of the world. Institutional print only subscriptions are $292 in the U.S, $332 in Canada and Mexico, and $366 in the rest of the world; electronic only subscriptions are $292 in all regions; combined print and electronic subscriptions are $335 in the U.S. and $375 in Canada and Mexico.

EDITORIAL CORRESPONDENCE should be sent to the Editor-in-Chief, Arthur M. Cohen, at the Graduate School of Education and Information Studies, University of California, Box 951521, Los Angeles, CA 90095-1521. All manuscripts receive anonymous reviews by external referees.

New Directions for Community Colleges is indexed in CIJE: Current Index to Journals in Education (ERIC), Contents Pages in Education (T&F), Current Abstracts (EBSCO), Ed/Net (Simpson Communications), Education Index/Abstracts (H. W. Wilson), Educational Research Abstracts Online (T&F), ERIC Database (Education Resources Information Center), and Resources in Education (ERIC).

Microfilm copies of issues and articles are available in 16mm and 35mm, as well as microfiche in 105mm, through University Microfilms Inc., 300 North Zeeb Road, Ann Arbor, MI 48106-1346.

CONTENTS

EDITOR'S NOTES

Sounding a clarion over a decade ago (Shults, 2001), calls of a leadership crisis in community colleges prompted attention to developing future leaders for two-year colleges. To aid in preparing potential leaders, the American Association of Community Colleges (AACC) initiated their Leading Forward program to help identify what skills and knowledge future leaders required. A series of summits occurred over a two-year period in which experts in community college leadership gathered to discuss and create a set of best practices from the field; ultimately, this information resulted in a report titled *A Competency Framework for Community College Leaders* (AACC, 2004). A year later, the AACC published *Competencies for Community College Leaders* (2005), which included a set of six competencies deemed critical for community college leaders: organizational strategies, resource management skills, communication skills, a willingness to collaborate, advocacy skills, and professionalism. The intention was that the competencies would guide leadership development, both for individuals and through formal training venues. What remains unknown, however, is how the competencies operate in practice.

Though a number of dissertations have begun to use the competencies as a framework for evaluation or guidance for future leaders (Duree, 2007; Haney, 2008; Hassan, 2008; Schmitz, 2008), scant publications are available on the topic for practitioners (Eddy, 2010; Hasson, Dellow, and Jackson, 2010; McNair, 2010; McNair, Duree, and Ebbers, 2011; Sinady, Floyd, and Mulder, 2010). Furthermore, although the *Competencies* report was well received by community college leaders and scholars, a recent survey showed that leadership development and training programs were not yet addressing these skill areas (AACC, 2008).

If the AACC competencies indeed provide a framework to guide development of future leaders, how are they being used by individuals to prepare for the demanding roles of community college presidents and other institutional leaders? As a framework, the competencies by their very nature are broad based and all encompassing. Thus, the application of the skills may differ for those in rural areas relative to urban locales, for those leading institutions with localized challenges that may range from financial exigency to burgeoning enrollments of new immigrants, and for women leaders relative to men. Likewise, placement along the career pathway may make a difference in how the competencies are applied. New leaders may find immediate need for skills in resource management or organizational strategy, whereas seasoned leaders may have more call for expertise in collaboration and advocacy. What remains clear is the need to help support and encourage talented individuals to seek top-level positions in community colleges.

An underlying premise for the AACC competencies is that learning about leadership is a lifelong endeavor. As adult learners, community college leaders tie in their new learning with past experiences, ultimately expanding their understanding of leadership. It therefore becomes critical to think about the types of leadership development that occur along the leadership pipeline and how aspiring leaders acquire the requisite competencies to lead in these challenging times. Recently, Wallin (2010) edited a volume of *New Directions for Community Colleges* that reviewed leadership in an era of change. Wallin's volume focused on a range of issues dealing with leadership development, but did not address the role of the AACC competencies and the implication of the competencies in practice. The broad foundation of leadership development provides a showcase for how the competencies are interpreted, thus allowing us to learn what is really working in practice.

Recent advances in leadership theory underscore the need for collaborative leadership (Hickman, 2010). Shifts away from hierarchical leadership models (Kezar, Carducci, and Contreras-McGavin, 2006) to more inclusive leadership (Hickman, 2010) require different skills and approaches to leading. Even though the competencies include collaboration as a skill set, current conceptions of this skill apply predominantly to outside collaborations versus working collaboratively within the institution to share leadership. The question then becomes how the existing competencies might be reinterpreted to accommodate for shifts in practice and the need for contextual competencies among leaders (Eddy, 2010).

Today's leaders need to be innovative as they work to meet the challenges facing their institutions, leveraging resources and personnel to realize greater outcomes (Alfred, Shults, Jaquette, and Strickland, 2009). Strategic leadership becomes the mode of operation. Yet the needs and context of challenges vary among colleges. This volume seeks to document the ways in which the AACC competencies have been applied in practice, to investigate the utility and range of the competencies, and to suggest next steps for revisions of the competencies to help improve leadership development.

The inclusion of empirical data in the chapters showcased for others a variety of ways to apply the competencies in their own settings. Those involved in leadership development, aspiring leaders, and institutional leaders can use the chapters to guide training and development opportunities within community colleges. Researchers and policymakers will find utility in the information presented to advance leadership theory and policy implementation to meet the needs of changing demographics and conceptions of community college leadership.

Chapter One, by Nan Ottenritter, provides a context for the establishment of the competencies. She outlines the historic backdrop that included an extensive data-gathering process, which resulted in the creation of the six competencies. Lessons learned fall into two domains: (1) designing and implementing a national project inclusive of a wide range of voices, and (2) current approaches and thinking about leadership in community colleges.

Chapter Two, by Desna Wallin, describes how the AACC leadership development programs utilize the competency framework. Preparing community college leaders for an uncertain future is a daunting task. In the plethora of available leadership programs, serendipity seems to be the dominant theoretical underpinning. Ideally, a meaningful leadership development program should be based on foundational principles that have proven to be both valid and reliable over time. In the development and subsequent revisions of the structure and curriculum of the AACC Future Leaders Institute and the Future Leaders Institute/Advanced, the AACC competencies are interwoven throughout each presentation, activity, and reflection to provide a foundation for training. The result is a comprehensive and coherent leadership development opportunity for rising leaders in America's community colleges.

Chapter Three, by Pamela Eddy, argues for the use of clusters in thinking about the competencies. Four clusters are presented: inclusivity, framing meaning, attention to the bottom line, and systems thinking. Overarching these clusters is the need for contextual competency in which leaders align their approaches based on their college's context.

Chapter Four, by Chris Duree and Larry Ebbers, provides data from a national survey of community college presidents regarding their views of the competencies. In particular, the research points out what competencies are viewed as most critical, what competencies require more professional development, and what competencies receive less prominence in practice. The chapter concludes with advice for sitting and aspiring presidents on targeted critical areas for development.

Chapter Five, by Brent Cejda, reviews the types of challenges facing rural community college leaders in particular. Repeated references in the leadership literature regarding how mission, location, culture, and constituencies influence an institution also suggest that there are differences between rural community colleges and their urban and suburban counterparts. This chapter focuses on the impact of location on the interpretation and development of the leadership competencies.

Chapter Six, by Regina Garza Mitchell, explores how community college presidents make tough decisions that meet the demands of internal and external constituents while maintaining the delicate balance between personal and professional ethics, mission, and vision. Ethical decision making is woven into assumptions of many of the current AACC competencies.

Chapter Seven, by Kristin Bailey Wilson and Elizabeth Cox-Brand, provides a review of the competencies using the lenses of gender and race for analysis. The chapter reviews the AACC competencies using discourse analysis to determine if underlying assumptions are made regarding who can lead in community colleges and what is the most appropriate manner of leading.

Chapter Eight, by Delores McNair and Dan Phelan, builds on interviews with six current presidents in which the presidents were asked to reflect on their pathway to the corner office and to review which of the competencies they have found to be most valuable in their practice. In addition, the participants were asked to address how they are building leadership development opportunities for their own staff and what competencies are highlighted in this training.

Chapter Nine, by George Boggs, presents suggestions for the competencies into the future. During his presidency at AACC, it was Dr. Boggs who initiated the study about the impending turnover in leadership in community colleges and was the steward of the process resulting in the competencies. In this chapter, Boggs argues that the competencies are not static. He discusses emerging challenges for colleges and reviews what leadership competencies will be needed to address these challenges.

Chapter Ten, by Richard Alfred, explores the countervailing forces inside and outside of colleges that demand skills and competencies unlike those required of earlier leader generations. This chapter describes the competencies leaders need to develop and deploy in colleges striving for abundance—a state achieved by institutions when their resources are leveraged to a level beyond reasonable expectation.

In summary, this volume provides information that will allow the reader a better understanding of the formation of the AACC competencies, their use in leadership development programs and in practice, and possible changes to the listing in the future. In particular, readers will understand better the thinking behind the construction of the competencies and how their use in practice emphasizes those most critical to leaders and those that leaders need more support to master. In addition, the changing environment of higher education places new demands on leaders, and as a result, the AACC competencies must expand and adjust to reflect this new climate. Each chapter includes campus-based examples, offers best practices, or covers implications for practice and policy in using the competencies in the field. New and seasoned leaders can transfer the information and best practices presented within this volume to their institutions. Likewise, leadership development programs can implement the concepts as they strive to train the leaders of the future.

Pamela L. Eddy
Editor

References

Alfred, R., Shults, C., Jaquette, O., and Strickland, S. *Community Colleges on the Horizon: Challenge, Choice or Abundance.* New York: Rowman & Littlefield, 2009.

American Association of Community Colleges. *A Competency Framework for Community College Leaders*. Washington, D.C.: American Association of Community Colleges, 2004.

American Association of Community Colleges. *Competencies for Community College Leaders*. Washington, D.C.: American Association of Community Colleges, 2005.

American Association of Community Colleges. *Leading Forward Report*. Washington, D.C.: American Association of Community Colleges, 2008.

Duree, C. A. "The Challenges of the Community College Presidency in the New Millennium: Pathways, Preparation, Competencies, and Leadership Programs Needed to Survive." Unpublished doctoral dissertation, Iowa State University, 2007.

Eddy, P. L. *Community College Leadership: A Multidimensional Model for Leading Change*. Sterling, Va.: Stylus, 2010.

Haney, R. J. "Illinois Community College Administrators' Perceptions of the American Association of Community Colleges Six Competencies for Community College Leaders." Unpublished doctoral dissertation, University of Illinois at Urbana-Champaign, 2008.

Hassan, A. M. "The Competencies for Community College Leaders: Community College Presidents' and Trustee Board Chairpersons' Perspectives." Unpublished doctoral dissertation, University of South Florida, 2008.

Hassan, A. M., Dellow, D. A., and Jackson, R. J. "The AACC Leadership Competencies: Parallel Views From the Top." *Community College Journal of Research and Practice*, 2010, *34*(1–2), 180–198.

Hickman, G. R. *Leading Change in Multiple Contexts: Concepts and Practices in Organizational, Community, Political, Social, and Global Change Settings*. Thousand Oaks, Calif.: Sage, 2010.

Kezar, A. J., Carducci, R., and Contreras-McGavin, M. "Rethinking the 'L' Word in Higher Education: The Revolution of Research on Leadership." *ASHE-ERIC Higher Education Report, 31*(6). San Francisco: Jossey-Bass, 2006.

McNair, D. E. "Preparing Community College Leaders: The AACC Core Competencies for Effective Leadership and Doctoral Education. *Community College Journal of Research and Practice*, 2010, *34*(1–2), 199–217.

McNair, D. E., Duree, C. A., and Ebbers, L. "If I Knew Then What I Know Now: Using the Leadership Competencies Developed by the American Association of Community Colleges to Prepare Community College Presidents." *Community College Review*, 2011, *39*(1), 3–25.

Schmitz, G. R. "Leadership Preparation and Career Pathways of Community College Presidents." Unpublished doctoral dissertation, Iowa State University, 2008.

Shults, C. *The Critical Impact of Impending Retirements on Community College Leadership*. Leadership Series Research Brief no. 1. Washington, D.C.: American Association of Community Colleges, 2001.

Sinady, C., Floyd, D. L., and Mulder, A. E. "The AACC Competencies and the PhD Completion Project: Practical Implications." *Community College Journal of Research and Practice*, 2010, *34*(1–2), 218–226.

Wallin, D. L. (Ed.). *Leadership in an Era of Change*. New Directions for Community Colleges, no. 149. San Francisco: Jossey-Bass, 2010.

PAMELA L. EDDY *is associate professor of higher education in Educational Policy, Planning and Leadership at the College of William and Mary.*

1

This chapter examines the development of the AACC competencies by providing a historical backdrop of their development and the specific steps involved in their creation. Also, a review of current leadership demands offers an opportunity to reflect on the application of competencies for today's leaders.

Historic Overview of the AACC Competencies

Nan Ottenritter

In summer 2003, the W. K. Kellogg Foundation awarded a grant to the American Association of Community Colleges (AACC) to address the national need for community college leaders. An extensive data-gathering process, part of the AACC Leading Forward project, resulted in the creation of the AACC competencies for community college leaders. This chapter examines the driving forces behind the initiative and the development of the competencies. Lessons learned fall into two domains: (1) designing and implementing a national project inclusive of a wide range of voices, and (2) current approaches and thinking about leadership in community colleges.

Driving Forces

Conditions. There were a variety of driving forces behind the Leading Forward project, not the least of which was the intense investment and pride in the community college segment of higher education found in those who work in and lead it. Occupying a distinct and important place in American higher education, community colleges have a culture of their own that is based on the democratic values of open access and community engagement. Retiring leaders wanted to assure a smooth transition of their institutions to those who did not share the history of their development, the culture of supporting second chances for students, and their passion of advocacy of the community college mission. While the desire of these

New Directions for Community Colleges, no. 159, Fall 2012 © 2012 Wiley Periodicals, Inc.
Published online in Wiley Online Library (wileyonlinelibrary.com) • DOI: 10.1002/cc.20022

leaders to maintain this culture was never explicitly stated, an anthropologist could look beneath the surface and find that pride and continuance of institutional identity were major drivers. Another unarticulated driver regarding the creation of the competencies that emerged over time was the lack not only of a cohesive curriculum for aspiring community college leaders, but also of formal leadership training for those currently leading community colleges. Further influencing the Leading Forward initiative were some clear demographic, cultural, and AACC-related factors.

AACC is a presidential membership organization whose efforts are focused in five strategic action areas: Recognition and Advocacy for Community Colleges; Student Access, Learning and Success; Community College Leadership Development; Economic and Workforce Development; and Global and Intercultural Education (AACC, 2006, www.aacc.nche.edu/About/Pages/mission.aspx). The goal of leadership development was traditionally met through a series of leadership events such as the Presidents Academy Summer Institute and the Future Leaders Institute and through publications. As the AACC *Competencies for Community College Leaders* publication ultimately concluded, "proactive leadership development [is] a central focus of its mission" (AACC, 2005, p. 1). Prior to this time, however, the AACC had not stepped back and looked in a deeply reflective manner at its leadership agenda. The Leading Forward project offered just that opportunity.

Simple demographics predicted a leadership vacuum as the Baby Boomer cohort began to retire—at least from their traditionally structured work lives (Shults, 2001). The tenure of presidencies and upper-level management positions appeared, at least from anecdotal evidence, to be shortening. The causes were many: greater geographic mobility; a shifting in roles (for example, the increased emphasis on fundraising for community college presidents) leading to less job satisfaction for some; the expansion of the range of skills needed due to technology changes; increased accountability; the perceived challenges of serving a more diverse student population; and, more recently, the increased enrollment experienced by shifts in the economy. The predicted mass exodus of community college presidents has been somewhat abated by retiring leaders serving as interim presidents or consultants or by delays in retirement due to the downturn of retirement investments as well as to presidents' desire to remain involved in an active work life. These factors might to some degree ameliorate the predicted leadership vacuum.

Beliefs and Values. The Leading Forward project employed a competency-based approach in describing leadership development needs. ACT, an organization well versed in competency assessment, in part because of their work with the American College Testing program and WorkKeys (a jobs skills assessment), was engaged by AACC to support the competencies development part of the project. One approach to leadership traditionally taken by many development programs was the anecdotal/modeling format in which guest leaders shared their experiences. Many of these programs, however, while inspirational, suffered from a lack of a coherent curriculum based in the reality of the community college experience. It was believed that a competency-based approach could significantly strengthen leadership program curricula.

The final competency document itself was designed to be flexible, allowing for change as needed. This flexibility to conform to time and context was a core value held in the design and development of the framework. A continual challenge in the refinement of the competencies was balancing the degree to which they were to be defined as opposed to being broad enough to encompass many different circumstances. Hence, a three-part approach emerged to include: (1) having a general category of competence, accompanied by (2) a statement about an effective community college leader in that category and (3) examples to enhance understanding of it. The belief was that this level of broadness and detail would be helpful to individuals charting their career; to human resources departments hiring, firing, rewarding, and recommending professional development for personnel; and to leadership program developers designing programs.

A competency-based approach to leadership implies, by its very existence, that leadership can be learned. In addition, leadership can come from many different levels in the organization, and the relative weighting of skills can vary by different hierarchical positions within the college. The dichotomy of "management vs. leadership" was embraced, acknowledging that they often occur together and thus are presented together in the competency framework. The amount of emphasis on each of these areas will differ depending on the leader's position in the institution and career stage. The process of learning leadership skills is lifelong and can flourish in a learning-centered college that embraces lifelong learning for faculty and staff as well as students. Finally, an array of strategies and delivery of leadership development should be used, including one strategy universally claimed to be important—an experiential component in which the learner has the ability to be deeply involved in a leadership experience, either at their own or at another college. That experience is to be accompanied by authentic reflection in which theories are applied and outcomes and personal reactions are examined.

The Development of Leading Forward

Even though leadership development had always been a part of AACC's programming, the driving force behind the Leading Forward initiative started in March 2001 and resulted in AACC's convening a leadership summit in that year. An AACC board–led Leadership Task Force emerged from the summit, providing the impetus for: (1) the establishment of a new Future Leaders Institute; (2) the creation of a web-based catalog of university-based community college programs and courses; (3) a series of research briefs on leadership; (4) a new CEO workshop; and (5) a series of "how to" publications geared to community college administrators. In 2002, the AACC board of directors endorsed the following document (AACC, 2003):

Effective Community College Presidents

- First, an effective 21st century community college leader **understands and implements the community college mission**, understands how the college fits in its community, develops a strong positive orientation toward community colleges, values and promotes diversity, knows how to create a student-centered environment, and promotes teaching, learning, and innovation as primary goals for the college.
- Second, an effective leader is an **advocate** who can work with legislators, understand fundraising and development, and use data and research effectively.
- Third, an effective leader is a **skilled administrator** who can master board, union, and employee relations; who understands organizational development; who promotes diversity and is committed to implementing a campus climate that values diversity and assures a positive work environment for all; who can assume the role of chief executive officer (CEO) and understand trends in students and student learning; who understands professional development needs of faculty and staff; who can use research and data for planning, decision making, responding to accreditation standards, and assessing institutional effectiveness; who can manage finances and facilities, understand legal issues, and know how to use marketing programs; who can manage technology to promote innovation and success in teaching and learning and organizational efficiency; and who can manage relations with the media.
- Fourth, an effective leader must be skilled in **community and economic development**, able to build partnerships with business, industry, government, K–12 schools, and universities, and able to encourage civic engagement and develop strategies for community and workforce development.
- And finally, an effective community college leader possesses **personal, interpersonal, and transformational skills** that enable him or her to work with staff to promote the college's vision, values, and mission; to maintain a code of personal ethics; to project the confidence and competencies of a leader; to model diversity and succeed in any environment; to interview and evaluate personnel effectively and fairly; to understand institutional politics and pick battles wisely; to possess flexibility and negotiation skills; to have public speaking and writing skills, including the ability to be articulate and circumspect with the media; and finally, to function in a way that demonstrates self-mastery and a high level of personal transformation.

(Adapted from report of the AACC Leadership Task Force, 2002)

The AACC argued that it was perfectly positioned to lead this work on leadership development because of its role as a "convener and catalyst"

(AACC, 2003, p. 4), due to its far reach through membership, commissions, and affiliate councils.

Leading Forward was funded as a planning grant and considered the first phase of a larger leadership initiative. The vision for the first phase of Leading Forward stated: "By virtue of their leadership excellence, community colleges will meet the needs of learners, communities, and the nation in academic, workforce, and community development" (AACC, 2003, p. 7). The goal of the initiative sought for "[p]lanning activities [to] produce an integrated plan, endorsed by all stakeholders, that addresses the national need for new community college leaders by putting into place by the end of 2005 training strategies that can annually move 1,500 individuals up one or more steps in their community college career ladder" (AACC, 2003, p. 7). The first objective of Leading Forward was to lay a strong foundation for leadership development by building consensus through the establishment of a national advisory panel and convening leadership summits. Developing, conducting, and synthesizing the data from the leadership summits was a story unto itself.

The AACC convened four summits to understand current and diverse thinking in the field about approaches to community college leadership. Summits were designed and facilitated by America*Speaks*, an organization highly regarded for providing interactive meetings on a wide range of topics. The summits included personnel from the following groups: (1) AACC-affiliated councils, (2) universities offering graduate studies in community college administration, (3) colleges or consortia offering "grow-your-own" leadership development programs, and (4) underserved community colleges. The goal was to reach the following outcomes:

- Understand how to work collaboratively to develop a more comprehensive and integrated national road map of leadership development offerings and curricula that will assist future community college leaders of all types in charting out their leadership paths.
- Inventory the offerings and map knowledge, skills, and values for effective leadership.
- Design strategies to create or modify existing leadership development programs (AACC, 2003, p. 9).

The first summit conducted to achieve these goals was the AACC Leadership Summit of Affiliated Councils, held in Washington, D.C., on November 18, 2003. The following description of the process and products of the AACC affiliated councils summit is used as an example and demonstrates the process used with all four summits.

Prior to the summit, attendees submitted their thoughts concerning leadership development by responding to the following prompts:

- What is leadership development? What does it encompass?
- How can leadership development be delivered?
- How can leadership development be measured?

Attendees also reviewed and commented on a description of their group's leadership development program, if they had one, taken from the affiliated council's website. The collective responses to all of the above requests were sent as "pre-meeting" materials for all to review prior to the meeting and thus allowed the group to begin the face-to-face summit with some grounding in their own as well as others' leadership development thinking and programming.

The actual summit was divided into small- and large-group work focused on four areas of inquiry and discussion:

1. Knowledge, skills, and values for effective community college leaders.
2. A working definition of leadership development and the most effective ways of developing leaders.
3. A reflection upon the inventory of council leadership programs, including an examination of the niches served, who was served, and any overlaps or gaps between the programs that might provide fertile ground for collaboration.
4. A discussion concerning creating a national framework for community college leadership built on the guiding principles of comprehensiveness, real choices, and usefulness.

The evaluation of this summit revealed that the participants were quite satisfied with the thoughtfulness and organization of the meeting and regarded it as a good and timely start to a national community college initiative on leadership. Questions concerned not only lessons from the day but areas of possible collaboration between the groups and thoughts concerning the role of AACC in leadership development for the community college sector.

On January 9, 2004, the AACC Leadership Summit of Grow-Your-Own Programs was held. This summit focused on short-term, noncredit programs offered by colleges or state/regional consortia, often addressing local or regional needs. The same "pre-meeting" information as in the affiliated councils summit was collected, compiled, and distributed to all attendees before the meeting. The same question protocol was followed for the actual summit. Evaluations were collected and compiled.

On January 21, 2004, the AACC convened the Summit on Leadership in Underserved Areas. It was originally conceptualized as a summit for rural and tribal community colleges but was deliberately expanded to include the voices and thoughts of those community college leaders dealing with issues of place—often impoverished place. The same protocols were followed.

On March 16, 2004, the fourth and last summit, the AACC Leadership Summit of University Programs, was held. It focused on graduate-level programs offered by universities. As in the previous summits, the pre-meeting materials were disseminated prior to the meeting and the format of the day remained constant. Discussions concerning the role of AACC were rich and touched upon one of the areas of ongoing discussion throughout the project—credentialing, a natural for this group. To provide some degree of closure to the summit part of the process, ACT submitted an AACC-commissioned report in 2004, *A Qualitative Analysis of Community College Leadership*. The broad picture of the competencies culled from reams of data generated from the summits was refined and contextualized to fit more closely with the community college environment.

In December 2004, the AACC distributed a survey to all summit participants and the Leading Forward National Advisory Panel to ensure that critical leadership competencies for community college professionals had been addressed in the first draft of the leadership competencies. Out of 125 surveys, 95 were returned, a response rate of 76 percent. All respondents noted that each of the six competencies was either "very" or "extremely" essential to the effective performance of a community college leader. Respondents also provided suggestions for minor modifications in wording. A lower response was given to the question regarding how well the respondents had been formally trained to apply each competency. Leadership program designers also gave a low response regarding how well their program prepared participants to apply the competencies. In other words, the survey respondents, who make up a significant percentage of U.S. community college leaders and leadership development program personnel, felt that each of the six competencies was essential to community college leadership but that the integration of these competencies was not as well established. These findings supported the need to promote the competencies in the curricula of community college leadership programs.

This creation process for the competencies culminated in the unanimous approval of the competencies document by the AACC board of directors on April 9, 2005. The summit participants were acknowledged on the Leading Forward website and the AACC publication *Competencies for Community College Leaders* was made available online (www.aacc.nche.edu/Resources/leadership/Pages/publications.aspx; AACC, 2005). This work was then available to all for the wide range of users stated above. It was also hoped that even further validation of the competencies would occur as doctoral students and faculty researchers integrated the competencies into their research on community college leadership. As program designers began building curricula with the competencies in mind, evaluation of the use of the competencies in practice could occur.

Lessons Learned

Inclusion.   Designing and implementing a national project that included a wide range of voices and perspectives was complex. A metaphor of a living, breathing organism helps to visualize the process. The development of the competencies for community college leaders, like living systems, involved the notion of taking in information, pushing out findings, taking in feedback, and pushing out revisions—a very iterative process. As described above, the Leading Forward effort began with the taking in of the AACC board's Leadership Task Force information as well as the thinking of current leaders in the field. Those thoughts, beliefs, and values were pushed out to the W. K. Kellogg Foundation in the form of a grant proposal. Upon receipt of the grant and of Kellogg feedback, a National Advisory Panel was established that provided feedback at regular intervals on the project. A plan was made for the summits, the major "taking in" part of the grant. After each summit, information was collected not only on leadership in community colleges but also on the summit process itself. This assessment helped inform subsequent summits. The massive amount of data collected at the summits was pushed out to the attendees and to the public through the ACT report of July 2004, presentations, and articles of the next time period (Ottenritter, 2006). An online survey then followed. Tweaking and adjustment of the competencies occurred during every step of the process. Finally, the AACC board of directors unanimously approved the final list of competencies and associated examples on April 9, 2005. Built within the document was also the dynamic nature of the competency framework that included flexibility in application and openness to changes over time. Not only was this reiterative process used in the development of the competencies, it was also built into the life of them. Indeed, this *New Directions* publication reflects on the recursive nature of the competencies.

The Leading Forward project dovetailed into and benefited from the already energized mission of the AACC around leadership: aligning a national project inclusive of a wide range of voices into current strategic initiatives of the association. Synergy resulted due to the coordination of these processes focused on leadership development. The Leading Forward initiative also did its best to consider and involve as many stakeholders in the field as possible. Key players involved with university programs, affiliate council programs, grow-your-own programs, and programs in underserved areas were invited to participate. If particular leaders could not come, their representatives were welcomed. Attendees were involved in a well-articulated and organized data-gathering and community-building summit that treated the information provided by each group as equally valuable. The question protocol and agendas for each summit were the same. The goal of the process was clear—to sustain the community college mission through the development of competent, caring, and college- and community-focused leaders.

The value of outside consultants cannot be overstated here. External consultants were used to guide the overall competency-development part of Leading Forward as well as the summit process. Attendees were very satisfied with the summits and appreciated the organization and facilitation of these meetings. The mission of the project, as well as the goals of the summits, was clearly articulated and very inclusive. For example, attendees responded to several questions before the summit began and their responses were collected into one document (which included not only their responses but names and affiliations) and shared with the entire group a week prior to the summit. This underscored the role of inclusivity and community building as well as good meeting management. When the summits were started, the thinking "pump was primed," thus saving time in creating shared understanding and allowing participants to reach a greater depth of discussion in the limited time available at the summits.

Additionally, the process was transparent, a critical factor in building buy-in among all stakeholders. The use(s) of the competencies was left open to the field. For example, a discussion about credentialing and the possible role of the AACC in a credentialing process emerged. Any competency framework can be used on a continuum of weighting, ranging from "low-stakes" to "high-stakes" use. A low-stakes approach, for example, would involve recommending the use of the competencies to leadership program developers; a medium-stakes approach could involve using the competency rubric in an employee evaluation process; while a high-stakes approach could require an employee to obtain a particular score on a validated instrument that assesses the competencies. The AACC could have taken any one of these approaches and, ultimately, took a low-stakes approach in providing the competencies as guidelines versus dictating any type of requirements associated with the listing. Even though this stance clearly builds more buy-in from the field, it also ultimately risks the low use and marginalization of the competencies. Part of the purpose of this *New Directions* publication is to examine the effects and impact of that low-stakes choice.

Contemporary Thoughts. Community college personnel have always prided themselves on the individuality of their institutions and community-directed missions. One way this individuality is reflected is through their workforce and credit program offerings' alignment to local culture and community needs. Leadership is no exception. Programs to develop, support, and sustain leaders must take this individuality into account. This leadership orientation is one reason for the low- to medium-stakes approach in using the competencies for leadership development. The guiding thought behind the recommended competencies was that they were critical for all community college leaders to either possess themselves or take into account when forming their college leadership team. The list represents a comprehensive core of functions required of community college leaders. However, how they become operationalized, their use, the weighing of one over another, and their relative importance are unique in each situation. This balance of unique (context) to universal (core elements transcending context) must be carefully navigated.

Both leadership and its delivery are highly contextualized. Modalities of delivery should be multiple and opportunities abundant. As the world moves to 24/7 delivery, perhaps community college leadership development could move that way as well. Specifically, people want what they want when they want or need it. It is conceivable that a community college leader might encounter a crisis in the organizational strategy domain and, in some sleepless hours, might want to learn more about how to think about it. An online module could meet that need versus general surfing of the Internet. Not only are online resources accessible 24/7, but focused modules could save time by targeting needed information in an approachable format. In this case, the leader's learning can have depth through authentic reflection, rich case histories, and other tools providing a detailed exploration of the situation and not necessarily breadth. In our Internet-dominated world, individualized content and individualized learning become paramount.

Contemporary society supports the value of collective learning, hence the popularity of cohort-based models of leadership development programs. In this case, leadership development is enhanced through collaborative learning and networks and strategic alliances are formed. These cohort programs also tend to cover the entire range of competencies, fulfilling the hope stated above that the competencies will be used for curricula in these programs. In this face-to-face delivery of leadership development, there is more breadth and less depth, with the social aspect of learning being prominent. The value of the collaborative learning and of the professional relationships that continue long after the program has ended cannot be understated.

Institutional and national mentoring programs are also helpful, although they are more difficult to organize and maintain. The social affiliation and modeling parts of these programs are powerful and often mitigate the isolation that leaders, particularly upper-level leaders, sometimes feel. The AACC encourages connections between graduates of their leadership programs through reunions at the national convention and by sharing updated contact information and tracking and publicizing participants' career advancements. These mentoring programs can also provide links with peers not available on an individual leader's campus, and these connections can provide an opportunity for authentic personal reflection. In the same way an external consultant can provide a more objective view, a mentor who is external to the institution often provides objectivity as well as knowledge about practices at other institutions.

This chapter has deliberately not focused on the career/job seeking aspect of leadership development. Good interviewing skills, presentation of self, and professional ties and networks are all important, of course, and should be found in the range of leadership development opportunities. During the creation of the competencies, there was also some discussion about the use of electronic portfolios to present one's work to others, a form of presentation of self. However, it is the stance of this author and the focus of this chapter that leadership development should focus primarily on leadership itself and not on how to acquire positions of leadership, hence the focus on the competencies themselves.

Takeaways

In addition to the uses previously described, the AACC competencies for community college leaders can be most useful as a practical and deep reflection tool to guide systemic change on an organizational level, as well as career development on an individual leader level. They could be used as a framework for environmental scanning or as a rubric for self-assessment. They provide an anchor for periodic assessment as well as a common language for discussion, networking, and shared problem solving. To name something is to give it life. The naming of the competencies ultimately serves to provide focus, direction, and, ultimately, success to the community college mission, students, and communities.

Conclusion

In summary, and in acknowledgment of the paradoxical importance of leadership development programs, I'd like to pay heed to Dwight D. Eisenhower's comment, "In preparing for battle I have always found that plans are useless, but planning is indispensable." Eisenhower had no way of knowing that the seas would be choppy on the night of June 5, 1944, but his planning for D-Day paid off. Likewise, a community college leader has no way of knowing what the next phone call will bring, but understanding the lay of the land, having a firm foundation in the range of skills needed, having good problem-solving abilities, being fully engaged in the experience, and having the necessary confidence will serve leaders well. It is the most and the least that we can expect from our community college leaders.

References

American Association of Community Colleges. *President's Report on AACC Strategic Action Areas and Initiatives.* Washington, D.C.: American Association of Community Colleges, 2002.

American Association of Community Colleges. *Leading Forward: The Community College Opportunity Planning Grant.* Washington, D.C.: American Association of Community Colleges, 2003.

American Association of Community Colleges. *A Qualitative Analysis of Community College Leadership.* Washington, D.C.: American Association of Community Colleges, 2004.

American Association of Community Colleges. *Competencies for Community College Leaders.* Washington, D.C.: American Association of Community Colleges, 2005.

American Association of Community Colleges. "Mission Statement." 2006. Retrieved Dec. 27, 2011, from www.aacc.nche.edu/About/Pages/mission.aspx.

Ottenritter, N. "Competencies for Community College Leaders: The Next Step." *Community College Journal*, February/March 2006, 15–18.

Shults, C. *The Critical Impact of Impending Retirements on Community College Leadership.* Leadership Series Research Brief no. 1. Washington, D.C.: American Association of Community Colleges, 2001.

NAN OTTENRITTER, *former manager of the Leading Forward project at the AACC, currently serves as the director of professional development for the Virginia Community College System.*

2

This chapter describes the development of the Future Leaders Institute and the Future Leaders Institute/ Advanced, highlighting the role of the AACC's Competencies for Community College Leaders in providing a framework for professional development. The competencies are built into each session's topics and activities.

Future Leaders Institute: Rising Leaders and the AACC Competencies

Desna L. Wallin

The overall mission of the American Association of Community Colleges (AACC) is "Building a Nation of Learners by Advancing America's Community Colleges." A significant component of this mission statement involves the development of leadership. Further, one of the core values of AACC states that "AACC promotes the development of community college leaders at all levels," and a focus of the AACC is to develop leaders to advance the work of community colleges around the nation. To accomplish this goal, a strategic action area for AACC is leadership development.

In short, the AACC believes that leadership can be learned and is committed to supporting and growing leaders: "While [leadership] can be enhanced immeasurably by natural aptitude and experience, supporting leaders with exposure to theory, concepts, cases, guided experiences, and other practical information and learning methodologies is essential" (AACC, 2005a). Leaders can learn new skills and competencies to be more effective in their current roles and to be prepared to assume additional responsibility as they move up the organizational ladder. In order to design leadership development programs that are effective for adult learners, an appreciation of how adults learn is crucial to the process.

Note: I am indebted to George Boggs, Margaret Rivera, Courtney Larson, and Lynn Barnett for their assistance in developing and sustaining the Institutes as well as providing background information for this chapter.

This chapter reviews the AACC competencies and how they have been integrated into the Future Leaders Institute (FLI) and the Future Leaders Institute/Advanced (FLI/A). The following topics will be discussed: understanding adult learning principles, designing the initial institutes, developing the leadership competencies, interpreting and integrating the competencies, and summary and reflection.

Understanding Adult Learning Principles

Adults learn differently than children. Pedagogy, the art and science of teaching children, "assigns to the teacher full responsibility for making all decisions about what will be learned, how it will be learned, when it will be learned, and if it has been learned. It is teacher-directed education, leaving to the learner only the submissive role of following a teacher's instructions" (Knowles, Holton, and Swanson, 2005, pp. 61–62). Adults, however, bring to the learning situation a variety of rich life experiences that affect their learning in a new situation. Thus, when planning a leadership development initiative for adults, it is important to consider basic principles of adult learning and the concept of andragogy in providing a framework. Andragogy is the "art and science of helping adults learn" (Knowles, Holton, and Swanson, 2005, p. 60); it encompasses the methods and techniques used to teach adults. The andragogical model is based on several assumptions that are different from the pedagogical model framing children's learning. These assumptions are important to understand when building a leadership development program:

- Adults need to understand why they need to learn something before they are willing to learn.
- Adults come into a learning activity with a far different set of life experiences than do children. They have accumulated more and different experiences that impact both their aptitudes and attitudes toward learning. Those experiences can be validated through participation in group discussions in a leadership-development program.
- Adults become ready to learn those things that they need to know to cope with their real-life situations. Thus, when they have decided that they want to move up in their organizational responsibility, they are ready to learn.
- Adults tend to be task-centered or problem-centered in their learning needs. New learning in skills or understanding is most effective when linked to a specific context that is meaningful. In planning a leadership-development program for community college leaders, it is important to situate the components of the program in the context of real issues in a community college.
- While adults are motivated by some external factors, such as the opportunity for promotions and better salaries, their primary motivations are

linked to internal factors such as increased job satisfaction and self-esteem. Most likely when they come to a leadership development opportunity, they are motivated to improve themselves, their effectiveness, and their opportunities for professional advancement (Knowles, Holton, and Swanson, 2005, pp. 64–69).

Keeping in mind these basic understandings of how and why adults learn, the initial Future Leaders Institutes were developed with an emphasis on linking learning to specific contexts and examples that showcased real issues in community colleges.

Designing the Initial Institutes

The AACC established the FLI in 2003 as a response to the growing number of actual and anticipated retirements of community college presidents and other community college leaders. While there were limited leadership development opportunities available both nationally and locally, the AACC board and member presidents felt that the AACC had a responsibility to develop leaders with skills specific to community colleges. AACC, through their own and others' research (Shults, 2001; Vaughan and Weisman, 1998), determined a need for new professional development opportunities and pathways to leadership positions. Realizing the impact of Baby Boomer retirements, the AACC board of directors supported the idea that AACC should create its own leadership development institute for rising community college leaders. In late 2001, given this directive, George Boggs, president and CEO of AACC, asked me, as a recently retired community college president and former board member who had been active in leadership development, to partner with the AACC in developing this new institute. An advisory committee of presidents and vice presidents from across the nation was selected to work with AACC staff and me in developing and implementing this new program. After some discussion, the program was given the name Future Leaders Institute (FLI) to accurately portray the goals and planned outcomes of the effort.

The first FLI was held in Pittsburgh, Pennsylvania, in 2003. In 2004, two more FLIs were held, the first in Long Beach, California, and the second in Baltimore, Maryland. In 2005, AACC published *Competencies for Community College Leaders,* after which many participants who had completed FLI, as well as those in second-tier positions, noted a need for a more advanced program that would help participants gain additional exposure to the expectations outlined in the competencies. AACC staff, working with me, created FLI/A to meet the professional development needs of community college leaders who were ready to take the next step in pursuing a college presidency and offered the first Future Leaders Institute/Advanced in Boston in 2005. In an effort to make both of the institutes as geographically accessible as possible, the location alternated between the eastern and western parts of the

United States. To more efficiently utilize facilities and presenters, the institutes for midlevel leaders and for advanced leaders were held simultaneously at the same location. Locations in subsequent years were Long Beach, Houston, Boston, Savannah, Portland, Jacksonville, San Francisco, Ft. Worth, Providence, Chicago, Newport Beach, and Baltimore.

Over 700 rising leaders participated in the FLI and the FLI/A in the classes from 2003 to 2011. In the FLI, targeting those whose next step would be at the second or third level (dean, director, VP), the 565 participants included 251 males and 314 females. The FLI/A, which began in 2005, targets those whose next step may be at the CEO level, president, provost, or chancellor. Of the 172 participants to date in FLI/A, 89 were male and 83 female (AACC, Courtney Larson, personal communication, November, 2011). Many of the participants in the FLI program have subsequently participated in the FLI/A program as they understood the need to further develop their own leadership competencies and sought out new responsibilities and challenges in a potential presidency.

While the first institutes were developed with attention to adult learning principles and research from the extant literature, it was not until the AACC competencies were developed in 2005 that specific agreed-upon skills, values, and knowledge were integrated purposefully into the AACC Future Leaders Institutes.

Developing the Competencies

As outlined in Chapter One, the concern over future leadership development for community colleges resulted in the Leading Forward initiative and the subsequent publication of the agreed-upon six competencies derived via consensus. Respondents in the AACC forums were also asked how well they were trained to apply the competencies in their own work or how well the leadership programs with which they were involved prepared participants in the application of the competencies. Their responses were considerably lower than their responses to the importance of the competencies:

> In other words, these respondents, who make up a significant percentage of
> U.S. community college leaders and leadership development program per-
> sonnel, feel that each of the six competencies is essential to community col-
> lege leadership but that the development of these competencies is not as well
> established. These findings provide evidence for the crucial need to establish
> this framework and to promote these competencies in the curricula of com-
> munity college leadership programs. (AACC, 2005b, para. 5)

Summarized, the six competencies are as follows:

1. *Organizational strategy*—strategically improves quality, protects long-term health, promotes success of students, and sustains the community college mission.

2. *Resource management*—equitably and ethically sustains people, processes, information, and physical and financial assets.
3. *Communication*—uses clear listening, speaking, and writing skills to engage in honest, open dialogue at all levels of the college and community.
4. *Collaboration*—develops and maintains responsive, cooperative, ethical, and mutually beneficial internal and external relationships.
5. *Community college advocacy*—understands, commits to, and advocates for the mission, vision, and goals of the community college.
6. *Professionalism*—works ethically to set high standards for self and others.

These six competencies now provide the framework for the design and development of the curriculum and the selection of presenters and facilitators for both the FLI and the FLI/A.

Interpreting and Integrating the Competencies

The skills, knowledge, and competencies required of contemporary community college leaders are much different than they were even a decade or two ago. The demands and the expectations of community college leaders have grown exponentially with the complexity of the responsibilities and increased public scrutiny and accountability (Vaughan and Weisman, 1998; Wallin, 2002, 2007). In an age where one misstep can result in a YouTube video that portrays both the leader and the college in a negative light, it is more important than ever that leaders internalize the skills and competencies of exemplary, ethical leadership.

The AACC competencies now provide the framework for the FLI and the FLI/A. Sessions are planned with the competencies in mind. Facilitators and presenters are selected who exemplify and have acknowledged experience in particular competencies.

Integrating the Competencies in FLI.   While the sessions are somewhat different for each subsequent institute program, based on feedback and evaluations from both the presenters and the participants, the embedding of the competencies is consistent. For example, FLI usually begins with a session led by the president and CEO of AACC. This general session touches on all the competencies, but emphasizes two: competencies 1 (organizational strategy) and 5 (community college advocacy). The CEO emphasizes the importance of organizational mission and creating a positive campus environment for both staff and students. The introduction also highlights the idea of advocacy, which underscores the role of community college leaders at all levels in understanding and advocating for the mission, vision, and goals of the community college.

Competency 2, resource management, deals with fiscal management and accountability, as well as supporting an effective human resource development system. In FLI, this vital competency is embedded in sessions dealing with community college law, use (and misuse) of resources, and management of conflict and change within the college. Presenters, either singly or as panels, are individuals who have experience in resource management, time management, and conflict management within their own institutions.

A session on collaboration emphasizes competency 4. The presenter(s) discuss and provide examples of the importance of collaboration with business and industry, K–12 education, universities, and other community resources and agencies as well as the nature of collaboration within the institution with faculty, staff, and students. The competency also suggests that an effective leader will "develop, enhance, and sustain teamwork and cooperation" (AACC, 2005a). The collaboration competency further emphasizes the ability of effective leaders to "embrace and employ the diversity of individuals, cultures, values, ideas, and communication styles . . . [as well as] cultural competence relative to a global society" (AACC, 2005a). In the midlevel FLI, a session is always included that focuses on the leader and equity, as well as a session on global change, both of which integrate the important competency of collaboration.

Communication and professionalism (competencies 3 and 6, respectively) are emphasized in FLI through a specific session dealing with the leader and ethics. To lead this session, a current president is invited who has experienced and overcome ethical challenges in his or her career. Sharing examples and working through case studies provides ample opportunity for participants to practice communication skills and strategies as well as to determine appropriate responses to ethical dilemmas.

Integrating the Competencies in FLI/A.   While the competencies remain the same, the application and emphases in the FLI/A are substantively different. The audience in FLI/A is composed of seasoned leaders who are aspiring to the presidency or chancellorship and are looking to fine-tune their leadership skills and anticipate some of the challenges they might face as an institutional CEO.

The introductory overall general session presented by the CEO of AACC, while briefly reviewing all the competencies, concentrates on competencies 1 (organizational strategy) and 6 (professionalism). When addressing the FLI/A participants, the AACC CEO makes a strong case for the leadership required to sustain "the community college mission, based on knowledge of the organization, its environment, and future trends" (AACC, 2005a) as a primary responsibility of the college president. Similarly, the importance of professionalism in all aspects is presented as a key factor in the success not only of a president, but also of the college. Participants are reminded of the importance of demonstrating "transformational leadership through authenticity, creativity, and vision" (AACC, 2005a). Ethical leadership is discussed as the foundation for all decisions. Finally, the importance of supporting lifelong learning for themselves as well as for others is identified as a cornerstone of professionalism.

The second competency (resource management) is embedded in sessions that revolve around such topics as "Leading in Adverse Economic Times." Contemporary community college presidents will face financial and budgeting decisions that are much more complex and challenging than they were a decade or two ago, when more resources were available. Resource management at the presidential level also involves finding alternative funding sources and engaging in entrepreneurial partnerships. Although a decade or more ago, fundraising responsibilities were not seen as a high priority for community college presidents, in a recent survey 36 percent of presidents indicated that fundraising was included in their contract as a specific responsibility (Wallin, 2007). Thus, sessions on external funding are appropriate and useful to potential presidents who may have had little or no experience with foundations, planned giving, grant writing, or "making the ask."

The third competency, communication, is interwoven throughout the sessions; particular emphasis, however, is placed on the president as communicator in media relations and crisis management in a targeted session dealing with the president as communicator. The buck stops with the CEO when there is a crisis on campus, regardless of how closely involved he or she is with the particular incident. How to communicate with both internal and external constituencies, and specifically with the media, is a skill that is developed over time; however, the new president needs to be aware of how to deal effectively with the press in times of crisis as well as how to communicate clearly to those within and outside the institution who are looking to the CEO for leadership in difficult situations. Leslie and Fretwell (1996) emphasize this point: "In some cases, institutions simply have no time and very few options: presidents and boards have to act swiftly and responsibly. In real crises, few would begrudge the leaders the right and duty to make decisions for which they will be held accountable" (p. 189). However, they go on to say that when possible, it is far better to foster cooperation and to engage in consensus decision making. Regardless of the situation, both internal and external communication skills are essential competencies.

Collaboration, the fourth competency, is embedded into discussions about shared governance, faculty input, union relationships, and board oversight. Leadership is not a solo act—a leader cannot accomplish goals without the willing efforts of others. As Kouzes and Posner (2007) realized from their research and studies, "You simply can't get extraordinary things done by yourself. Collaboration is the master skill that enables teams, partnerships, and other alliances to function effectively" (p. 242).

Regardless of the type or size of the institution that a new president is leading, the role of the governing board is critical to the success of the president and the smooth running of the college. A session led by experienced board chairs and presidents deals with maintaining positive relationships through collaborative leadership and provides an introduction to the importance of board/CEO relationships. Collaboration, whether with faculty, external agencies, governing boards, or donors "is a critical competency for achieving and sustaining high performance" (Kouzes and Posner, 2007, p. 224).

Because the presidential role in advocacy (competency 5) is a major responsibility of a CEO, a panel discussion is devoted to this issue. A panel of community college presidents and staff from AACC who have been deeply involved in advocating for community colleges present the topic from a national, state, and local perspective. Participants have the opportunity to see advocacy from a much broader viewpoint than they have understood previously.

While all the competencies are integrated into the sessions in both FLI and FLI/A, the emphases are necessarily different depending on the career stage of the participants. The principles of adult learning underscore how training must link to participant experience; thus, those involved in the FLI/A come to the sessions with a different knowledge base and background given their time in leadership. However, similarities still exist across the institutes. In both institutes, early sessions introduce participants to the importance of self-understanding in effective leadership. Understanding emotional intelligence and the role it can play in a leader's success, as well as professional assessments of leadership strength through a variety of instruments, is critical to helping participants understand their own strengths and challenges. In both institutes, participants reflect on their own leadership using role-play interview experiences to give them some feel for the types of questions that might be asked in an interview.

Career counselors play an important role in both FLI and FLI/A. Depending on the class size, two or three former presidents who have been very successful in their respective tenures spend dedicated one-on-one time by appointment with each participant. Prior to the institute, the counselor receives the resume and career goal statement of the participant; when the two meet, the counselor is well prepared to help the participant see any gaps in the resume and suggest possible opportunities that may increase the chance of attaining the stated career goal. Ultimately, the career counselor becomes a part of the participant's professional network. This activity is aligned with adult learning principles, including the desire for increased job satisfaction and self-esteem. The career counselor is able to respond to one of the important assumptions of adult learning—that adults become ready to learn those things that they need to know to cope with their real-life situations. The career counselor is the right person at the right time to support the participants as they explore their current situation and compare that with their long-term professional goals. The conversation between the career counselor and the participant also models the competency of professionalism and emphasizes the need for continual self-improvement and lifelong learning.

NEW DIRECTIONS FOR COMMUNITY COLLEGES • DOI: 10.1002/cc

Reflection and Summary

The Future Leaders Institute and the Future Leaders Institute/Advanced have provided a leadership development opportunity to over 700 rising leaders. Of those participants, 81 have become community college presidents and more than 400 have moved up to more senior-level positions since participating in one of the institutes. New presidents and other senior-level leaders who have completed FLI or FLI/A provide a valuable resource for organizers of AACC leadership development experiences on their campuses. Development of institutional-based training sessions can expand the scope of reach of the training and development efforts. It is clear from feedback provided by participants that the competencies have been helpful in understanding and meeting the challenges of contemporary community college leaders. However, the competencies should not be regarded as static; they need to be constantly reinterpreted and reevaluated in response to changing external and internal environments. Similarly, the leadership programs and sessions of FLI and FLI/A need to be continuously reevaluated to be sure they are meeting the needs of today's leaders. While the competencies provide a solid foundation for leadership development, the emphases within each competency need to be carefully considered and adjusted as necessary in relation to specific financial, political, and cultural conditions, which will likely differ among colleges, systems, and regions of the country.

The AACC's *Competencies for Community College Leaders* has provided a framework for the development of a dynamic and relevant curriculum that addresses challenges faced by contemporary community college leaders. The strong foundation of the leadership competencies, coupled with an understanding of adult learning principles, enables the Future Leaders Institute and the Future Leaders Institute/Advanced to continue to provide a coherent and comprehensive leadership-development program for rising leaders in America's community colleges. This framework can be replicated for campus-based leadership development programs as well.

References

American Association of Community Colleges. *Competencies for Community College Leaders*. Washington, D.C.: American Association of Community Colleges, 2005a.

American Association of Community Colleges. *Leading Forward Development Process: November 2003–April 2005*. Washington, D.C.: American Association of Community Colleges, 2005b.

Knowles, M. S., Holton, E. F., and Swanson, R. A. *The Adult Learner: The Definitive Classic in Adult Education and Human Resource Development*. Burlington, Mass.: Elsevier, 2005.

Kouzes, J. M., and Posner, B. Z. *The Leadership Challenge*. San Francisco, Calif.: Jossey-Bass, 2007.

Leslie, D. W., and Fretwell, E. K. *Wise Moves in Hard Times: Creating and Managing Resilient Colleges and Universities*. San Francisco, Calif.: Jossey-Bass, 1996.

Shults, C. *The Critical Impact of Impending Retirements on Community College Leadership.* Research brief, Leadership Series No. 1. Washington, D.C.: American Association of Community Colleges, 2001.

Vaughan, G. B., and Weisman, I. M. *The Community College Presidency at the Millenium.* Washington, D.C.: Community College Press, 1998.

Wallin, D. L. "Professional Development for Presidents: A Study of Community and Technical College Presidents in Three States." *Community College Review,* 2002, *30*(2), 27–41.

Wallin, D. L. *The CEO Contract: A Guide for Presidents and Boards.* Washington, D.C.: Community College Press, 2007.

DESNA L. WALLIN, *a former community college president in Iowa and North Carolina, currently serves as associate professor in the Department of Lifelong Education, Administration and Policy at the University of Georgia and is a contributing faculty in the Higher Education and Adult Learning doctoral program of Walden University.*

NEW DIRECTIONS FOR COMMUNITY COLLEGES • DOI: 10.1002/cc

This chapter argues for the use of clusters in thinking about the AACC competencies. Four clusters are presented: inclusivity, framing meaning, attention to the bottom line, and systems thinking. Overarching these clusters is the need for contextual competency in which leaders align their approaches based on their college's context.

A Holistic Perspective of Leadership Competencies

Pamela L. Eddy

The passage of time since the creation of the six competencies by the American Association of Community Colleges (AACC) allows for critical reflection of the original list. This chapter reviews data collected from twelve community college presidents and a variety of campus members (Eddy, 2010). The data for this study included interviews with each of the case site presidents, members of the leadership team, and faculty leaders, for a total of seventy-five interviews. The dozen presidents in this study lead a variety of types of institutions, ranging from small rural campuses to large, multicampus urban colleges. The presidents differed as well on the number of presidencies they held and their years of service in the top-level position. The only variable of consequence for how the presidents implemented the competencies was their length of tenure as president (Neumann and Bensimon, 1990). The longer their service, the greater breadth they had in using the competencies given their experiences and resulting learning due to feedback from their actions.

As noted in chapter one, in 2005 AACC published a set of six competencies created by consensus to target skills central to leading the community colleges of the future. This listing provided individuals seeking top-level positions a road map for development and helped institutions target areas in training topics for in-house grow-your-own leadership programs. As with any type of listing, however, an inherent danger is devolution to a mere checklist versus viewing the competencies as a general

New Directions for Community Colleges, no. 159, Fall 2012 © 2012 Wiley Periodicals, Inc.
Published online in Wiley Online Library (wileyonlinelibrary.com) • DOI: 10.1002/cc.20024

starting point. The next section reviews how the presidents in this study used the individual competencies.

The Competencies in Action

Each of the presidents in this study utilized the AACC competencies to some extent. In particular, organizational strategy, with its focus on management issues and operations, was an area frequently addressed first when the presidents initially arrived on campus. Visible outcomes were apparent as new presidents implemented new organizational reporting structures or created strategic plans. Often, the creation of a new reporting arrangement established a more hierarchical structure that embedded power more centrally with the president (Morgan, 2006). The strategic planning activities, however, served to underscore collaboration and consensus building. As one president commented, "Our strategic planning sessions were interactive, more of a dialogue and smaller groups." These sessions fostered openness and a connection for the campus members with the outcomes. Campus members saw these types of efforts as most successful, however, when plans resulted in actual changes in practice versus planning exercises whose final planning documents sat on a shelf. Existing campus culture and college history influenced how the operationalization of plans occurred and how staff reacted.

The challenges of fiscal constraints facing the colleges resulted in all the presidents focusing on resource management skills. How leaders manage personnel and physical plant operations relies heavily on ethical leadership. Presidents must account for use of funds and support their decisions of resource allocation. The expansion of college missions coupled with the simultaneous cuts in state funding resulted in case site presidents making tough decisions. How presidents framed this situation, however, differed among those in the study (Neumann, 1995). In essence, approaches focused on the glass as either half-empty or half-full. As one president reflected, "Focusing on dealing with the budget crises in such a way that everybody is kind of focusing on a bigger picture, not just the 'oh poor me, they took my money away and I can't travel' but the fact that we have an important job to do and the college needs us, we're going to serve our students and so forth." Another president also referenced the need to frame the situation for others: "My role is to probably help people here understand that even though we've got to tighten our belt and we're having to do these undesirable things, it's going to be okay." Countering these examples, campus members on one campus noted constantly being asked to do more with less and seeing no relief in sight. The manner in which the presidents spoke of resources on campus influenced campus reactions (Neumann, 1995).

How leaders communicate within the campus and with outside constituents matters. A critical element in communication is the art of listening

(Hoppe, 2006). The first opportunity a leader has to communicate is during the initial job interview. Clues are given during these interactions with campus staff, board members, and community constituents. Sitting presidents were often able to note in retrospect the messages they missed during this first visit on campus and to understand more clearly in hindsight how the first campus visit presented aspects of the campus's culture. As one president reflected, "Sometimes you have to put four, five, six pieces together. You talk to different people and then you put it all together." Seeking out divergent perspectives helps create a richer understanding of campus realities. Communication styles varied among study participants, with some favoring writing to connect their ideas to the campus and others preferring to talk with groups, either in small group settings or with larger groups. Consistency in the messaging was critical to ultimate success. On some campuses, messaging was successful as several campus members could articulate the strategic plan and mission of the college using similar metaphors and stories (Bolman and Deal, 2008).

Decreases in funding for community colleges make partnering with others enticing. Collaborations, however, have brought in a wider range of stakeholders that include universities, industry, and community agencies. Indeed, many state policymakers include collaborations in their planning to reform educational practices and efforts to link educational sectors across the P-16 continuum (*Closing the Expectations Gap,* 2011). External collaborations for the participants involved linking with businesses to fulfill training needs, working on regional economic development initiatives, or working with local school districts to establish educational ladder programs. Equally important for leaders were internal collaborations. One new president noted the challenges she faced when first arriving on campus: "All these deans had carved off their little fiefdoms. And they were all fighting with one another and their staff were fighting with one another." She worked to build a collaborative culture, which required good communication skills as well as an ability to work well with individuals.

Advocacy, espoused by participants as a critical competency, was inherent in the work of both new and seasoned presidents. Advocacy was apparent in both the words and actions of the presidents. Many of the participants used strategic planning as an opportunity to support the missions of their institutions. College websites also served as a vehicle for advancing the college's mission. Presidents were visible at community events and used these opportunities to network with various stakeholders to garner more support. As one president commented, "The college typically views itself as being apart from the region, and I'm trying to build the image in the minds of our faculty and staff that we are the region. And without us, it will not change." For rural colleges in particular, links to the community were heightened due to their small population, which resulted in everyone's knowing one another. Advocacy in these instances differed from urban locales in which competition for public attention was harder to obtain.

The final AACC competency is professionalism. As college spokespersons, the presidents always represented more than merely themselves as college leaders. Indeed, they *were* the college for many they encountered. This public spotlight resulted in a closer inspection, especially for the presidents of color and female presidents. Leadership development and mentoring served a critical role in preparing presidents for their role, and in turn influenced how these sitting leaders helped train others on their campuses. Leaders modeled expectations and helped in developing the next generation of community college leaders. As one female minority president noted of her advisement to others, "Develop a confidence that you can do it. I think white males are raised that way. I think it is a kind of entitlement. I've never been in a position to feel or think I can achieve just because it's an entitlement; I've had to work for everything." Central to this mentoring is developing what one president referred to as "survival skills." A critical component in this skill bank was a professional network. As noted in Chapter Two, national leadership development training programs embed mentoring and networking as part of their programs. Seeing how others lead and learning from the mistakes of others provide valuable learning opportunities. Visits to other campuses also help illustrate a range of ways to solve problems and illustrates how problems on any one campus are not unique.

Despite the comprehensive skill set outlined in the AACC competencies, missing from the list is the importance of environment. I have argued that the current AACC competency listing needs to include cultural competency (Eddy, 2010). Here, competency requires understanding the college culture and reading the context of what is valued. This concept is different than historic notions of cultural competency that deal with issues of diversity, so, to avoid confusion, I will refer to this now as *contextual competency*. Knowing more about the campus culture allows for the creation of organizational strategies aligned with existing frameworks of what works and acknowledges the history of the institution.

A sense of fit between the college and the leader emerged during the site visits. A good fit might exist due to a leader's past experiences and skill set and the current demands on the college. Some campus members noted the need to hire a "go-getter" to initiate institutional changes. Others sought to counteract the type of leadership exhibited by the last president.

Leaders who possessed a competency for reading and interpreting the campus context and culture hit the ground running. In part, acknowledging and recognizing campus traditions and history helped to engage the campus in change. One campus member described her campus as a "dysfunctional family," which underscored for the new president a need to build community and to start new traditions. Two of the male presidents who had long careers as leaders could best be described as "good ole boys." Part of the reason for their success on their new campuses was the level of participation they elicited from campus members and how they valued leadership throughout the institution. But, at the end of the day, it was clear that these leaders understood that they were responsible for making the tough decisions on campus. Knowing the culture and context of the campus helps leaders achieve desired changes. Because many community colleges are part of larger district cultures, leaders often must figure out how to work within the culture of their own college as well as that of the larger system.

The Competencies as Clusters

In the analysis of the data from this study, it became apparent that many of the competencies operated in tandem, and patterns of alignment came forward. For instance, the competency of resource management often aligned with organizational strategy, and communication aligned with collaboration. Present in all of the clusters was the application of contextual competency. Viewing the competencies more holistically provides a different perspective and approach to leadership development and leadership enactment on campus. In many ways, these connections to campus context harken to notions of situational leadership. What differs in this case is that the focus is no longer on how best to address a campus context by selecting the appropriate leader for the time, but rather on how to recognize that individual leaders can acquire a wider range of leadership approaches to allow for expansion of existing schemas that provide more frames to guide their actions (Bolman and Deal, 2008). Viewing leaders from a multidimensional perspective (Eddy, 2010) provides more complexity to aid understanding of leadership in what is now a more complicated campus environment.

Inclusivity.   The cluster of inclusivity builds on the skills of communication and collaboration. Here, collaboration moves beyond merely asking campus members for contributions on ad hoc teams toward relationships that involve shared leadership. Communication changes from dyadic exchanges to shared dialogue. One of the study presidents who utilized this cluster referenced a team metaphor to illustrate the concept, but was clear in his intention for inclusivity when he stated, "I'm not a team owner. It's ours. We are all in this together." The president's description underscored how roles change on the team, in particular the role he played. He did not view himself as the sole arbitrator for the group; rather, he saw his role shifting depending on the needs of the group. This changing role highlights the contextual competency he drew upon in his leadership. His notion of inclusivity built on a platform of mutual values, which harkens to ideals associated with transformational leadership.

Associated with the inclusivity cluster is the ideal of organizational learning. Drawing on the expertise of multiple campus and external stakeholders assumes that communication venues are using feedback loops that allow organizational leaders an opportunity to test assumptions about operations and to change campus direction based on this feedback. One campus member described operations on her campus that used consensual decision making. She stated, "We have 'imagine luncheons,' which are vision luncheons where the president updates us and she praises particular initiatives, individuals, pins new faculty and employees who have come on." This person added how quick the president was in responding to e-mail, which contributed to the feeling of transparency in communication on campus. This process helped support organizational learning on this campus and made campus stakeholders feel included in the process.

Framing Meaning.   Framing, as the name implies, involves campus leaders helping to make sense and interpret campus events for others. Here, one might imagine a president using a picture frame to focus campus attention on a particular view or perspective. Undergirding the cluster of framing meaning are competencies in organizational strategy, communication, collaboration, and advocacy. Contextual competency is included, as it is in the other clusters, but here the role of understanding campus needs and the culture is pivotal to the cluster. Knowing what the campus needs helps the president decide on what is most important to frame. Framing communicates the overarching organizational strategy to campus members, and this strategy is developed collaboratively.

One of the new presidents in the study found herself on a fractured campus in which faculty held little trust in administration, ethical issues emerged during a campus self-study, and deans sought to operate as silos within the larger institution. The president's first action was to change organizational reporting to both symbolize and frame a different orientation to campus operations. She created a new organizational reporting structure that showed more cohesiveness of operations and instilled new reporting routes. This action allowed the campus to "see a change." Next, the president worked with a cadre of faculty to build trust and better understand the culture of the institution. This relationship building and collaboration created an environment more conducive to operationalizing the campus's strategic plan.

Two other leaders who operated using the framing meaning cluster needed to rebuild trust on their campuses. They sought to frame meaning by conducting a series of one-on-one or small group meetings with faculty and staff. This exercise let these new leaders quickly get a sense of what was important to the campus community and to gauge the best mechanisms for relaying messages about future direction. While both leaders were careful to acknowledge the past history of the campus, they realized that in order to make progress in the future, the campus environment needed to change. Framing meaning for the campus meant creating a new image of how campus members would interact, both with each other and with larger system offices.

Framing meaning involved presenting a vision for the college that was based on collaboration and dialogue with campus stakeholders. Here, listening was central to the communication process (Hoppe, 2006). Leaders also served as internal advocates for their campus members and external advocates for their colleges. An important element in the framing process was a consistent message and shared understanding of organizational strategy. In many ways, this singular messaging represented cohesiveness on campus and focused the attention of campus actors to move in the same direction.

Attention to the Bottom Line.   The current national context of fiscal exigency creates internal challenges for many community college campuses. For some colleges, extreme resource constraints drive all other decisions as campuses struggle to meet their multiple obligations and missions. Central to this cluster are the competencies of resource management, organizational strategy, and advocacy. Contextual competency focuses on understanding the fiscal climate and on how limited resources may align with the college's largest demands. Decisions are driven by an attention to bottom-line costs and achieving the greatest outcomes possible with the limited resources.

One of the campus leaders using this cluster orientation led a campus that had been historically underfunded and was part of a larger system. He advocated within the system structure for more resources and used these resources to attend to the direst needs. Campus perception was that "we got the short end of the stick." Ultimately, the president was able to secure additional resources for his campus; by his account, one of the reasons he was successful in this endeavor was that he had prior presidential experience and was able to draw upon his wider network and the competencies acquired over time to achieve this outcome. He also understood the need to develop a campus vision and organizational strategy to help in deciding how resources could be spent best. Once this vision was crafted, he advocated for resources that focused on achieving the central initiatives of the strategy.

For one of the other campus leaders, financial problems were also an issue. Here, the president worked to educate her campus on techniques to increase resources without significantly changing operations. Namely, she advocated for students to take a full-credit load of course work each semester. The funding formula in the state rewarded campuses with higher student credit hours, and communicating this operational strategy to faculty advisors provided a quick fix. The president regularly communicated with campus members to enhance their understanding of the resource issues and thereby build consensus in final decisions as stakeholders understood the rationale behind them. Seeing success in the changes advocated on campus provided immediate feedback and built trust on campus as well.

Systems Thinking.   The final cluster of systems thinking also has a focus on organizational strategy and communication, but additionally includes professionalism. A higher-order organizational perspective allowed those using this orientation ways to see connections between actions and reactions, even when not most evident. Longer-serving campus presidents used this cluster most often. Not only did previous experience help guide these presidents, but they also possessed an understanding of cause and effect within the campus organizational system.

The longevity of these leaders also meant that they had favored schemas for their own leadership approaches (Eddy, 2010). One president operating from this perspective turned to the use of technology in teaching and learning as a mechanism to advance the campus mission. His background in the business community also meant that he valued an entrepreneurial approach to academics for both faculty and students. Even though he had this vision for the campus, he sought to build broad-based consensus for the proposed programming. He relied on building his professional network and his own orientation to learning to help support this campus change. His system view of problems allowed him to see connections between academics, campus operations, student learning, and community outreach. This type of connective thinking provided the campus with various means to achieve the vision for the college.

Another president utilizing this perspective used the college's mission statement as a vehicle to advocate and promote the changes he envisioned. Built into the mission statement was a commitment to lifelong learning opportunities and innovative partnerships, which clearly links to the AACC competencies of professionalism and collaboration. Using the agreement and buy-in for the mission statement, a five-year strategic plan was devised. Unlike typical strategic plans that sit on a shelf, this campus actively used their plan in making decisions and marking progress. Because of the detail in accountability and reporting on progress throughout the year, campus members could see clear links with actions and outcomes. Monthly leadership meetings provided the opportunity for feedback into the system and better recognition of how actions by various campus entities were connected. The campus was readily positioned to advocate its mission and strategy as it had a television station on campus. This venue allowed the president ready access to college stakeholders and served as a vehicle for advocacy with both external and internal stakeholders.

A Look to the Future

The creation of a new way to think about the AACC competencies is illustrated in Figure 3.1. In this model, contextual competency resides as a core element and is present in all of the cluster approaches. Contextual competency links to individuals' past experiences and emerges from underlying leadership schemas (Weick, 1995). How leaders learn to lead is based on what they know has worked for them in the past and how they naturally operate given their individual preferences (Eddy, 2010). For instance, some individuals are natural networkers and enjoy connecting people and ideas, whereas others are drawn to analytical investigation of problems and strategies. Despite these natural inclinations, all leaders can learn (AACC, 2005).

Figure 3.1. Holistic Competencies

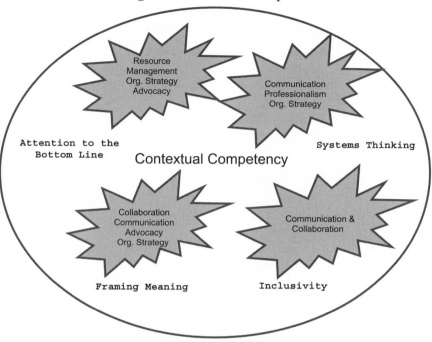

Each of the clusters in the model utilizes two or more of the original AACC competencies. Natural connections emerge among several of the groupings, such as resource management/organizational strategy and communication/advocacy. Because the groupings share many of the individual competencies, leaders can move among the various clusters with relative ease once they have done an environmental scan of the college context to determine what is needed. Thus, it is erroneous to say that one of these clusters is more valued than another. Instead, the best approach by a leader depends on the situation they face. As Neumann and Bensimon (1990) found when researching college presidents, a multiple-framed view of organizations by leaders develops with experience and with need. They found that community college leaders in their study were most likely to use more than one organizational frame of operations, as were senior leaders.

Seasoned leaders draw from their previous experiences of what worked and what did not as they arrive on a new campus. Here, they make adjustments based on the new setting and on feedback to their actions. New leaders, however, test the waters differently given their limited experience base in the top-level position. Moreover, leaders may see the clusters operating differently when viewed through the lens of race and gender as others may have stereotyped or prescribed roles ascribed to particular leader character-

New Directions for Community Colleges • DOI: 10.1002/cc

istics. Campus perceptions of leadership actions are viewed based on expectations of how women or leaders of color should act (Griffin, 1992).

Using a more holistic approach to the competencies affords an opportunity to expand thinking about leadership in community colleges. Instead of narrow definitions of leadership, this broad perspective creates a chance for picturing a variety of types of leaders as options to lead two-year colleges. Thus, the anticipated turnover in community college leaders due to retirements (Weisman and Vaughan, 2007) may make way for more presidents of color and women to ascend to these top-level positions.

Leadership developers and graduate program faculty can take note of this broader conceptualization of the AACC competencies and embed ideals of connections among the competencies into their training and classes. For instance, as Wallin points out in Chapter Two, the Future Leaders Institute already builds its training development from the existing competencies. Inserting scenarios for the participants to think about how to mix and blend the competencies based on campus needs and on the individual's leadership orientation would help new leaders when they arrive on campus. Realizing in advance how the competencies operate in clusters can contribute to a faster learning curve for leaders and provide a more complex analysis of any given situation. The increased complexity of today's community colleges requires adaptations by leaders to this changing environment and a more holistic view of the competencies required in leading.

Preparing to use the competency clusters in practice requires a sense of self-awareness and reflection on which of the initial six competencies one aligns with. Next, an understanding of the current environment aids in determining which of the clusters is most effective. The following points serve as an initial guide to using the clusters in practice:

- Identify your go-to competencies from the AACC listing (organizational strategy, resource management, communication, collaboration, community college advocacy, professionalism).
- Conduct environmental scanning of your current/new institution to determine the type of competency cluster required based on the current context and desired change.
- Assess which of the competencies you must augment to make your competency cluster most effective. For instance, if you determine that a framing cluster is required, but you note that your personal orientation relies on organizational strategy and advocacy, work on becoming more skilled in the areas of collaboration and communication.
- Build competencies in your staff through professional development to help support the overall cluster in practice at the institution and to create capacity. All campus members serve as emissaries of the college in the community and with stakeholders, thus it is critical to prepare them to represent your agenda well.

NEW DIRECTIONS FOR COMMUNITY COLLEGES • DOI: 10.1002/cc

References

American Association of Community Colleges. *Competencies for Community College Leaders.* Washington, D.C.: American Association of Community Colleges, 2005.

Bolman, L. G., and Deal, T. E. *Reframing Organizations: Artistry, Choice, and Leadership* (4th ed.). San Francisco: Jossey-Bass, 2008.

Closing the Expectations Gap. Washington, D.C.: Achieve, American Diploma Project Network, 2011.

Eddy, P. L. *Community College Leadership: A Multidimensional Model for Leading Change.* Sterling, VA: Stylus Press, 2010.

Griffin, B. Q. "Perceptions of Managers: Effects of Leadership Style and Gender." Paper presented at the Annual Meeting of the Southeastern Psychological Association, Knoxville, Tenn., 1992.

Hoppe, M. H. *Active Listening: Improve Your Ability to Listen and Lead.* Greensboro, N.C.: Center for Creative Leadership, 2006.

Morgan, G. *Images of Organizations.* Thousand Oaks, Calif.: Sage, 2006.

Neumann, A. "On the Making of Hard Times and Good Times." *Journal of Higher Education,* 1995, *66*(1), 3–31.

Neumann, A., and Bensimon, E. M. Constructing the Presidency: College Presidents' Images of Their Leadership Roles, a Comparative Study. *Journal of Higher Education,* 1990, *61*(6), 678–701.

Weick, K. E. *Sensemaking in Organizations.* Thousand Oaks, Calif.: Sage, 1995.

Weisman, I., and Vaughan, G. *The Community College Presidency: 2006.* Washington, D.C.: American Association of Community Colleges Research Brief No. AACC-RB-07–1, 2007.

PAMELA L. EDDY is an associate professor and area coordinator in Educational Policy, Planning, and Leadership at the College of William and Mary in Williamsburg, Virginia.

4

This chapter reports on research on presidential perceptions of the AACC competencies. In particular, the research points out what competencies are viewed as most critical, what competencies need further professional development, and what competencies receive less prominence in practice.

The AACC Competencies in Action

Chris Duree, Larry Ebbers

The U.S. community college system educates nearly half of all students enrolled in higher education and sustains a responsibility and commitment to educate the underserved. The popularity of the community colleges has also created renewed attention about the conception of the role of the president. Levin (1998) concluded that community college presidents have significant influence on the organization and are perceived to be the primary players in creating a culture of change. Yet it is important to distinguish between the type of skills required to lead community colleges, as these institutions have different missions and core values relative to their four-year college counterparts. The heightened attention on the community college sector means that presidents will have the opportunity to create educational programs and services that will greatly affect the lives of students and the communities in which they reside.

Perhaps one of the greatest challenges facing community colleges in the new millennium is filling the leadership pipeline with individuals who possess the necessary skills and traits to be successful and are committed to upholding the community college core values and mission. Many of the community college presidents, upper-level administrators, and faculty who began their jobs during the advent of the community colleges in the 1960s and 1970s are nearing the end of their careers. Pointedly, a recent survey found that 84 percent of current presidents indicated they intended to retire by 2016 (Weisman and Vaughan, 2006). The amount of history, experience, and commitment to the community college mission that will be lost with their retirement is immeasurable.

New Directions for Community Colleges, no. 159, Fall 2012 © 2012 Wiley Periodicals, Inc.
Published online in Wiley Online Library (wileyonlinelibrary.com) • DOI: 10.1002/cc.20025

The problems resulting from turnover of chief executive officers and other senior-level administrators due to retirement are compounded by key administrative positions attracting smaller numbers of applicants considered to be well qualified. Additionally, numbers of experienced faculty who might be interested in assuming leadership roles are shrinking. Negative perceptions of leadership positions may be a determining factor in a person's decision to prepare academically for community college leadership positions. Adding to the growing concern of a leadership shortage are significant shortfalls of student enrollments in graduate programs designed for community college administration.

Clearly, the anticipated increase in chief executive officer retirements along with an identified shortage of qualified candidates to fill these vacancies has created a high level of concern throughout the community college system. To address this situation, the American Association of Community Colleges (AACC) board of directors approved the *Competencies for Community College Leaders*, specifying a set of six competencies to be used as a framework for community college leadership development (AACC, 2005). Although 100 percent of the respondents for the initial review of the list rated each of the six competencies as "very" or "extremely" essential to effectively performing in the various roles expected of community college leaders, responses to questions about how well their formal training prepared them to meet these competencies was not encouraging. Further, Amey (2005) suggested that it remains unclear whether any of the graduate school leadership development models sufficiently provide what the next generation of community college leaders actually needs to learn. A better understanding of how presidents learn the skills and develop the traits and competencies necessary to be successful transformational leaders is needed to help resolve the leadership crisis as talented pools of potential candidates are identified.

Data findings from the *Community College Presidency Demographics and Leadership Preparation Survey* (Iowa State University) addressed leadership preparation, career pathways, and perceptions about the AACC competencies (Duree, 2007; McNair, Duree, and Ebbers, 2011). This chapter reviews what competencies need more personal development to master and what competencies receive less prominence in practice. The advocacy of transformational leadership within community colleges and within the AACC competencies provided the conceptual framework for analysis for this study.

Critical Community College Leadership Traits, Skills, and Competencies

Recent studies on the AACC's *Competencies for Community College Leaders* indicate that sitting presidents and board trustees support the application of the skill set in the field and as a framework for leadership development

NEW DIRECTIONS FOR COMMUNITY COLLEGES • DOI: 10.1002/cc

(Hassan, Dellow, and Jackson, 2010). Eddy (2010) applied the AACC leadership competencies as a bedrock for the foundation of her multidimensional leadership model. These studies highlight the agreement regarding attention to developing a skill set for community college leaders.

As outlined in earlier chapters in this book, the six competency domains include organizational strategy, resource management, communication, collaboration, community college advocacy, and professionalism. The AACC competency document (2005) described each competency domain in detail, including a description of the domain and illustrations of specific competencies within each domain. Even though there is consensus on the overarching skills in the competency listing, Goff (2003) noted, "It begs the question of how one individual can obtain and master all the traits and behaviors provided in the literature" (p. 17). Thus, the findings drawn from the Duree study (2007) provide new insight about the pathways, preparation, competencies, and leadership programs needed to face the challenges of the community college presidency in the new millennium.

Brief Portrait of the Community College Presidency

The number of female presidents continues to grow (Weisman and Vaughan, 2006), although the annual increase has slowed considerably since 2001 when the number of female presidents was reported to be 28 percent (Weisman and Vaughan, 2006) and may be plateauing. This figure is in stark contrast to the majority of women students attending community colleges. If the nation's community colleges are to embrace diversity and continue to take pride in their claims to be the "open-door" institutions of the higher education community, then trustee boards should not be satisfied with a ratio of approximately two male presidents to every one female. Ongoing development and preparation of competent female professionals in the leadership pipeline should continue to be a priority. Furthermore, opportunities should be provided to advance to the presidency on a pathway free of gender-biased roadblocks.

Even more striking in the survey data is the lack of significant increase in the number of presidents of color. Vaughan and Weisman (1998) reported a race/ethnicity breakdown of community college presidents as: 85.6 percent Caucasian, 5.2 percent African American, 4.9 percent Hispanic, 1.9 percent Native American, and 1.5 percent Asian American. A little more than a decade later, results from our study reveal the race/ethnicity stratification as: 80.7 percent Caucasian, 8.2 percent Black/African American, 5.8 percent Hispanic/Latino, 2.2 percent Native American, and 1.9 percent Asian/Pacific Islander (Duree, 2007). Again, the presidential ranks do not mirror the student body of community colleges in which 34 percent of students are non-white. Promoting greater diversity in the leadership ranks should be of utmost concern. Increasing numbers of minority leaders may also be one way to ensure that organizational structures are not creating barriers that discourage the advancement of underrepresented populations into leadership positions in the future.

Current Presidents' Perceptions of Competency Preparation

Overall, presidents indicated they were prepared for their first CEO position; however, findings revealed areas in which leaders felt less prepared than others (Duree, 2007). The following sections present a review of perceptions for each of the six domains. These findings help inform those responsible for leadership development.

Organizational Strategy.   Current community college presidents indicated they were most prepared to develop a positive work environment that supports innovation, teamwork, and successful outcomes. Yet, the presidents also reported they were not well prepared in skills required to maintain and grow college personnel, to oversee fiscal resources and assets, or to use a systems perspective to assess and respond to the needs of the communities. Fundraising was identified by some presidents as their greatest organizational challenge and highlights the need for aspiring leaders to develop a working knowledge of community college finance.

The survey findings also indicated a need for leaders to be well prepared to strategically engage with constituents regarding community workforce and economic development. Presidents who serve as mentors for those who have been targeted as potential leaders should be aware of these results and seek opportunities to directly involve protégés in the strategic planning processes.

Resource Management.   Overall, current community college presidents think they are well prepared in resource management competencies. However, approximately two out of five respondents did not rate themselves prepared or well prepared to take an entrepreneurial stance in seeking ethical alternative funding sources. Whether current presidents are rating their preparation in growing the college's fiscal assets under the organizational strategy domain, or seeking alternative funding sources under the resource management domain, there appears to be a similar theme. The findings of the study suggest that there has been a shortfall in leadership preparation that adequately develops the competencies essential to effectively address funding-related issues (Duree, 2007).

Communication.   In general, most current community college leaders rated themselves prepared or well prepared in the communication competency set. The respondents felt prepared or well prepared to articulate and champion a shared mission, vision, and values to constituents. As the literature suggests, leaders must be able to inspire a shared vision through values shared by the group to become effective transformational leaders. Thus, the survey results are encouraging as leaders feel they possess a strong skill set in the communication domain.

Collaboration.   In contrast to their ratings of preparation in the communication competency set, survey respondents did not rate themselves as well prepared in skills associated with successfully developing a sense of collaboration. One-third of the survey respondents did not rate themselves as prepared or well prepared in demonstrating cultural competence in a global society when they assumed their first presidency (Duree, 2007). Yet we know that transformational leaders in the community college setting must be able to understand the various roles that are played in resolving issues and to empower others to take an active part in making decisions, managing conflict, and working effectively with constituents (Roueche, Baker, and Rose, 1989). Further, as institutions proclaiming commitment to fostering multicultural environments that embrace diversity, community colleges have failed to actually provide it (Rendon, 1999).

A lack of cultural competence in the top leadership position does not bode well for students who discover that "their cultural capital (cultural knowledge) and academic preparation does not facilitate movement through the educational pipeline" (Trujillo and Diaz, 1999, p. 128). The time has arrived for all community college leaders to competently demonstrate a working knowledge and ongoing awareness of how traditional monolithic organizational structures are counterproductive to the success of the diverse constituencies served by the institution. An effective set of skills in collaboration must include being prepared to acknowledge the importance of cultural competence by embracing diversity and bringing individuals with different cultures, values, and ideas into the organization.

Community College Advocacy.   Approximately four out of five current community college presidents reported that they were prepared or well prepared in the community college advocacy competency. This finding is encouraging when the community college mission includes attention to the promotion of equity and open access. However, one out of five presidents in the study did not rate themselves prepared to value and promote diversity, inclusion, equity, and academic excellence. Approximately one out of five also indicated they were not prepared to demonstrate commitment to the mission of community colleges and student success through teaching and learning. To continue the advancement of the community college mission, all community college leaders will need to be competent in this particular set of competencies if they hope to be a congruent fit for the job.

Professionalism.   Not unlike presidents' ratings of preparation in the other five sets of competencies, community college leaders responding to the survey rated themselves prepared overall in the competency set for professionalism. However, even though more than 80 percent of the responding presidents self-identified as transformational leaders, only slightly more than two-thirds rated themselves prepared to competently demonstrate transformational leadership when they assumed their first presidency. Indeed, this would appear to substantiate one of the founding principles of transformational leadership theory that leadership can be learned. Perhaps, as Eddy (2005) suggested, leadership is developed through stages of cognitive development that occur over a period of time and a range of experience.

These findings suggest that learning experiences from multiple sources may contribute to development as a transformational leader over time. Regardless, formal education programs preparing the community college presidents of the future should consider revisiting how transformational leadership theory is presented in the curricula. Providing real-life learning experiences that introduce aspiring leaders to the processes of transformational leadership could possibly assist in the development of the critical competencies prior to entering the presidency.

Links Between Highest Degree Earned and the Competencies

Studies conducted in the last decade have found that approximately 90 percent of community college presidents have an earned doctorate (Weisman and Vaughan, 2006). However, fewer than half earned their doctorates in higher education with an emphasis in community college leadership, which opens the question about how different educational pathways impact the preparation for the community college presidency (Duree, 2007).

Based on the data from our study, one cannot conclude that surviving the doctoral journey through the completion of a terminal degree is the only source of preparation for the presidency. Formal education, while important, is not the only pathway to the competencies necessary for the presidency. Individuals need to develop a sense of competence in handling the job responsibilities of the chief executive officer through plural inputs.

Although nine out of ten presidents possess a doctoral degree, the presidents in this study felt they were unprepared in several of the competency domains when they assumed their first presidency. However, the findings should not be interpreted to diminish the importance of the contributions to an individual's leadership development that come as a result of scholarly work, but, rather, that doctoral programs focused on community college leadership should include intentional links with the AACC competencies. Although an earned doctorate appears to serve as a passport to the presidency, a terminal degree is not a final solution to the overall development of future community college leaders (Duree, 2007).

Overall Preparation for the First Presidency

The conceptual framework for this study used transformational leadership theory (Roueche, Baker, and Rose, 1989) and the AACC competencies (2005). The analysis of the data from the study reported here suggest there were four aspects of leadership development and preparation that influenced how current community college presidents rated their level of preparation for their first presidency. Specifically, formal education programs for the highest degree earned, formal leadership programs outside of education, and preparation in the two AACC competency constructs related to organizational strategy and resource management were identified as critical to the first leadership position.

Both the competency of organizational strategy and resource management reflect critical elements within the transformational leadership model (Roueche, Baker, and Rose, 1989). In this study, the organizational strategy and resource management competency sets were directly associated with the skills needed to face the major challenges identified by current presidents. For example, the ability to maintain college personnel, fiscal resources and assets in the organizational strategy domain is a critical competency needed to address funding issues. Implementing financial strategies and being entrepreneurial in fundraising are competencies essential to address fundraising challenges and concerns.

In some respects, a dilemma exists regarding leadership development training and doctoral programs. On the one hand, these programs educate leaders on the full range of leadership theories and applications. On the other hand, awareness of the scope of leadership may highlight lack of knowledge by the participants and result in a negative perception of preparation for top-level positions. Further, if participation in a terminal-degree program of study and in a formal leadership development program occurs after assuming a presidential appointment, the activities would only add to an exhausting list of responsibilities and thus could possibly be perceived as a negative experience.

When possible, aspiring community college presidents should complete the terminal degree before assuming their first presidency. At the same time, these individuals should seek doctoral programs that can clearly document attention to the development of the AACC competencies in course syllabi. Learning more about organizational strategy and resource management prior to ascending to top-level positions may occur through mentoring, job experiences, and leadership development programs.

Leadership development opportunities should be pursued that include specific elements identified in this study as having had significant influence in how current leaders felt prepared for their first presidency. A recommended checklist for leadership preparation should include:

- Involvement in leadership programs outside of formal education prior to the first presidency.
- Completion of a terminal degree before assuming the first presidency.
- Participation in leadership programs, academies, conferences, and seminars specifically intended to prepare current and future leaders in the AACC competencies.
- Development and participation in in-house leadership opportunities that strengthen competencies in organizational strategy and resource management.

By considering these recommendations for leadership development, individuals should be better prepared with the necessary tools to survive the challenges they will face as transformational leaders in the twenty-first century.

Advice to Aspiring and Sitting Community College Presidents

An earned doctorate continues to be the educational passport to a seat in the office of the community college president; experience in academic administration is most common prior to assuming the first presidency; and current presidents are more involved with the sponsorship of in-house leadership development programs than their predecessors when they were preparing for the position.

Formal Educational Preparation.   An earned doctorate continues to be the highest degree earned for the majority of community college presidents. Results from this study revealed 87 percent of the survey respondents had either a PhD (43 percent) or an EdD (44 percent), mirroring other survey findings (Weisman and Vaughan, 2006). One noteworthy difference was the percentage of presidents reporting a community college leadership emphasis as their major field of study in the highest degree earned. Results from this study revealed that 38 percent of the current presidents earned their doctorates in higher education with a community college leadership emphasis, in contrast to findings from Amey and VanDerLinden (2002) that found less than 2 percent of presidents specifying a degree with emphasis on community college administration.

Position Prior to the First Presidency.   Of the 415 current community college presidents responding to the study survey, 47 percent had traveled to the CEO position through an academic pathway, and 11 percent had held a provost position prior to assuming their first presidency. Twenty-four percent had held a position in central office administration; examples of these latter positions would include directors, vice presidents and chancellors of personnel, business, administration, development, legal affairs, institutional planning, physical plant operations, and chief financial officers. Eight percent of respondents reported having been involved with student affairs. Although the trajectory to the position of president is diversified, the most popular path leading to the presidency continues to be through prior experience in the academic ranks. This finding would suggest that finding individuals who know and understand the concerns of the faculty remains a primary concern when institutions find themselves searching for a new institutional leader.

Leadership Preparation Programs Outside of Formal Education.   More than half (57 percent) of the survey respondents indicated they had participated in leadership development programs prior to assuming the first presidency. These programs included a variety of institutes, academies, and seminars. For example, presidents indicated they had participated in programs sponsored by the AACC, the American Council for Education, Association of Community College Trustees, Harvard University, Iowa State University, the League for Innovation, W. K. Kellogg Foundation, and numerous other state and private organizations. Nearly two out of five respondents reported having participated in similar programs after assuming their first presidencies. This finding would suggest that whether presidents take the opportunity to participate in leadership programs before or after they begin the job, these programs address an obvious need for training beyond the scope of what is made available through formalized education programs and background experiences.

Grow-Your-Own Leadership (GYOL) Programs. One solution designed in response to the community college leadership crisis has been the creation of in-house staff development programs. In a recent study, Wesiman and Vaughan (2006) found that 43 percent of current presidents sponsor a GYOL program on their campuses. Based on the survey results reported from the Duree (2007) study, however, only one out of ten current community college presidents participated in a GYOL program prior to their first presidency. Even though the study presidents had not participated in a GYOL program, 44 percent have helped orchestrate GYOL initiatives on their present campuses. Indeed, this finding suggests that current community college leaders are beginning to acknowledge and address succession planning in order to start filling the leadership pipeline with a strong pool of candidates who will be qualified to replace positions left vacant as a result of the forthcoming retirements.

Mentor–Protégé Relationships. According to the survey results, approximately half of all current community college leaders participated in a mentor–protégé relationship as a protégé before assuming their first roles as presidents. More important, in the context of preparing future leaders for the presidency in the new millennium, more than 85 percent are now participating in either a formal or informal mentor–protégé relationship as a mentor. Studies have suggested that mentoring may have significant impact on the learning process (VanDerLinden, 2005) and contribute to the complexities of cognitive leadership development for the next generation of community college presidents. Findings from this study would strongly suggest that current community college presidents have embraced the concept of mentorship on their campuses by the employment of both formal and informal approaches to building the mentor–protégé relationship.

Challenges in the New Millennium

When asked to identify the most challenging issues confronting their institutions at present time, the five most challenging issues for community college presidents, ranked in order of the importance, were fundraising, student enrollment and retention, legislative advocacy, economic and workforce development, and faculty relations.

The issues identified by the study participants resonate with other study findings. Vaughan and Weisman (1998) reported six major issues identified from the results of a survey of community college presidents conducted in 1996, including funding, technology, leadership and governance, interacting with change, accountability and mission, and workforce development. Amey and VanDerLinden (2002) differentiated between external and internal issues. Their findings revealed state financial support for programs and teaching, linkages with business and industry, and meeting community needs were the top three external issues facing community college leaders. Student retention, creation of new program delivery systems, and student recruitment and marketing were consistently noted as the top three internal issues.

Leaders in the new century must have the skill set to competently face issues related to funding, governance, economic and workforce development, and legislative advocacy. As if these expectations were not enough, findings from the responses of current community college presidents indicate that institutional leaders must also be able to provide the leadership necessary to foster and support new initiatives that have become pervasive issues of conversation such as the focus on the community college completion agenda and student success and completion agenda.

Those who have broad oversight of formal leadership development programs are advised to review the expected learner outcomes of the curricula to ensure participants are building a strong foundation of competencies designed to tackle these challenges in the field. Additionally, the findings from this study strongly suggest that current presidents should consider intentionally developing these types of skills in protégés. By gaining awareness prior to moving up into a presidential position, individuals can be deliberate in their search for professional growth opportunities that develop the competencies necessary to effectively confront the challenges that await them.

Since very few presidents actually hold doctorates with a concentration on community college leadership, and given the anticipated number of presidents beginning their exodus from the field, university-based programs will continue to play a critical part in the development of successful transformational leaders in the new millennium. Furthermore, it would seem rather clear that programs delivering curricula embedded with the essential characteristics and competencies identified by the AACC will be best suited to meet the charge coming as a result of a leadership crisis expected to last several more years.

The evolution of the modern-day community college has required generations of leaders to evolve as well. As community colleges and leadership roles become more complex, perceptions of issues and challenges may differ between chancellors and presidents. Critically examining these differences may influence leadership development and preparation needs.

The AACC and college/university preparation programs need to identify new and leading-edge training resources to provide the best background in the competency skill sets. Helping future leaders to chart the most effective pathway in preparation for the job is the responsibility of current presidents, mentors, researchers, and thought leaders.

Ultimately, both current and future leaders must be prepared to fit the identified needs and culture of the organizations in which they find themselves. At the time of this writing, there is discussion within the AACC that the competencies need to be revisited and revised to serve as a tool for those preparing for the presidency. As the blueprint for the community college of the future unfolds (AACC, 2012), the identification of new leadership competencies for the next decade will undoubtedly emerge.

Even with the heavy burden of many responsibilities on the shoulders of the CEO, this period in community college history can only be viewed as a very exciting time to be involved with higher education. Challenging oneself to advance one's skills using these frameworks to make a positive difference in the lives of people who would not otherwise have access to higher education will undoubtedly continue to be the driving motivation of the community college president in the new millennium.

Individuals interested in advancing in leadership positions should consider the following points:

- Completing the doctoral degree prior to assuming a presidency.
- Holding academic leadership positions within the community college setting.
- Participating in institutional, regional, or national leadership development programs.
- Working with a mentor to guide progress along the leadership pipeline.
- Gaining experience in fund development and fundraising prior to assuming a presidency.
- Honing communication and relationship-building skills to effectively navigate legislative advocacy, board of trustee relationships, and building of workforce development partnerships.
- Understanding how to use data to document student learning progress and completion and to use data for organizational decision making.

References

American Association of Community Colleges. *Competencies for Community College Leaders*, 2005. Washington, D.C.: American Association of Community Colleges.

American Association of Community Colleges. *The AACC 21st-Century Initiative: A Future Vision for Community Colleges*. Washington, D.C.: American Association of Community Colleges, 2012. Retrieved February 3, 2012, from www.aacc.nche.edu/Pages/default.aspx

Amey, M. J. "Editor's Notes." *Community College Journal of Research and Practice*, 2005, 29(9–10), 683–688.

Amey, M. J., and VanDerLinden, K. E. *Career Paths for Community College Leaders*. Research Brief Leadership Series, No. 2, AACC-RB-02-2. Washington, D.C.: American Association of Community Colleges, 2002.

Duree, C. A. "The Challenges of the Community College Presidency in the New Millennium: Pathways, Preparation, Competencies, and Leadership Programs Needed to Survive." Doctoral dissertation, Iowa State University, 2007.

Eddy, P. L. "Framing the Role of Leader: How Community College Presidents Construct Their Leadership." *Community College Journal of Research and Practice*, 2005, 29, 705–727. doi: 10.1080/10668920591006557

Eddy, P. L. *Community College Leadership: A Multidimensional Model for Leading Change.* Sterling, Va.: Stylus Publishing, 2010.

Goff, D. G. *What Do We Know About Good Community College Leaders: A Study in Leadership Trait Theory and Behavioral Leadership Theory.* Report No. JC 030 281, 2003. Tampa, Fla.: Hillsborough Community College. (ED476456)

Hassan, A. M., Dellow, D. A., and Jackson, R. J. "The AACC Leadership Competencies: Parallel Views From the Top." *Community College Journal of Research and Practice*, 2010, 34(1), 180–198. doi: 10.1080/10668920903388172

Levin, J. S. "Presidential Influence, Leadership Succession, and Multiple Interpretations of Organizational Change. *Review of Higher Education*, 1998, 21(4), 405–425.

McNair, D. E., Duree, C. A., and Ebbers, L. "If I Knew Then What I Know Now: Using the Leadership Competencies Developed by the American Association of Community Colleges to Prepare Community College Presidents." *Community College Review*, 2011, 39(1), 3–25.

Rendon, L. I. "Toward a New Vision of the Multicultural Community College for the Next Century." In K. M. Shaw, J. R. Valadez, and R. A. Rhoads (eds.), *Community Colleges as Cultural Texts: Qualitative Explorations of Organizational and Student Culture*, 1999, 195–204.

Roueche, J. E., Baker, G. A., and Rose, R. R. *Shared Vision Transformational Leadership in American Community Colleges.* Washington, D.C.: Community College Press, 1989.

Trujillo, A., and Diaz, E. "Be a Name, Not a Number." In K. M. Shaw, J. R. Valadez, and R. A. Rhoads (eds.), *Community Colleges as Cultural Texts: Qualitative Explorations of Organizational and Student Culture* (pp. 125–151). Albany: State University of New York Press, 1999.

VanDerLinden, K. E. "Learning to Play the Game: Professional Development and Mentoring." *Community College Journal of Research and Practice,* 2005, 29(9–10), 729–743.

Vaughan, G. B., and Weisman, I. M. *The Community College Presidency at the Millennium.* Washington, D.C.: Community College Press, 1998.

Weisman, I. M., and Vaughan, G. B. "A Profile of Community College Presidents." [Special issue] *Chronicle of Higher Education*, Oct. 27, 2006, B16.

CHRIS DUREE *is chancellor of the Iowa Valley Community College District.*

LARRY EBBERS *is university professor of higher education in the Department of Educational Leadership and Policy Studies at Iowa State University.*

NEW DIRECTIONS FOR COMMUNITY COLLEGES • DOI: 10.1002/cc

5

Although many of the issues facing community colleges are similar, rural community colleges face additional leadership challenges due to limited resources, geographic isolation, and static economies. This chapter focuses on the impact of location on the interpretation and development of the leadership competencies. The chapter concludes with suggestions for developing leaders in the heartland.

Competencies in the Heartland

Brent Cejda

In a 2007 volume of the *New Directions for Community Colleges* series that focused on issues facing rural areas, Fluharty and Scaggs (2007) stressed that rural community colleges are directly linked to the rural communities that they serve. Although all community colleges share the mission of serving their communities, rural community colleges often act as community and cultural centers for their service areas and are among the largest employers in their regions. Rural America can be described as large in size and small in population, representing 85 percent of the geography of the United States but containing only 15 percent of the population (Miller and Kissinger, 2007). Rural community colleges follow this pattern to a lesser extent, representing 59 percent of all community college campuses but enrolling only 34 percent of community college students (Hardy and Katsinas, 2007). Clearly, differences exist between rural community colleges and their suburban and urban counterparts.

The purpose of this chapter is to consider the American Association of Community Colleges (AACC) leadership competencies in light of the rural context. The chapter begins with an overview of rural America and rural community colleges. The literature on the impact of location on the interpretation and development of the AACC leadership competencies is reviewed, and the chapter concludes with suggestions for developing leaders in the heartland.

Overview of Rural America

For the purposes of this chapter, counties will be defined as metropolitan or nonmetropolitan. Metropolitan counties are counties with one or more

New Directions for Community Colleges, no. 159, Fall 2012 © 2012 Wiley Periodicals, Inc.
Published online in Wiley Online Library (wileyonlinelibrary.com) • DOI: 10.1002/cc.20026

urbanized areas (a minimum population of 50,000 or more) and outlying counties that are economically connected as measured by work commuting. Nonmetropolitan counties are outside the boundaries of metropolitan areas. Miller (2009) found that, between 2000 and 2007, 85 percent of the counties that lost population were nonmetropolitan counties. This population exodus within rural areas resulted in significant demographic changes. Whites account for the largest racial and ethnic category in rural areas of the United States, but rural areas now have more Hispanics and African Americans moving in. Rural America is also aging. The median age of nonmetropolitan residents is greater than metropolitan residents, and nonmetropolitan areas have a greater percentage of population aged 65 and over (Miller, 2009).

A rural–nonrural gap in educational attainment continues to exist in our country, especially with respect to postsecondary enrollment and attainment. Younger adults in rural areas are less likely than their counterparts in nonrural areas to attend college and thus earn a college degree (Gibbs, 2003). In 1970, 5 percentage points separated the most and least educated regions in the United States, but that gap had grown to 13 percent in 2000. The Northeast region of the United States, with greater percentages of metropolitan areas, has the highest level of educational attainment, and the Southern region, with greater percentages of nonmetropolitan areas, has the lowest level of attainment.

Rural regions have had higher rates of poverty compared to urban areas since the 1960s, the first time that poverty rates were recorded. In the past thirty years there has been a decrease in the gap between nonmetropolitan and metropolitan poverty rates. It is important to note, however, the persistence of poverty in rural America. Counties are defined as persistently poor if, over the past thirty years, 20 percent or more of the population meets the definition of poverty. In 2000, the most recent year that county-level data are available, 88 percent (340 of 386) of the persistent poverty counties in the United States were nonmetropolitan counties.

Overview of Rural Community Colleges

Rural community colleges represent 59 percent of all community college campuses and enroll 34 percent of community college students (Hardy and Katsinas, 2007). Almost three-fourths (72 percent) of rural community colleges are located in the regions served by the north central and southern regional accrediting agencies (Hardy and Katsinas, 2007). In comparison to their urban and suburban counterparts, rural community colleges serve broader geographic areas (Green, 2003) and are more likely to include an intercollegiate athletic program (Casteneda, 2004) and provide on-campus housing (Moeck, Hardy, Katsinas, and Leech, 2007).

Using data from 2000–2001, Hardy and Katsinas (2007) provide the most comprehensive comparison between students that attend rural, suburban, and urban community colleges. Rural community colleges have average enrollments that are lower than suburban and urban community colleges; 2,100, 5,433, and 6,288, respectively. The pattern of enrollment is also different among these institutions, as larger percentages of full-time enrollment are found in rural (41 percent) relative to suburban (32 percent) or urban (31 percent) community colleges. Although the male–female ratio of students is similar across rural, urban, and suburban community colleges, there are significant differences in the race and ethnicity of students. White students comprise 45 percent of urban, 54 percent of suburban, and 74 percent of rural community college enrollments.

Challenges Facing Rural Community College Leaders

The literature identifies a number of issues facing rural community colleges. The lack of economies of scale is a substantial challenge to these colleges, especially in regard to the comprehensiveness of curricular offerings. There is consensus that rural community colleges are struggling with the comprehensive mission of community colleges (that is, transfer, vocational, continuing and professional education, developmental), especially in providing higher-cost vocational programs at institutions with smaller enrollments (Hardy and Katsinas, 2007).

The aforementioned connection between the rural community college and its communities also presents challenges. Miller and Kissinger (2007) stressed that rural community colleges often serve as the cultural and community center for their communities. Fluharty and Scaggs (2007) emphasized that place-based community and economic development activities are not funded in a programmatic fashion similar to more traditional credit-generating programming. As a result, community and economic development has not been included in state plans, and the limited funding that has been allocated is unstable. In a survey of approximately 300 rural-serving community colleges, Green (2003) found that slightly more than one-half (51 percent) reported that their campus delivered a business service project during the 2000–2001 academic year. These services included strategic planning, assessment of worker skills, and leadership training. Although most of these services were not large scale, the community colleges offering these programs received no funding to provide the services.

These challenges are not new. Almost 20 years ago the Commission on Small/Rural Community Colleges (1992) identified inadequate funding and maintaining curriculum breadth as primary challenges facing rural community colleges. In describing challenges facing the leadership of rural community colleges, Cohen and Brawer (2008) stress institutional contexts that included fewer resources with greater economic constraints, fewer faculty to uphold the same mission as larger colleges situated in urban environments, and greater demands to aid community and economic development.

NEW DIRECTIONS FOR COMMUNITY COLLEGES • DOI: 10.1002/cc

Rural Community Colleges and the AACC Leadership Competencies

There is not yet a significant body of research that has examined the AACC competencies from the perspective of rural community college leaders. Eddy (in press) found that certain competencies are most often enacted in rural areas, namely, advocacy, collaboration, and communication. Although these competency areas were identified as critical, the authors were not able to identify how they developed skills and abilities in these areas. More general evidence in the literature points to the relationship between the competencies and effective community college leadership without regard for location.

Kools's (2010) dissertation study considered the views of presidents from small, single-campus rural community colleges and large, multicampus urban community colleges. He questioned whether a difference would exist in the perceptions of leaders regarding the importance of the competencies in these different settings. The findings reveal that both rural and urban presidents considered each of the six core competencies to be either very important or extremely important to effective community college leadership. To analyze differences in perceptions, Kools developed a survey that included the forty-five dimensions that are subcomponents of the six core competencies. Statistically significant difference between the rural and urban respondents was found between only two of the dimensions. The first dimension with significant difference based on college location is from the organizational strategy competency: Use a systems perspective to assess and respond to the culture of the organization, to changing demographics, and to economic, political, and public health needs of students and the community. The second dimension with significant difference was from the professionalism competency: Manage stress through self-care, balance, adaptability, flexibility, and humor. In both instances participants from urban institutions rated the dimension significantly higher than their rural counterparts. In terms of the first significant difference, Kools suggested that the size of the organizations, the greater population of students, and greater diversity at urban community colleges could serve as explanations for the greater emphasis among urban participants.

Kools (2010) turned to the qualitative portion of the study to address the second significant difference, positing that leaders of urban, multicampus settings expressed a greater amount of stress, as well as a greater need for multitasking skills and flexibility, than did their rural counterparts. There were differences, however, between the ratings of "very important" and "extremely important." When considering the combined mean scores, rural community college leaders perceived community college advocacy and resource management to be of greater importance than did their urban counterparts.

NEW DIRECTIONS FOR COMMUNITY COLLEGES • DOI: 10.1002/cc

Relationship of Other Literature to the AACC Competencies

Leist (2007) questioned whether different geographic locations require professional qualities markedly different from one another. From the responses of fifteen rural community college presidents who were identified as exemplary leaders by their peers, he found that the expectations of external constituencies in a rural setting required a president to possess three special traits and characteristics: situational awareness, telling the story, and rural roots. Leist described these traits and characteristics as understanding and then assimilating into the local culture, understanding the rural belief system, advocating for the traditions that distinguish the quality of life in rural settings, exposure to or understanding of rural life and the challenges facing rural America, and support in sustaining and improving the community through the activities of the community college. These traits and characteristics could easily serve as descriptors for the organizational strategy, communication, and professionalism competencies. Because of the relationship between rural community colleges and their communities, the importance of advocating for and supporting rural life could also be viewed within the resource management and community college advocacy competencies.

Eddy (2007) found that rural community college leadership required a high level of cooperation and that rural presidents spent a considerable amount of time building and maintaining relationships. Michael Chipps, president of Mid Plains Community College in Nebraska, concurred. He stressed that the multiple communities that his institution served required careful attention to cooperation and collaboration between multiple entities and indicated that he spent a considerable amount of time on relationship development. Although not grounded in examinations of the AACC competencies, both of these sources point to the collaboration competency.

Developing Leadership Competencies in the Heartland

Although limited in scope, research supports the AACC competencies as a foundation to prepare leaders for rural community colleges. Yet, we must recognize that different situations and environments might emphasize certain competencies or the dimensions that form these competencies. A one-size-fits-all philosophy to leadership development is inappropriate.

There is consensus that leadership competencies are acquired through multiple paths that include on-the-job experiences, doctoral education, mentoring and networking, and both formal and informal professional development experiences (Amey and VanDerLinden, 2002). Formal professional development programs, including grow-your-own leadership programs as well as state and national programs provide opportunities for aspiring leaders to develop skills and network with other community college professionals. Mentoring and doctoral studies are an additional means to develop leadership competencies. Two studies have indicated, however, that rural community college leaders had not utilized these multiple paths of professional development.

Kools (2010) asked participants to identify the leadership development experiences that were most beneficial in the development of the AACC competencies. Among the respondents from rural community colleges, the four experiences with the highest frequency of response were (1) challenging job assignments (12 percent), (2) progressive administrative responsibilities within the community college (11 percent), (3) networking with colleagues (10 percent), and (4) graduate programs (9 percent). Eddy (forthcoming) found that rural community college leaders did not reference training as the means for developing competencies but pointed to previous job experiences and, in the case of advocacy, previous familiarity with the rural environment.

Rural community colleges are smaller-sized institutions, in terms of the number of students, faculty, and administrators. The sheer lack of numbers of professional staff needs to be considered when suggesting strategies to develop leaders for rural community colleges. For example, Eddy (2007) noted that peer networks are often smaller in rural settings and found that new community college leaders relied heavily on previous experiences in leading in their new environments. This supports the findings of Kools (2010) regarding the importance of challenging job assignments and progressive administrative responsibilities as experiences that were perceived as beneficial in developing the AACC competencies among rural community college presidents. These examples point to the importance of the institution and current administrators in identifying potential leaders.

Not all individuals aspire to become leaders and often seek leadership positions only as a result of being mentored or identified by someone in a higher-level position. A number of studies have concluded that community colleges constitute an occupational internal labor market (OILM), in which careers exist among firms or organizations that are similar in nature (Amey, VanDerLinden, and Brown, 2002). Geographic boundaries have created OILMs within the community college labor market. Two studies have demonstrated that more than the majority of job movements among community college administrators occurred within the same state, moved to a neighboring state, or moved within the same geographic region (Cejda and McKenney, 2000; Clark, Twombly, and Moore, 1990). There is also limited evidence that rural community colleges can comprise either an OILM or a firm internal labor market, where individuals move to increasing levels of responsibility in the same organization (Allen and Cejda, 2007). In a study of rural community college presidents and vice presidents/deans of instruction, Eddy (forthcoming) found that a greater number of participants were promoted from within the organization in comparison to national norms. Strategies to identify and encourage individuals at the local level to apply to leadership vacancies may well serve rural community colleges that are strategically planning for leadership succession.

NEW DIRECTIONS FOR COMMUNITY COLLEGES • DOI: 10.1002/cc

Geographic distance must also be considered in terms of the use of graduate programs and professional development activities as a way to develop leaders. Sitting presidents have indicated the regret that they did not complete the doctorate prior to assuming office (McNair, Duree, and Ebbers, 2011); thus, rural community colleges and the university preparation programs that serve community colleges need to provide access to and support for the completion of doctoral study. Technology and social networking are strategies that have been used to support new K–12 principals in rural states (see the new principals program coordinated by the Nebraska Council of School Administrators at www.ncsa.org/ for an example) and may also prove effective in facilitating leadership development for rural community colleges.

Economy of scale is an additional reason to suggest regional professional development offerings and the use of technology in developing leaders. The board of directors of Claremont University's community college leadership development initiative recommended that community colleges adopt a regional approach to draw from a broader pool of potential leaders. The MidSouth Partnership for Rural Community Colleges serves as a specific example of a regional collaboration to develop rural leadership. A number of state systems and community colleges have also developed grow-your-own leadership programs. A recent study of rural community college leaders supports the regional or local approach, as Eddy (forthcoming) found that greater numbers of leaders sought formal training on a state or regional level and only a few participated in nationally recognized programs.

Finally, the rural context and characteristics of rural community colleges described earlier in this chapter must be considered in light of the AACC leadership competencies. Rural America has experienced an outmigration of younger individuals and, in some instances, immigration of more diverse populations. Although recently reduced, both educational and income gaps continue between rural and metropolitan locations. Understanding the rural context in general, and more specifically, recent demographic and economic changes within respective states and service areas are crucial to each of the six leadership competencies identified by the AACC. The broad geographic areas served by rural community colleges, the increased likelihood of on-campus housing and intercollegiate athletic programs, and the enrollment characteristics of greater numbers of full-time students and a lack of diversity are important considerations in the preparation of individuals who will provide leadership in twenty-first-century rural community colleges.

Additional research on the AACC leadership competencies as applied to rural community colleges is warranted. Hardy and Katsinas (2007) point to differences among rural community colleges by the size of the institution (that is, small, medium, or large enrollment). Just as we have discovered differences between rural community colleges and their suburban and urban counterparts, there may be differences among the rural communities as determined by enrollment size. The fact that rural community colleges represent 59 percent of all community colleges and the continued projections for significant numbers of presidential retirements emphasizes the importance of continued attention to the development of leaders for this unique type of community college.

More important, however, is to improve leadership preparation by moving from the general agreement of the desirability and applicability of the AACC leadership competencies to investigations into competency development. University, professional association, state system, and grow-your-own leadership development programs all may hold potential. Eddy (forthcoming) stressed the importance of identifying those competencies that are critical to the rural community college as an initial step in improving the preparation of rural community college leaders. It is now time to examine how leaders learn and develop the competencies necessary to provide effective leadership in the heartland.

References

Allen, N., and Cejda, B. D. Career patterns of chief academic officers in rural community colleges. *Community College Journal of Research and Practice,* 2007, *31,* 261–269.

Amey, M. J., VanDerLinden, K. E., and Brown, D. F. "Perspectives on Community College Leadership: Twenty Years in the Making." *Community College Journal of Research and Practice,* 2002, *26,* 573–589.

Casteneda, C. "A National Overview of Intercollegiate Athletics in Public Community Colleges." Unpublished doctoral dissertation, University of North Texas, 2004.

Cejda, B. D., and McKenney, C.B. "Boundaries of an Administrative Labor Market: The Chief Academic Officer in Public Community Colleges." *Community College Journal of Research and Practice,* 2000, *24,* 615–625.

Clark, B. C., Twombly, S. B., and Moore, K. M. "Inter-institutional Job Mobility in Two-Year Colleges and Institutional Characteristics." *Community College Journal of Research and Practice,* 1990, *14,* 371–380.

Cohen, A. M., and Brawer, F. B. *The American Community College* (5th ed.). San Francisco: Jossey-Bass, 2008.

Commission on Small/Rural Community Colleges. *Forgotten Minorities: Rural Americans and the Colleges That Serve Them.* Washington, D.C.: American Association of Community Colleges, 1992. (ED 351 054)

Eddy, P. L. "Grocery Store Politics: Leading the Rural Community College." *Community College Journal of Research and Practice,* 2007, *31,* 271–290.

Eddy, P. L. "Developing Leaders: The Role of Competencies in Rural Community Colleges." *Community College Review,* forthcoming.

Fluharty, C., and Scaggs, B. "The Rural Differential: Bridging the Resource Gap." In P. L. Eddy & J. Murray (eds.), *Rural Community Colleges: Teaching, Learning, and Leading in the Heartland.* New Directions for Community Colleges, no. 137, 19–26). San Francisco: Jossey-Bass, 2007.

Gibbs, R. *Rural Education at a Glance.* Rural Development Research Report Number 98. Washington, D.C.: U.S. Department of Agriculture, Economic Research Service, 2003. Retrieved March 4, 2010, from http://www.ers.usda.gov/publications/rdrr98/rdrr98_lowres.pdf

Green, G. *Community Colleges in Rural America*. Community Economics Newsletter, no 312. Madison, Wis.: University of Wisconsin–Madison/Extension, 2003.

Hardy, D. E., and Katsinas, S. G. "Classifying Community Colleges: How Rural Community Colleges Fit." In P. L. Eddy & J. Murray (eds.), *Rural Community Colleges: Teaching, Learning, and Leading in the Heartland*. New Directions for Community Colleges, no. 137, 5–18. San Francisco: Jossey-Bass, 2007.

Kools, J. M. "Leadership Competencies for College Leaders of Public Small, Rural, Single-Campus and Large, Urban, Multiple-Campus Colleges." Unpublished doctoral dissertation. University of South Florida, 2010.

Leist, J. "'Ruralizing' Presidential Job Advertisements. In P. L. Eddy & J. Murray (eds.), *Rural Community Colleges: Teaching, Learning, and Leading in the Heartland*. New Directions for Community Colleges, no. 137, 35–46. San Francisco: Jossey-Bass, 2007.

McNair, D. E., Duree, C. A., and Ebbers, L. "If I Knew Then What I Know Now: Using the Leadership Competencies Developed by the American Association of Community Colleges to Prepare Community College Presidents." *Community College Review*, 2011, *39*(1), 3–25.

Miller, K. *Demographic and Economic Profile: Nonmetropolitan America*. Columbia, Mo.: Rural Policy Research Institute, 2009.

Miller, M. T., and Kissinger, D. B. "Connecting Rural Community Colleges to Their Communities." In P. L. Eddy & J. Murray (eds.), *Rural Community Colleges: Teaching, Learning, and Leading in the Heartland*. New Directions for Community Colleges, no, 137, 27–35). San Francisco: Jossey-Bass, 2007.

Moeck, P. G., Hardy, D. E., Katsinas, S. G., and Leech, J.M. On-campus housing at rural community colleges. *Community College Journal of Research and Practice*, 2007, *31*, 327–337.

BRENT CEJDA is professor and chair of the Department of Educational Administration at the University of Nebraska–Lincoln.

6

This chapter explores the relationship between leadership style, ethical orientation, and the AACC competencies. A glimpse of the competencies in practices is provided through the results of interviews with thirteen community college presidents. The findings presented here are culled from a larger study of presidential decision making during difficult times (Garza Mitchell and Hornak, 2010; Hornak and Garza Mitchell, 2010) that was funded by a Faculty Research and Creative Endeavors grant from Central Michigan University.

Doing the Right Thing: Ethical Leadership and Decision Making

Regina L. Garza Mitchell

A popular approach to leadership holds that "Managers are people who do things right and leaders are people who do the right thing" (Bennis and Nanus, 2003, p. 20). The American Association of Community Colleges' (AACC) *Competencies for Community Colleges Leaders* (2005) also took the approach about leaders doing the right thing. For example, the competencies note: "Take an entrepreneurial stance in seeking ethical alternative funding sources" (p. 4); "Respond responsibly and tactfully" (p. 5); "Use influence and power wisely" (p. 6). These guidelines echo current leadership literature that encourages leaders to be ethical and to "do the right thing." However, the definition of the "right thing" varies depending on an individual's ethical approach. While leaders are expected to be familiar with and apply the ethics of the profession, the interpretation of those principles in practice is heavily influenced by a person's personal code of ethics.

In this chapter, *ethics* refers to the moral principles that govern an individual's behavior. These principles are developed throughout a person's life and influence their schema (Harris, 1994), which ultimately impacts leadership style (Eddy, 2010). Researchers have indicated linkages between ethical perspective and leadership style (for example, Groves and Larocca, 2011; Kanungo, 2001; Preskill and Brookfield, 2009). Thus, it is possible to have two leaders who "do the right thing" but who make different decisions on an issue based on their individual ethical perspectives. This chapter examines how ethical perspectives affect leadership and decision making of community college presidents.

New Directions for Community Colleges, no. 159, Fall 2012 © 2012 Wiley Periodicals, Inc.
Published online in Wiley Online Library (wileyonlinelibrary.com) • DOI: 10.1002/cc.20027

63

Ethics, Leadership, and Decision Making

The current climate faced by community college leaders is rife with financial constraints, increased expectations from stakeholders, and governmental mandates. Where once it was assumed that community colleges and their communities would interact in a demand–response scenario (Gumport, 2003), increasingly limited resources have resulted in college leaders being more selective in their responses to stakeholder needs. The types of decisions faced by leaders today require a delicate balance of stakeholder need versus college resources, mission, vision, and values. The manner in which presidents share information with others inside and outside the organization, frame the information that is shared, and interpret the college mission and their own role as leader all stem from one's ethical perspective. These leadership attributes align with several of the AACC competencies, including organizational strategy, resource management, communication, and collaboration. Thus, interpretation of the "right thing" by leaders is key to a college's survival and growth.

Theoretically, institutional decision making and leadership are conducted in conjunction with the college's mission and values. Much is dependent, however, on how a leader interprets the mission and values and the importance of multiple mission components. Decision making is highly influenced by a leader's cognitive schema, which is itself based on an individual's personal values system (Eddy, 2010; Harris, 1994). A president's leadership style is grounded within her or his own core values and beliefs, which guide decisions made in regard to organizational and external constituencies' needs and demands. Institutional decisions made during tough times are more likely to be made at the top ranks (Leslie and Fretwell, 1996) and are therefore more likely to reflect the leader's personal belief structure.

Additionally, leadership styles have been linked to ethical perspectives. Starratt (2005) proposed five domains of ethical responsibility that are central to educational leadership: responsibility as a human being, as a citizen and public servant, as an educator, as an educational administrator, and as an educational leader. Each domain has its own key elements that link leadership with ethical values related to the common good rather than individual gain. In describing their idea of learning as a way of leading, Preskill and Brookfield (2009) stated that their view of leadership encourages change for social good and that the "underlying ethic of leadership is change for a more humane and just world" (p. 3). A recent study (Groves and LaRocca, 2011) tested the often-espoused theory that particular leadership styles correspond to particular ethical perspectives. Results of the study supported the notion that deontological ethical values such as altruism, universal rights, and Kantian principles were strongly associated with transformational leadership, while teleological ethical values such as act and rule utilitarianism were associated with transactional leadership.

NEW DIRECTIONS FOR COMMUNITY COLLEGES • DOI: 10.1002/cc

Essentially, the findings from this study illustrated that transformational leadership was associated with moral reasoning that considered "universal principles rather than self-interest or adherence to rules and laws" (Groves and LaRocca, 2001, p. 524). This perspective of focus on group benefits supports the link between transformational leadership and an ethical orientation that leans toward social rather than individual good.

Current leadership literature tends to be linked to deontological ethical values, as the majority of leadership emphasizes collaboration and the social good. However, traditional notions of leadership that tend to be more authoritarian and transactional are still upheld as good models. The ethical values expressed by these forms of leadership tend to focus more on rules and the organization than the individuals within the institution or the external community. This is not a judgment on either type of leadership, but it is important for leaders themselves to be aware of the ethical underpinnings of their own leadership styles, particularly during times of great change, so that they can explain their decisions to stakeholders and so that they better realize why they make the decisions that they do.

Competencies in Practice

Data reported in this chapter were culled from interviews with thirteen community college presidents in one Midwestern state. The state was selected because it had a declining economy, high unemployment rate, and no statewide system of higher education. Thus, presidents of these colleges had great latitude in decision making. Presidents who participated in the study were selected using a purposeful sampling approach in an attempt to gain participation from the greatest variety of institutional type and size. The presidents in this study (eleven men and two women) represented a range of colleges, including tribal, very small rural, very large suburban, and multicampus urban institutions. Their number of years as president and years in current position also varied greatly; at the time of the interviews, four participants had been in their first presidency for less than three years and one was in the first year of his first presidency. Eleven held a terminal degree. Table 6.1 highlights characteristics of the presidents who participated in this study. Interview transcripts were coded for themes, and the results are presented here to highlight several of the AACC competencies. While not all of the presidential participants are directly quoted in this chapter, the quotes provided reflect the overarching themes that emerged from data analysis.

Balancing Resources, Values, and Mission.   All presidents in the study cited resource management as the most critical area of decision making. All colleges had experienced steady growth in the number of students and credit hours, so presidents faced decisions regarding how to shift resources, which programs to grow or cut, and what new programmatic areas should be explored. Not all colleges had experienced significant

Table 6.1.   Participant Characteristics

	Gender	Years in Office	Highest Degree	Institution Type
1	M	10	Doctorate	Large Suburban
2	M	6	Doctorate	Medium Rural
3	M	1*	Master's	Small Rural
4	M	9	Doctorate	Large Rural
5	M	2	Doctorate	Very Large Rural
6	M	1.5	Doctorate	Large Urban
7	F	9	Doctorate	Medium Rural
8	M	<1*	Doctorate	Medium Urban
9	M	11	Doctorate	Large Urban
10	M	9	Doctorate	Large Rural
11	M	2*	Doctorate	Very Large Suburban
12	M	6	Doctorate	Very Small Tribal
13	F	2*	Master's	Medium Rural

* In first presidency for less than 3 years at time of study.

funding cuts from state or local sources at the time of the interview, but all presidents expected that they would face severe cuts in state-level funding within a period of one to three years.

Several participants mentioned developmental education as a particular area of concern because of its high cost to the college. Richard, the president of a large rural college, discussed some of the issues associated with developmental education at his institution:

> I've got people coming in testing in at fifth-grade math. You know, how do . . . how do I spend money for a fifth-grade-level mathematics? The intensity and dollars I would have to spend with faculty and tutors and mentors and all that to get a fifth grader or fourth grader in math up to collegiate-level ready takes more time and effort than one faculty member speaking to a classroom of thirty math students, so dollar for dollar, I'm better off going with the masses. So at what point do the needs of the many outweigh the needs of the few? . . . Those are the difficult choices that I'm having to make and I don't like them. And they wake me up at three o'clock in the morning.

Richard believed that developmental education was necessary for the students served by the college, but the choice to continue remediation at current levels required more resources than the college had to spare. In this president's view, his mission was "serving other people," and he was ethically obligated to do so, but there was great concern about how to continue doing so.

Alfonso, the president of a medium rural college, had a similar outlook in which being ethical meant serving those in the greatest need. Rather than looking at return on investment (ROI) in terms of money, his focus was "What's the return to the individual that we're investing in?":

I think we have a social responsibility to those who are underrepresented and the programming we offer to make this a more attractive place for [them] because in some instances they're not represented proportionally, and so it's not a very attractive place. So that comes more out of probably my bias than it does any kind of, you probably wouldn't necessarily find something like that in the institutional mission statement.

Alfonso felt that the greater good lay in assisting developmental students as opposed to honor students because they received the greatest ROI. "I suspect the honors students have other options. . . . It's not essential programming. [The college] wouldn't like to hear me say that, but . . ."

Kevin, the president of a large suburban institution, viewed ROI from a strictly financial perspective. His decision-making process focused purely on resources:

In the end, you have to, again, not a popular thing to say, but you have to make money. You know, people do expect to be paid and so, if it doesn't make money in and of itself or have value to the totality of your operation, because some things lose money, obviously . . . then you shouldn't be doing it.

In Kevin's view, developmental education was not a purview of the college and was not a good ROI. Likewise, Philip, who ran a very large urban college, felt that ROI was important, as was providing a quality education. In discussing potential budget cuts, he explained:

And, if it gets down to, well, it's about a student being in the classroom taking the curriculum. And everything else is incidental. You can let a lot of people go. Keep my financial aid folks around, keep my admission folks around, keep my registrar around, keep my accounting people here, my HR people, but Student Affairs and everything you do, we don't need you. Developmental support programs, mentoring programs, tutoring programs, labs, we don't need you. I mean, well, yeah, we kind of need that, but we can still, well . . . wait a minute, we're helping them outside of the classroom, so how, you know, how are you going to set criteria to make those decisions. I'd rather just say let's learn to live with what we have to work with and continue to offer quality.

In contrast, Chuck, the president of a large urban college, viewed ROI from a financial perspective but did his best to balance that with the needs of the students. Chuck also had a financial perspective in regard to ROI, but he felt that the college had other obligations that trumped financial returns. "We have a large developmental program," he stated. "I can't imagine any community college abandoning their developmental program, because so many students come to us and need to improve their English language skills or their writing skills or math skills." His college had cut some developmental education offerings, yet he looked for innovative solutions to the issue such as providing free classroom space for a local literacy foundation in exchange for free one-on-one tutoring with students.

As evidenced from the preceding examples, the presidents in this study were astute in the areas of organizational strategy, resource management, and community college advocacy. However, each president approached these areas from a slightly different ethical orientation, placing different levels of importance on the college's social responsibility and what it meant to equitably and ethically sustain his or her college.

Planning and Collaboration.   Each college in the study was required by its accrediting agency to have a strategic plan on file. The extent to which the plan was used, how it was developed, and how it was shared with the rest of the college provided insight into the competencies of organizational strategy and communication. Chuck, who had been in office for eleven years, noted that his college did not have an official strategic plan until the Higher Learning Commission mandated it. At that point, he relabeled the college's goal statement as a strategic plan and created a ten-year financial plan, five-year facility plan, three-year technology plan, and yearly unit goals. Chuck then created four to five strategic goals and included them in the financial plan.

> Basically, it's me. There is not some master plan where we all sit around in a room and put sticky notes on a wall. I have never found that this big huge group hug that people like to think of as strategic planning has ever accomplished anything, so this is what I think we need to do for the next year, and they are usually pretty simple, pretty straightforward.

From Chuck's perspective, decision making was a rational process and was the purview of the president. He felt that the bulk of decisions should be made in regard to what was best for the college (from his perspective) and what would bring the greatest ROI for the college. Thus, strategic planning was guided solely by the president as the only decision maker on key decisions.

At the opposite end of the spectrum was Joseph, who was in his first year of office and was in the process of moving away from a strategic plan and toward a strategic agenda that was developed by representatives from the college and the community. The agenda would identify three to five core values of the college, and all decisions would be determined by how well they fit those values, as the president felt that funding was too uncertain to develop a strategic plan. The strategic agenda would function as "a set of values that you can use to measure your response to the changing environment." Further, Joseph added,

> The strategic agenda is something that you can keep in front of you all the time. The other part is, frankly, and I think many of us in education have

done this, we've participated in strategic plans and have really nice documents that fill spaces on bookcases and we may not look at those very often, so the purpose of the strategic agenda is what we do value.

It was important to Joseph that the college and the community know what was most salient for the college so that their focus could be maintained, even during times of financial strife. It was important that the college maintain values that guided decision making if the budget was unable to continue supporting current activities.

Personal Values.   Each president described how their own personal values affected decision making, and each president held different values. One president, Cathy, who was in the second year of her first presidency, felt that people were the most important element of a college. She shared how this value framed the way she made personnel decisions:

> Another personal value is that in terms of employees I really, really believe that there are very few people in the world that can't do a good job, but I think that they need to be trained or I think that they need to have the job that best fits them. . . . Some of my colleagues who you are going to meet in the very near future just went in and fired half of the place. And, you know, life might be easier that way for some people . . . but, when I know that that person has talents and abilities and is loyal to the institution and all of that, I work really hard to try to keep them here in a place that respects their talents. And that takes time and it takes trust and it sometimes takes some ambiguity where people don't know what I am doing, because you can't go out and discuss people's performance with everybody and announce this is why I am making this decision. So you have to try and maneuver around and around and around until it gets to where the right people are in the right spot doing the right things. And, that's a value I have and I am very glad that the institution wasn't in crisis, that I didn't have to come in and just make wholesale changes.

Similarly, Joseph noted that his decisions were guided by core values:

> My dad once said, "What's right is still right and what's wrong is still wrong." I tend to judge those things that I do by those precepts and then look at what it is that's important to [the college]. What are our values? What's our mission and how do you make decisions that can be consistent with those?

Joseph was in his first year of the presidency but had been with the college for twenty-three years. He chose to lead the college in a manner that directly aligned his personal values with those of an institution that he knew well. Another president, Alfonso, concurred:

> There are times when the competing interests just fly in the face of what makes good business sense or even what makes good sense ethically to do

that, you know; you've got to stand up and say no and take the heat for whatever comes with it.

Each president's personal values and ethical code were integral parts of their college decision making, though some participants described their values more explicitly than others. All presidents talked about the need to lead an institution with similar values, and many provided examples of decisions that keep them up at night, the majority of which involved ethical decisions that adversely affected students, employees, or the community. Leader and institutional fit mattered.

Discussion and Recommendations

Three out of thirteen presidents in this study aligned with a classical, authoritarian style of leadership and decision making in which the president's decision was viewed as best and did not require much, if any, feedback from others. These presidents viewed decision making as a management tool that was a completely rational process and did not involve emotion or collaboration. These presidents felt that they were able to view issues and decisions from a more informed perspective due to their years in office and life experiences; thus, they were comfortable and confident in making those decisions with little to no input from others. Their ethical perspectives aligned with transactional leaders who place high value on rules and exchanges (Groves and LaRocca, 2011). Likewise, those presidents who valued collaboration and social change placed the greatest emphasis on gathering input and ensuring that all voices, particularly those that might be overlooked, were heard prior to decisions being made (Preskill and Brookfield, 2009).

The leadership style and ethical perspective of the presidents in this study greatly influenced how they interpreted various areas of the AACC competencies (2005), the college mission, and their own role as leader. One challenge in determining how leaders enact the competency areas was the vast amount of overlap among the different areas. For example, the area of organizational strategy corresponded with both communication and resource management. Those presidents who led from a teleological/authoritarian perspective tended to place the highest value on financial ROI to the college, whereas those who led from a deontological standpoint placed higher value on the ROI to the neediest students, though they also recognized the need to seek other areas in which to strengthen the college's finances.

Though at times these different ethical perspectives appear to be at odds, with one group placing higher value either on rules and experience and the other favoring broader, humanistic concerns, both sets of leaders can be viewed as making ethical decisions. All presidents noted the importance of making decisions that adhered to the college's mission. However, the mission of the college was viewed and interpreted through the president's personal lens or schema (Harris, 1994).

The AACC competencies (2005) do not state specific preferred ethical values, but they do lean toward more inclusive, collaborative, and entrepreneurial approaches to leadership. However, individual ethical perspectives influence every aspect of leadership, including decision making. A recent study of corporate leadership found that transactional and transformational leaders were driven by divergent ethical values, which also influenced follower attitudes toward corporate social responsibility (Groves and LaRocca, 2011). Thus, the impact on followers must also be considered when evaluating a leader's values. Followers within the college will use those values that are prized and modeled by leaders. The influence of leaders on the organization continues to privilege views of hierarchical leadership despite the ways in which the competencies forefront collaboration.

Conclusion and Implications for Practice

In summary, a leader's ethical perspective and its influence on choices stem from a lifetime of experiences (Eddy, 2010) and are influential in all aspects of leadership and decision making. Ethics influence the behavior of both leaders and followers within an organization, and the intentions behind and implications of personal ethics should be visible. The multiple intersections of ethics, leadership, and decision making should be considered carefully:

- Consideration of how ethical elements are embedded within leadership programs is key to ensuring that future leaders gain the ability to develop and understand their own personal ethical and leadership perspectives. What ethical perspective(s) are promoted? Why? What are the implications in regard to participants' organizational mission, vision, and values? Are leadership programs promoting leadership styles that align with the AACC's (2005) implied values?
- Leaders must take time to step back and reflect on their own personal ethics, consider how those ethics align with their organization and their profession, and identify personal blind spots in regard to decision making.
- How well does a leader's personal ethical perspective align with institutional stakeholders? Will decisions made be viewed as radical or necessary? Leaders must consider how they frame the rationale behind decision making to ensure that others understand the reasoning behind decisions.
- Ethics behind decisions made in regard to resource management must receive particular attention. Rather than bifurcating decisions between human needs or organizational resources, leaders may opt to look for decisions that attempt to balance multiple ethical perspectives.

- Search committees must consider their college's unique needs when evaluating a presidential candidate's ethical and leadership styles. Which style is better suited to helping the college move in the preferred direction?

References

American Association of Community Colleges. *Competencies for Community College Leaders.* Washington, D.C.: American Association of Community Colleges, 2005. Retrieved June 10, 2012, from www.aacc.nche.edu/Resources/competencies/Pages/default.aspx

Bennis, W., and Nanus, B. *Leaders: Strategies for Taking Charge.* New York: Harper Business Essentials, 2003.

Eddy, P. L. Community College Leadership: A Multidimensional Model for Leading Change. Sterling, Va.: Stylus Publishing, 2010.

Garza Mitchell, R. L., and Hornak, A. M. "Difficult Decisions." Research paper presented at the Annual Conference of the Council for the Study of Community Colleges. Seattle, Wa., 2010.

Groves, K. S., and LaRocca, M. A. "An Empirical Study of Leader Ethical Values, Transformational and Transactional Leadership, and Follower Attitudes Toward Corporate Social Responsibility." *Journal of Business Ethics, 103*(4), 2011, 511–528.

Gumport, P. J. "The Demand–Response Scenario: Perspectives of Community College Presidents. *Annals of the American Academy of Political and Social Science,* 2003, *586,* 38–61.

Harris, S. G. "Organizational Culture and Individual Sensemaking: A Schema-Based Perspective." *Organizational Science,* 1994, *5*(3), 309–321.

Hornak, A. M., and Garza Mitchell, R. L. "Community College Leadership: Personal Values and Decision Making." Research paper presented at the Annual Meeting of the Association for the Study of Higher Education, Indianapolis, Ind., 2010.

Kanungo, R. "Ethical Values of Transactional and Transformational Leaders." *Canadian Journal of Administrative Sciences,* 2001, *18,* 257–265.

Leslie, D., and Fretwell, J. *Wise Moves in Hard Times: Creating and Managing Resilient Colleges and Universities.* San Francisco: Jossey-Bass, 1996.

Preskill, S., and Brookfield, S. D. *Learning as a Way of Leading: Lessons From the Struggle for Social Justice.* San Francisco: Jossey-Bass, 2009.

Starratt, R. J. "Responsible Leadership." *Educational Forum,* 2005, *69*(2), 124–133.

REGINA L. GARZA MITCHELL *is an associate vice president for student learning at Texas State Technical College in Harlingen, Texas.*

NEW DIRECTIONS FOR COMMUNITY COLLEGES • DOI: 10.1002/cc

7

This chapter uses a feminist lens to analyze the AACC's
Competencies for Community College Leaders *and*
concludes that the competencies are largely indifferent to
gendered ideologies within leadership.

Reading the Competencies Through a Feminist Lens

Kristin Bailey Wilson, Elizabeth Cox-Brand

In a 2004 article in the *Chronicle of Higher Education*, George Vaughan, a longtime community college advocate, called for greater diversity in community college leadership, seeing diversity as the antidote to inbreeding and the key to higher organizational functioning. The American Council on Education's (2012) newest study on college presidents provides a snapshot of current community college leadership demographics and finds that 33 percent of community colleges are led by women, and 13 percent are leaders of color. At institutions well known for their open access—nearly 60 percent of community college students are women and 45 percent of students are minorities—presidential leadership is still dominated by white men (American Association of Community Colleges [AACC], 2011). Diversity in leadership continues to be an elusive goal for community colleges.

The AACC has been a constant advocate for greater diversity in community college leadership. Along with other work to encourage diversity in leadership, the AACC brought together community college practitioners and scholars to develop a competency framework for community college leadership, *Competencies for Community College Leaders* (2005). The framework was intended to both guide current leaders and aspiring leaders by naming the sorts of abilities, activities, and beliefs central for community college leaders. It offers a somewhat complete description of community college leadership. Part of the motivation for writing the competencies was

NEW DIRECTIONS FOR COMMUNITY COLLEGES, no. 159, Fall 2012 © 2012 Wiley Periodicals, Inc.
Published online in Wiley Online Library (wileyonlinelibrary.com) • DOI: 10.1002/cc.20028

the lack of diversity among leaders and the belief that greater diversity would result in better organizational functioning. The reasoning was that by making obvious what is entailed in effective leadership, women and minorities would be able to seek the sorts of development activities that would make them competitive candidates for leadership positions. In addition, the framework offers a way of assessing current leaders so that beliefs about effectiveness are not tangled with gendered or racial notions of acceptable leadership. We wanted to better understand whether this reasoning was realistic. Could the competencies be an avenue for greater diversity in community college leadership?

In order to study the competencies, we employed discourse analysis because it is premised on the notion that language acts, like the competencies, guide people in shaping their perceptions of what they can do and become. Discourse analysis is also a way to read for predispositions; in this case, that predisposition was an equalitarian understanding of community college leadership using a feminist lens. We asked can or how can the competencies be read as an egalitarian description of community college leadership?

Our work with the competencies was guided by a long tradition of scholarship about community college leadership from a feminist perspective. Townsend and Twombly (2007) termed the majority participation of women faculty and students in community colleges as *accidental,* concluding that community college leadership did not deliberately work to create a culture of equity. Eddy and Cox (2008) noted that female presidents behave in male ways in order to gain support or acceptance as the college leader. One prevalent gendered role for leaders is that of the institutional "hero" or "great man," a status derived from holding a leadership position in an institution (Amey and Twombly, 1992; Eddy and VanDerLinden, 2006).

Recent scholarship has also noted a shift from seeing leadership choices as being gender driven to seeing choices as context or situation driven, meaning that men will use participatory strategies in certain contexts and women will use directive strategies in certain contexts (Eddy and VanDerLinden, 2006). The choice whether to use directive leadership or participatory leadership depends on the context or situation more so than gender.

Methodology and Methods

Operating from a constructionist paradigm, we employed the methods of discourse analysis, which functions on the theoretical assumption that language patterns or discursive practices teach humans about potential social identities and activities—certainly one purpose of the competencies.

Among discursive practices, those that seem natural are dominant discourses; however, dominant discourses produced and maintained in the public sphere can function as a male hegemonic practice. This may be true with community college leadership because so many presidents are white men. One risk with a document like the AACC's *Competencies for Community College Leaders* (2005) is that it may simply reinforce the current dominant discourse. The competencies were produced in a context of male dominance at the presidential level that privileges male norms of leadership.

For our analysis, we combined Gee's (2005) understanding of discourse with Iverson, Allan, and Gordon's (2010) feminist discourse analysis framework. Specifically, Iverson, Allan, and Gordon developed the ideal of discourse that occurs at the intersection between masculine and feminine. For example, the phrase in the competencies of "take an entrepreneurial stance in seeking ethical alternative funding sources" reflects masculine leadership qualities in that entrepreneurial acts are often autonomous and risky, whereas "value and promote diversity, inclusion, equity, and academic excellence" reflects feminine leadership qualities of doing for others. At the intersection of masculine and feminine discourse in the competencies was "facilitate shared problem solving and decision making," which seemed to embrace relational decision making where no individual is solely taking risks or making decisions as an autonomous actor.

We employed several coding and analysis techniques to read the competencies from a feminist lens. First, we discussed how the literature applied to the competencies. Then we each coded the illustrations of the competencies independently. We compared the codes and discussed differences. At times, coding was changed, but we did not seek to code identically. Many differences were left because we felt they illustrated the varied ways feminism can be understood. In general, verbs were the central coding cue, so when a verb indicated a directive or an autonomous action, it was coded as masculine (for example, act, build, solve), whereas when a verb suggested doing for others or supporting others, it was coded as feminine (for example, support, care, empower). At the intersection were verbs that recommended relationships (for example, champion, respond, promote). The differences between our codes and the differences between our ideas about how the competencies might be read led to more formal coding activities using qualitative coding software. We began to look at the parts of speech and how they were grouped together. We asked questions about what kinds of verbs and nouns were employed most often. These activities are described in greater detail below.

Gendered Competencies

Overall, our feminist reading of the competencies yielded five compelling findings: first, they conflate activities and identities in troubling ways; second, they are "contextless" or fail to address context; third, masculine verbs are often combined with feminine or intersection goals or outcomes; fourth, the mixed use of masculine and feminine verbs and adverbs seems to support directive leadership, even while many of the named goals and outcomes are participatory; and, fifth, the competencies are often silent on the role of followers or silent on how leadership behavior influences follower actions.

First, the competencies name six broad areas in which a leader should be competent, including organizational strategy, resource management, communication, collaboration, advocacy, and professionalism. Under each broad category, illustrations describe how the broad competency might be evidenced in a leader. For example, under collaboration, an illustration reads "develop, enhance, and sustain teamwork and cooperation." In other words, the competencies describe activities that leaders engage in and identities that they assume. For example, leaders "maintain open communications" and "maintain high standards of integrity." While the same verb is used for both, having open communications is a leadership choice or a leadership activity. A leader might choose open communications regarding potential curricular changes, while choosing closed communications regarding a disciplinary action for an employee. Given the context, choosing closed communications seems reasonable. By contrast, having high standards of integrity must be embodied; it is a core value. It cannot be chosen in some instances and disregarded in others, suggesting that integrity is more an identity than an activity, but integrity would also be evidenced via activities.

Activities and identities in the competencies seemed conflated, leading to articulated and unarticulated confusion about how to read and apply the competencies. The reader's gender, race, and ideology among other aspects of human identity would influence how the reader understands "open communication" to be evidenced in terms of activities. For example, one leader might view having a budget available when requested from the financial officer as an example of transparency or openness, while another leader might see openness as providing faculty and staff the budget book and working to explain what it means and how budgeting decisions are made as an example of transparency or openness.

Second, even though the competencies name specific activities and identities, they are nonetheless conceptual in that they are without situation or context: "contextless." For example, "Manage conflict and change by building and maintaining productive relationships" makes no reference to the sorts of context-specific conflicts whereby a leader might build a productive relationship. In addition, language choices in the competencies are discordant because the language, particularly verbs, seems to contradict: "make decisions," "facilitate shared problem solving," "employ time management," "convey information succinctly," "listen actively," "respond tactfully," and "embrace diversity." While these activities are not necessarily conflicting, they are potentially conflicting, and with no context it is difficult for a reader to recognize when to apply what activity.

This contextless nature of the language seems to suggest a certain intertextuality; in other words, the competencies appear to allude to a context, the community college context, which readers and users of the competencies will simply know. A leader will know when to make a decision and when to share decision making. We were challenged by this assumption, having brought to the reading a perception that the community college landscape is varied as are the leaders in it. We read the contextless nature of the competencies to be a silence, and with the dominance of white men in presidential positions, it seems to be a gendered hegemonic silence. Because language helps people imagine possible activities and identities, without a context, the competencies are unlikely to spur imagining of leadership roles on the part of minorities and women. These populations will not see their identity (values) and actions represented in them.

The competencies document lists the six main leadership competencies and under each one offers between six to eleven illustrations. These illustrations were coded using a variety of techniques, including each researcher engaged in independent coding. During this phase, Coder 1 tended not to code illustrations of competencies at the intersection (see Table 7.1), while Coder 2 often coded at the intersection. When we summed all the independent coding of illustrations by competency, we found that two competencies were coded primarily masculine (that is, organizational strategy and resource management); one competency was coded primarily feminine (that is, community college advocacy); and no competencies were coded primarily intersection (see Table 7.2). The other three competencies were divided between categories. Neither coder used the feminine code for the resource management illustrations, nor did either coder use the masculine code for the community college advocacy illustra-

Table 7.1.   AACC Competencies Coding by Masculine,
Feminine, and Intersection

Coding	Coder 1	Coder 2
Masculine	52%	29.5%
Feminine	29.5%	29.5%
Intersection	18%	41%

Table 7.2.   Coding by Competency and Masculine, Feminine, and
Intersection

Competency	Masculine	Feminine	Intersection
Organizational strategy	*		
Resource management	*		
Communication	*	*	
Collaboration		*	*
Community college advocacy		*	
Professionalism	*		*

tions. As we worked through this coding and our differing readings of the language, we were struck by the difficulty of attributing language in a clear way to gendered understandings of identities and activities.

Examining this coding led us to the third finding that often the illustrations combined masculine verbs with feminine or intersecting goals. This combination made it more subjective for us to identify the precise code for the text. Take, for example, the phrase "Build and leverage networks and partnerships." While the words *build* and *leverage* seemed masculine, the words *networks* and *partnerships* were generally synonymous with Iverson, Allan, and Gordon's (2010) conceptualization of language at the intersection as *negotiator.* The reader is left with acting like a man to do things like a woman or negotiator.

Because the competencies often combine an initial verb that seems masculine (for example, leverage) with intersection or feminine concepts, verbs, and adverbs (for example, networks), we decided to combine some numerical content analysis with our intuitive coding. Using qualitative coding software, we developed a definitive list of verbs used to describe leaders and leadership in the competencies (see Table 7.3). We coded verbs that seem to be performed autonomously or at others (for example, a directive) as masculine; verbs that seem to be performed for the benefit of others more than the self as feminine; and verbs that seemed to be performed in concert with others as intersection. Our list included fifty-six verbs; eight verbs appeared most frequently (four, five, or six times) in the document: *support(s), promote(s), understand(s), demonstrate, develop, sustain(s), maintain(s),* and *manage.* Taking into account the frequency of use, we calculated the percentage use based on each code: feminine, 28 percent; intersection, 21 percent; and masculine, 51 percent. In addition to the verbs listed above, we considered words that were acting as adverbs. In terms of usage, the adverbs coded intersection represented 31 percent of all usage, with feminine at 31 percent and masculine at 38 percent (see Table 7.4). The pattern that developed in this work was one where half the codes were masculine and half the codes were feminine and intersection. This caused us to wonder whether the intersection code was a distinct category or part of feminine descriptors.

Through this process of considering the verb usage in the competencies, we began to wonder if Iverson, Allan, and Gordon's (2010) third category of intersection made sense to us. Were the codes at the intersection illustrating a unique ideal or a feminist ideal? Our thought was that both doing for and with others embodied feminist ideals. We decided to challenge our initial assumption that coding at the intersection made sense in theoretical terms.

To better understand what we were thinking about coding at the intersection, we looked for language in the competencies around the intersection of negotiator. We identified words like *collaboration, cooperation, dialogue, discussion, empower, exchange, flexibility, inclusion, listen, networks,*

Table 7.3.   Verbs Appearing in the Competencies According to
Feminine, Intersection, and Masculine

Feminine	Intersection	Masculine
Support(s)	Promote(s)	Demonstrate
Understand(s)	Change	Develop(s)
Engage	Contribute	Sustain(s)
Accept	Respond	Maintain(s)
Advocate	Articulate	Manage
Care	Champion	Assess
Commits	Comprehend	Implement
Create	Convey	Improve(s)
Embrace	Disseminate	Plan
Empower	Exchange	Use
Fosters	Model	Work(s)
Listen	Process	Advance
Nurture	Represent	Employ
Protect(s)	Weigh	Ensure
Respect	Enhance	Assess
Learning	Facilitating	Act
Teaching	Influence	Align
	Facilitate	Analyze
		Build
		Catalyze
		Endorse
		Evaluate
		Fulfill
		Grow
		Impact
		Leverage
		Monitor
		Reward
		Solve
		Building
		Ensuring

Table 7.4.   Coding for Adverbs

Intersection	Feminine	Masculine
Ethically	Diplomatically	Strategically
Frequently (communication)	Equitably	Actively
Tactfully	Inclusively	Effectively
	Wisely	Succinctly

nurture, partnerships, relationships, and *shared.* In no instance did we feel the word should be coded as masculine, but in every instance the words seemed to align with our understanding of feminine choices versus seeing them at the intersection.

Once we reconsidered feminine and intersection coding, we concluded that the competencies appear balanced if not tending toward a leadership ethic that is participatory in their use of gendered terms; however, the construction of the illustrations has a masculine tendency in that masculine verbs often begin the illustrations and are combined with feminine nouns, like "build networks." If the assumed reader were operating from a directive view of leadership, "build networks" might feel more comfortable than "nurture professional relationships," yet these phrases are essentially synonymous notions. The first phrase, though, fits with our understanding of masculine leadership, whereas the second fits with our understanding of feminine leadership. Thus, language choice and ordering matters in interpretation and understanding. This led to our fourth finding that the mixed use of masculine and feminine verbs and adverbs leads to a reading of the competencies that seems to support directive leadership, even while many of the named goals and outcomes are participatory.

The final finding is that the competencies are often silent on the question of who should receive the leadership behavior (see Table 7.5). For example, one illustration under Resource Management reads, "Employ organizational, time management, planning, and delegation skills." Whose time should be delegated? When delegating the time of faculty members, a president would likely choose to lead differently than when delegating the time of board members. In order to better understand this finding, we again employed content analysis by looking at the frequency of the use of words

Table 7.5.   Groups or People Named in Competencies

Word	Frequency	Example
Audience	2	"... appropriately matching message to audience."
Board	1	"... as legislators, board members, business leaders, ...
Community	4	"... community members to work for the common good."
Constituencies	2	"... diplomatically with unique constituent groups ..."
Faculty	1	"Catalyze involvement and commitment of students, faculty, staff ..."
Leader(s)	6	"An effective community college leader ..."
Members	2	"... community members to work for the common good."
Others	4	"Support lifelong learning for self and others."
People	2	"... integrity, honest, and respect for people."
Personnel	1	"Maintain and grow college personnel ... resources ..."
Self	4	"Manage stress through self-care ..."
Staff	3	"... professional development and advancement of all staff."
Stakeholders	2	"... and facilitating discussion with all stakeholders."
Student(s)	6	"... promotes the success of all students ..."

NEW DIRECTIONS FOR COMMUNITY COLLEGES • DOI: 10.1002/cc

referring to specific groups or people. We found the words identifying groups often overlap; for example, when *board* was used, so was the word *members*. We took this into consideration. When the word *self* was used, it always referred to the reader of the competencies, and when the word *leader* was used, it generally referred to the reader of the competencies. Again, we took this into consideration. Overall, the named groups are vague or general, like *taxpayers*. In addition, many illustrations mentioned no group, which made the identification of impacted stakeholder an act of intertextual reading. In other words, the reader must bring to the reading act enough contextual knowledge of community college leadership to simply know who the impacted stakeholders might be.

Faculty members, cited by Birnbaum (1992) as the most important constituency group for leaders, are named only once in the competencies. The word *curriculum* is never used in the competencies, and the word *program(s)* is only used twice, both times in reference to student services rather than academic programs. Although a reader might assume that words like *staff, personnel, people, others, constituencies,* and *members* refer to faculty members in a broad sense, the discursive silence occurs when realizing that the various groups referred to by the word *staff* have an enormous variety of functions; therefore, leadership activities relative to the groups will vary greatly, but the competencies are silent on this.

Conclusions

In her book on female sexuality, Luce Irigaray (1985) writes that "sexual indifference . . . underlies the truth of any science, the logic of every discourse" (p. 69). She means this as a condemnation of science and discourse because humans are gendered and cannot escape a gendered reality. The combined findings noted earlier lead us to name the competencies indifferent to feminist ideology. While it is noteworthy that the competencies invoke language that is in keeping with a participatory leadership style, the construction of the illustrations and the silences suggested a type of patriarchal hegemony—an old boy's club.

Further, without a leadership context and language naming the groups receiving the leadership activities, leadership is a "storyless" activity. Work based in feminist theory is characterized by diverse narratives about what it is to be a member of an oppressed population based on the notion that story invites people to articulate self and construct self. So while the competencies might describe the sorts of skills every leader needs, narratives of female and minority leaders engaging those skills in a particular context with a named group will better invite the sort of diversity that Vaughan (2004) says is vital to the ongoing success of democracy's college.

How should individual leaders decode the competencies, particularly women and minorities? For us, it seems important to read the competencies as they are, both "contextless" and "storyless." They describe leadership in terms that are both directive and participatory; they describe skills and knowledge areas needed for leaders. But they cannot replace mentoring and storied descriptions of leaders in the media and in research. Growing leaders at community colleges and leadership programs focused on the community college context will continue to be critical avenues for encouraging participation in leadership by women and minorities.

How might governing boards use the competencies as a resource when seeking to hire women and minorities for leadership positions? In Malcolm Gladwell's (2005) book *Blink: The Power of Thinking Without Thinking*, he describes the use of screens by orchestras during auditions. The screens are used to reduce gender discrimination in auditions. A screen is placed in front of the player so the listener cannot see the gender, race, or age of the player. Because some instruments, like the trombone, are so commonly viewed as masculine, it can be difficult for maestros to hear a female playing the trombone accurately. The screens increase the likelihood that those hired to play will be the most talented. It seems to us that the competencies might serve as something like a metaphoric screen for governing boards. Because the competencies are largely balanced in the use of terms illustrating directive and participatory leadership, they offer a way of seeing leadership talent that is varied. Because they list skills and knowledge areas, they offer a way to read a leader's background without using a gendered lens. Processes that reduce gender bias in hiring will be intentional. It seems unlikely to us that the dominance of white men in presidencies will be changed without intentional actions by governing boards committed to gender and racial equity.

What can scholars do with the competencies to encourage greater participation by minorities and women? More work is needed that delineates between leadership activities and identities (or core values). Identities are illustrated by activities but only through interpretation. This interpretative work is central to leadership activities. Leaders are constantly considering how their activities will be viewed, so much so that choices are sometimes more a reflection of how the leader believes she or he will be perceived than it is a reflection of the leader's values. Greater understanding of how actions demonstrate values is needed. Researchers can also add the context and story to the competencies. How are leaders likely to act when faced with a budget crisis? How is it different than when they are faced with a media crisis? What are the storied understandings of these contexts?

What should the AACC do to make the competencies more useful in recruiting women and minorities to leadership positions? Because the AACC is a large professional organization, it can do more to intentionally capture the stories of leadership, particularly leadership by minorities and women. If there is to be broader participation in leadership by women and minorities then women and minorities need to see and hear themselves in leadership roles.

NEW DIRECTIONS FOR COMMUNITY COLLEGES • DOI: 10.1002/cc

References

American Association of Community Colleges. *Competencies for Community College Leaders*. Washington, D.C.: American Association of Community Colleges, 2005.

American Association of Community Colleges. *2011 Fact Sheet*. Washington, D.C.: American Association of Community Colleges, 2011.

American Council on Education. *The American College President—2012*. Washington, D.C.: American Council on Education, 2012.

Amey, M. J., and Twombly, S. B. "Re-Visioning Leadership in Community Colleges." *Review of Higher Education*, 1992, *15*(2), 125–150.

Birnbaum, R. *How Academic Leadership Works: Understanding Success and Failure in the College Presidency*. San Francisco: Jossey-Bass, 1992.

Eddy, P. L., and Cox, E. M. "Gendered Leadership: An Organizational Perspective. In J. Lester (ed.), *Gendered Perspectives on Community Colleges*. New Directions for Community Colleges, no. 142. San Francisco: Jossey-Bass, 2008.

Eddy, P. L., and VanDerLinden, K. "Emerging Definitions of Leadership in Higher Education: New Visions of Leadership or the Same Old 'Hero' Leaders?" *Community College Review*, 2006, *34*(1), 5–26.

Gee, J. P. *An Introduction to Discourse Analysis: Theory and Method* (2nd ed.). New York: Routledge, 2005.

Gladwell, M. *Blink: The Power of Thinking Without Thinking*. New York: Little, Brown, 2005.

Irigaray, L. *This Sex Which Is Not One*. Ithaca, N.Y.: Cornell University Press, 1985.

Iverson, S. V., Allan, E. J., and Gordon, S. P. "The Discursive Framing of Gendered Images of Leadership in the *Chronicle of Higher Education*." Paper presented at the 2010 ASHE Annual Conference of the Association of the Study of Higher Education, Tampa, Fla., November 2010.

Townsend, B. K., and Twombly, S. B. "Accidental Equity: The Status of Women in the Community College." *Equity & Excellence in Education*, 2007, *40*, 208–217.

Vaughan, G. B. "Diversify the Presidency." *Chronicle of Higher Education*, 2004, *51*(10), B14–B16.

KRISTIN BAILEY WILSON is the chief academic officer at Hopkinsville Community College in Hopkinsville, Kentucky.

ELIZABETH COX-BRAND is the director of communication and research at the Oregon Department of Community Colleges and Workforce Development, Salem, Oregon.

8

Interviews with current community college presidents showcase their reflections on their pathway to the corner office and review the competencies they have found to be the most valuable in their practice. The presidents also offer insights into what they are doing to help prepare future leaders at their institutions.

Reflections From the Field: Voices of Experience

Delores E. McNair, Daniel J. Phelan

To better understand the influence of the American Association of Community Colleges (AACC) competencies on practice since their formation, six community college chief executive officers (five presidents and one chancellor) were asked to reflect upon the enduring relevance of the competencies. They were also asked specifically how they acquired and developed these competencies, the ways they integrate them into their professional practice, and what components might be missing from the framework.

This chapter begins with an introduction of the study participants, including their path to the presidency, and an overview of how they developed the identified leadership competencies. Discussion then shifts to the competencies used in practice by describing how these presidents integrate the AACC leadership competencies into hiring, evaluating, and preparing future leaders. Finally, the presidents were asked to reflect upon the competencies specifically and to identify any areas that may be missing from the original framework. The chapter concludes with recommendations to improve the development process for future leaders.

Participant Overview

The six participant leaders come from different regions of the United States and have extensive backgrounds in community college leadership. In total,

NEW DIRECTIONS FOR COMMUNITY COLLEGES, no. 159, Fall 2012 © 2012 Wiley Periodicals, Inc.
Published online in Wiley Online Library (wileyonlinelibrary.com) • DOI: 10.1002/cc.20029

two women and four men were included in the study. Position titles ranged from president to chancellor, but for purposes of clarity, all of the participants are referred to as "president." The presidents were selected due to their reputations as exemplary leaders, their familiarity with the AACC leadership competencies, the type of college (that is, urban, rural, or suburban), and their geographic representation. Details on the participants and their leadership pathway are provided in Table 8.1.

Three of the participants are in their second presidency: Jack Becherer, Daniel Phelan, and Richard Sánchez; each served in their first presidency in a different state. Glenn DuBois, the one system chancellor in the study, has served in three states in leadership capacities. Two participants are in their first presidency: Laura Coleman is in the sixth year of her first presidency, and Thelma Scott-Skillman, who will retire this year, has served over ten years on her campus.

Table 8.1.   Leadership Pathways

Name and Current Position	College/District	Prior Position College/District
Jack Becherer, EdD President	Rock Valley Community College Rockford, Illinois (Midwestern United States)	President Wenachtee Valley College Wenachtee, Washington (Western United Sates)
Laura Coleman, PhD President	Bay de Noc Community College Escanaba, Michigan (Midwestern United States)	Executive Dean Bertrand Crossing Campus Lake Michigan College Benton Harbor, Michigan (Midwestern United States)
Glenn DuBois, EdD Chancellor	Virginia Community College System Virginia (Mid-Atlantic)	Commissioner/CEO New Hampshire Community Technical College System Concord, New Hampshire (Northeastern United States)
Daniel J. Phelan, PhD President	Jackson Community College Jackson, Michigan (Midwestern United States)	President Southeastern Community College West Burlington, Iowa (Midwestern United States)
Richard M. Sánchez, EdD President	Navarro College Corsicana, Texas (Southwestern United States)	President Grossmont College El Cajón, California (Western United States)
Thelma Scott-Skillman, EdD President	Folsom Lake College Folsom, California (Western United States)	Vice Chancellor California Community Colleges (System Office) Sacramento, California (Western United States)

NEW DIRECTIONS FOR COMMUNITY COLLEGES • DOI: 10.1002/cc

Pathway to the Presidency

Prior research suggests that while the common route to the presidency is through academic administration (Amey, VanDerLinden, and Brown, 2002; Weisman and Vaughan, 2002, 2007), practical reality suggests that there is no one specific route for aspiring presidents to follow (McNair, Duree, and Ebbers, 2011). The presidents described in this chapter reflect this diversity of pathways: two, Becherer and Scott-Skillman, have prior leadership experience in student services. Dubois, Coleman, and Phelan have had administrative experiences that crossed organizational boundaries, as leader of a statewide system, dean of an educational center, and vice president of educational and student services, respectively. Of the six, Sánchez is the only president to have followed a more typical progression through academic affairs, moving from a faculty position to academic vice president before assuming his first presidency.

Some of the participants knew early in their careers that they desired a top-level leadership position. Scott-Skillman shared that she intentionally sought key experiences to help her develop her skills:

> I wanted to understand all the operations and the mechanisms that go on at a community college. I started talking to mentors and going in different directions with different positions so I could feel confident that I had both instructional as well as student services experiences.

Holding a variety of campus positions and intentionally seeking new learning opportunities affords a practical means to develop critical knowledge and a wide range of the skills outlined in the competencies. Scott-Skillman not only worked at several colleges in California but also pursued opportunities that allowed her to engage with state-level policy issues. These experiences led her to the state system office as vice chancellor and later involvement with AACC that broadened her perspective to include national issues.

Currently serving in his second presidency, Sánchez also held positions in different colleges, at different levels in each organization, before becoming president of Grossmont College in California. He described how his experience in his first presidency helped prepare him for his current position as president of Navarro College in Texas:

> There was a lot of learning taking place all throughout my first presidency, but then when I came to Navarro I was mostly honing those skills that I had developed because I had already been tested by the fire, so to speak.

The presidents all agreed that the acquisition of a doctorate is important due to the skills one can develop through doctoral study, such as planning, organizational strategy, assessment methodologies, research, and resource management. Yet DuBois confirmed prior research findings (Hull and Keim, 2007; Townsend and Bassoppo-Moyo, 1997) when he noted that the doctorate alone may not be sufficient preparation for the presidency:

> Having a doctorate shows you can stick to something over a long period of time and pull it off. The doctorate helps a person develop good habits of the mind, but you need experience to go with this.

Phelan expanded on this as he noted that practical experience, mentoring, engaging in peer networks, continued professional development, reasonable risk taking, and hard work are essential ingredients beyond the degree.

Being able to bridge the theory acquired in a doctoral program to the practice acquired by experience provides for enhanced leadership development. This suggests that the doctorate is more than an important credential for community college presidents, but when used in combination with skill development is more likely to ensure the overall success of the president.

Development of the Competencies

Amey and VanDerLinden (2002) identified three key ways that community college leaders develop their knowledge, skills, and abilities: professional development activities, mentoring, and on-the-job experiences. When asked to reflect on how they acquired the skills outlined in the roster of AACC competencies, the presidents noted these same pathways. Working with mentors and participating in professional development opportunities provided a guide, to be sure. However, learning on the job, often by trial and error, offered an opportunity to understand what was required to be a successful president.

Becherer reinforced the importance of mentors: "Mentors play a key role in what we do because we do learn by imitation. I probably wouldn't be where I am without either of my mentors." The reality, though, is that the learning can be a solitary experience. As Phelan noted, "Much of my learning has come from experience . . . some of it, the hard way." Coleman described how each position she held prior to becoming president helped her develop the leadership competencies and build on them. She described how prior positions allowed her to learn all facets of running a college on a smaller scale. Coleman cited this experience as key in developing the competency of resource allocation, including financial as well as human resources. Other competencies, such as communication, she says, have "developed over my lifetime."

Drs. Becherer and Sánchez explained that what they learned in their first presidency helped them strengthen their skills in the second presidency. In the second presidency, they were no longer encumbered by learning what it meant to be president, which allowed them to better anticipate the demands of the position. Scott-Skillman described the ways she has benefited from feedback from others along her career path:

In the beginning of my administrative career, I had little guidance in terms of how to actually function, and there were times when I faltered because I didn't understand. Over time, as I conversed with more seasoned administrators, I got to really examine different parts of those areas that I was working on. I began to map out different steps that I could take in order to make what I considered to be more value-oriented types of decisions.

The presidents in this study each acquired their leadership skills along familiar routes. However, the acquisition and development of the competencies fit their unique learning context. Furthermore, these learning experiences have informed the development of competencies in ways that allow the presidents to integrate these aptitudes into their work.

AACC Leadership Competencies in Practice

Researchers have long described the complexity of the role of a community college president (Eddy, 2010; Pierce and Pederson, 1997; Vaughan and Weisman, 1998). Community college presidents must be able to manage multiple demands, changing student populations, increasing enrollments and decreasing budgets, and increased external accountability. Ongoing fiscal constraints require community college leaders to become more entrepreneurial, engage in more fundraising activities, and create new partnerships with businesses (Boggs, 2011). At the same time, new leaders need to "understand and value the unique role that community colleges play among the segments of higher education" (Boggs, 2011, p. 4).

Given the complexity of the role, community college presidents need a broad set of skills to be successful. Yet it may not be reasonable to expect one person to possess all of the skills embedded in the AACC competencies. It is more reasonable to expect that a president will possess many of the competencies and be stronger in some areas than in others. To be successful, Phelan recommended that presidents continue to participate in professional development activities:

> Experimentation, study, and application are vital to help fill any skill gaps that may be present. Ultimately, given the changing nature of the higher education industry, due to the marketplace, competition, student expectations, and governmental forces, a commitment to the regular development of a president's knowledge base, skills, and abilities is not only crucial, it is indispensable.

In this section the presidents discuss the relevance of the AACC leadership competencies and the ways they integrate the competencies into their professional experiences, including the hiring, evaluation, and development of leaders at their colleges.

Relevance of the Competencies.   Each of the presidents agreed that the AACC leadership competencies provide a global framework that

NEW DIRECTIONS FOR COMMUNITY COLLEGES • DOI: 10.1002/cc

encompasses the varied skill set community college leaders need to be successful. As Becherer observed:

> The competencies are excellent. Anyone who is aspiring to be a president or who is a president has to answer the question: How do the competencies apply to the community? You really have to meld the college and the community together to have the magic that happens with community colleges.

Drs. Coleman and Scott-Skillman agreed that the competencies are important to successfully do the work required of a president. Coleman suggested that if "people are not employing all of these competencies, or at least working the ones that are their major strengths, they're making a big mistake." Scott-Skillman noted that the competencies provide a solid foundation for the philosophical underpinnings of community college leadership: "They give a sense of stability and certainly an identity or purpose for how and why we exist as an institution."

Because the use of the essential competencies for success might vary according to context (that is, region, type of college, type of governance, gender or race), the presidents were asked to describe which of the competencies have been most useful in their current positions. While indicating that "resource management is great, communication is absolutely essential, collaboration is also important as are advocacy and professionalism," Sánchez suggested that organizational strategy has been the most useful for him because good skills in managing the organization drive the institution. Scott-Skillman agreed that organizational strategy is a key competency that allows her to "make sure that we have the functional elements to be able to operate effectively." Phelan echoed this sentiment, indicating that "visioning/environmental scanning (organizational strategy), listening (communication), and relationship building (collaboration)" have all been useful in his current presidency. Coleman added that "organizational strategies and resource allocation allow us to take resources and put them into something that is going to be productive and that is going to help the students be successful." She also explained how communication is becoming increasingly important due to the many ways people access and receive information:

> Communication is especially difficult right now because it used to be that we could communicate in one or two ways. Today we are bombarded with all kinds of communication—online, news, Twitter, Facebook, e-mails, and phone calls. There's just a zillion different ways that we communicate.

DuBois also stressed the importance of resource management in today's environment. He described the value of fundraising as well as "resource raising, along with good, very, very good people skills and political skills." The emphasis on these competencies reflects the context in which DuBois works—a community college system in a region dominated by fundraising and political relationships.

Although each of the presidents identified one or two competencies that are most useful in their professional experience, Becherer also noted that the importance of the competencies may be situational:

> Sometimes you really have to focus on resource management or college planning. There are times when things are shifting, so I might be a collaborator or I might need to be very systemic. Right now, advocacy for community seems so important. I think we're always dancing across these competencies and having to understand what is required for the next six months but also understanding these competencies might shift from your thinking about what's going to happen in two years.

Coleman summed up the sentiments of the presidents when she said "All of them are important; I couldn't do my job if I couldn't do all six of them."

Hiring and Evaluation.   Sitting presidents have another opportunity to shape the future by identifying, training, and supporting individuals in their organization who have the potential for leadership positions. In considering their approach to hiring, all of the presidents stressed the importance of communication, collaboration, and the ability to build good relationships in the organization. To attract and identify candidates with these competencies, some of the presidents include a description of these skills in position announcements. Others ask questions during interviews that allow candidates to illustrate their skills in these essential competencies.

As they evaluate staff, the presidents in this study adopt a coaching or mentoring approach that allows them to identify strengths, as well as areas for development. Because they hold high standards for themselves and those in the organization, they are candid about the feedback they offer college leaders, which provides opportunities for honest conversations about the competencies that need improvement.

Preparing Future Leaders.   Each of the presidents noted the importance of preparing future leaders. Their approaches to preparing leaders vary from individual mentoring to participating in professional development activities, such as national conferences, leadership development institutes, and doctoral studies. Each of the presidents stressed the importance of the AACC leadership competencies as a foundation for developing future leaders. Using the AACC competencies as a framework allows the presidents to work with future leaders to identify areas that might need refinement and concomitant activities that support the development of the competency. DuBois, for example, tells emerging leaders that "even though your job doesn't require you to do fundraising, get involved in your community and do it through your church, through other organizations." Becherer stated that in developing future leaders he wants to empower them to succeed—and to fail. I'm always looking to position people to do something they have not done before and I want to make sure the structure of support is there so that they can do it well.

At the same time, two presidents described the role presidents can take in encouraging others to consider executive leadership positions. Specifically, Scott-Skillman stressed that it is "important for me as an educator to help create the pipelines and at some point pass the baton. If we don't do it, it's not going to happen on its own." Sánchez suggested that presidents themselves need to

> convince potential leaders that being a leader at the community college is a very satisfying process. A lot of the lack of interest in succession for presidents is because we don't talk about the joys, about the reward that the presidency brings.

Missing Competencies.   Reflecting upon what will be required of future leaders, the presidents were asked to consider changes to the competencies. The presidents in this study stressed that the AACC leadership competencies are important and relevant. When asked if there were any competencies missing from the framework, the presidents offered thoughtful comments that can serve as a basis for future thinking about community college leadership. Their suggestions for adding to the competencies included three topical areas: entrepreneurial thinking about the future; commitment to diversity and equity; and taking a systems perspective. Specifically, developing visioning and/or scenario-planning skills could set the stage for potential innovations, which assumes an ability and willingness to take risks and challenge current assumptions. Demonstrating an obligation for student success builds on a commitment for equity and valuing of diversity. Finally, using system thinking helps in seeing connections, particularly when managing internal and external constituents.

Some of the previous suggestions are embedded in the current AACC competencies. For example, the competency of collaboration suggests, "An effective community college leader develops and maintains responsive, cooperative, mutually beneficial, and ethical internal and external relationships that nurture diversity, promote the success of all students, and sustain the community college mission" (AACC, 2005, p. 4). The illustrations for this competency include descriptions related to diversity and working with elected officials. However, the presidents in this study thought the missing competencies they identified need more of a presence in relation to their importance for effective leadership and should, perhaps, be stand-alone competencies.

Recommendations for Preparing Future Leaders

The six presidents interviewed share an unwavering optimistic, enthusiastic view of community college leadership. They acknowledge the current challenges facing community colleges, in particular the impact that decreasing fiscal resources may have on the community college mission. They also believe that these challenges offer exciting opportunities for innovation and new thinking about the ways community colleges support student success. Their comments suggest that the AACC leadership competencies provide a solid framework to help prepare future leaders even during times of uncertainty. During the interviews they emphasized the importance of including the competencies in doctoral programs so that graduates emerge with the skills necessary for executive-level leadership. They stressed the importance, for example, of integrating organizational strategy and resource management into doctoral course work and practicum experiences. In addition, the presidents proposed that doctoral programs would be enhanced by including specific courses and practicum components that address board relations, strategic planning, fundraising, union relations and collective bargaining, lobbying, community relations, advancing student success, managing construction and bond projects, instructional leadership, systemic leadership, and contracts. Skill in these competencies, the presidents observed, is essential regardless of context or environment.

The presidents also recognize that in times of declining resources it may be tempting to reduce support for professional development activities. Yet they continue to look for ways to provide opportunities to current and aspiring leaders. These opportunities include sending leaders to national conferences or bringing a national program to their campus. Coleman noted that the latter approach has been essential for her college, which is in a remote area. Bringing a national speaker to campus had additional benefits in that it was cost efficient, more people could attend the activity, and broad participation led to campus-wide engagement related to the event.

Comments from the presidents also reflect the need for each individual president to provide one-on-one professional development experiences for campus leaders. The presidents acknowledge the importance of identifying future leaders and creating the space for them to learn through on-the-job experiences, mentoring, professional development activities, and doctoral studies. Done well, as Phelan noted, this will "take time on the president's calendar, yet the rewards to the college, and the industry in general, will yield great dividends."

Summary

The voices of these presidents stand as a litmus test of the AACC competencies and illustrate how the competencies work in the lives of college presidents. The presidents clearly indicate that the competencies matter— in developing future leaders, in creating the context for work in the community college, and for value-driven decision making. Their stories also suggest that leadership is contextual: The competencies that are important in one environment may not be as important in another environment.

NEW DIRECTIONS FOR COMMUNITY COLLEGES • DOI: 10.1002/cc

Furthermore, using a specific competency may be situational, and presidents need the ability to quickly identify which competency is relevant in a given situation.

Embedding the competencies into hiring, evaluation, training, mentoring, on-the-job experiences, and professional development activities, including doctoral studies, allows current and future leaders to see the importance of both education and practice. The six presidents interviewed for this study also described the importance of intentionally developing these competencies in future leaders. Qualified new presidents are needed due to retirements and to movement of leaders to other community college presidential openings. The presidents agreed that each community college should be intentional about this effort and embed it into the way the college does business, including its incorporation as an element of succession planning.

References

American Association of Community Colleges. *Competencies for Community College Leaders.* Washington, D.C.: American Association of Community Colleges, 2005. Retrieved from www.aacc.nche.edu/Resources/competencies/Documents/compentenciesforleaders.pdf

Amey, M. J., and VanDerLinden, K. E. *Career Paths for Community College Leaders.* Research Brief Leadership Series. AACC-RB-02-2. Washington, D.C.: American Association of Community Colleges, 2002.

Amey, M. J., VanDerLinden, K. E., and Brown, D. F. "Perspectives on Community College Leadership: Twenty Years in the Making." *Community College Journal of Research and Practice,* 2002, *26,* 573–589. doi: 10.1080/10668920290102707

Boggs, G. R. *Community Colleges in the Spotlight and Under the Microscope.* New Directions for Community Colleges, no. 156,. San Francisco: Jossey-Bass, 2011. doi: 10.1002/cc.462

Eddy, P. L. Community College Leadership: A Multidimensional Model for Leading Change. Sterling, Va.: Stylus, 2010.

Hassan, A. M., Dellow, D. A., and Jackson, R. J. "The AACC Leadership Competencies: Parallel Views from the Top." *Community College Journal of Research and Practice,* 2010, *34,* 180–198.

Hull, J. R., and Keim, M. C. "Nature and Status of Community College Leadership Development Programs." *Community College Journal of Research and Practice,* 2007, *31,* 689–702. doi: 10.1080/10668920600851621

McNair, D. E., Duree, C. A., and Ebbers, L. "If I Knew Then What I Know Now: Using the Leadership Competencies Developed by the American Association of Community Colleges to Prepare Community College Presidents." *Community College Review,* 2011, *39*(1), 3–25. doi: 10.1177/0091552110394831

Pierce, D. R., & Pederson, R. P. (1997). *The Community College Presidency: Qualities for Success.* New Directions for Community Colleges, no. 98. San Francisco: Jossey-Bass, 1997.

Townsend, B. K., and Bassoppo-Moyo, S. "The Effective Community College Academic Administrator: Necessary Competencies and Attitudes." *Community College Review,* 1997, *25*(2), 41–56.

Vaughan, G. B., and Weisman, I. M. *The Community College Presidency at the Millennium.* Washington, D.C.: Community College Press, 1998.

Weisman, I. M., and Vaughan, G. B. *The Community College Presidency 2001*. Research Brief Leadership Series. AACC-RB-02-1. Washington, D.C.: American Association of Community Colleges, 2002.

Weisman, I. M., and Vaughan, G. B. *The Community College Presidency 2006*. Research Brief Leadership Series. AACC-RB-07-1. Washington, D.C.: American Association of Community Colleges, 2007.

DELORES E. MCNAIR is assistant professor of higher education leadership at University of the Pacific in Stockton, California.

DANIEL J. PHELAN is president of Jackson Community College in Jackson, Michigan, and a member of the AACC 21st Century Commission on the Future of Community Colleges.

9

This chapter describes the influence of emerging challenges on the AACC competencies that successful leaders must draw upon the most and why new competencies may be needed in the future.

Next Steps—Looking to the Future

George R. Boggs

Soon after assuming the presidency of the American Association of Community Colleges (AACC) in September 2000, I became concerned about what appeared to be a high rate of turnover in community college leaders and about reports of small applicant pools for presidencies. It was also alarming to read in national publications about leaders who were in trouble or who were losing their positions. For these reasons, I focused the Association on the imperatives of leadership preparation, support, and development. With support from the AACC board, I deployed staff and resources for a study that documented the extent and seriousness of the impending turnover in leadership due to the age of administrators and the likelihood of an insufficient number of qualified candidates because of the loss of most of the university-based community college leadership programs that began in the 1960s (Shults, 2001). The AACC's work and engagement of the field led to a renewed interest in community college leadership, resulting in the development and approval of the AACC leadership competencies (2005), the initiation of the Future Leader Institute and Future Leader Institute/Advanced, and the expansion of affiliated council, university-based, and "grow-your-own" institutional and state-based community college leadership programs.

As evident in previous chapters, the AACC leadership competencies have been widely studied and used. The relative importance of the six leadership competencies and how they are applied by leaders vary significantly, depending not only on the values and experience of the individual leader but also on the environment, values, and challenges of the institution.

New Directions for Community Colleges, no. 159, Fall 2012 © 2012 Wiley Periodicals, Inc.
Published online in Wiley Online Library (wileyonlinelibrary.com) • DOI: 10.1002/cc.20030

Search firms often indicate the importance of finding the right match between the competencies of a candidate and the needs of an institution. Even for a single institution, however, required leadership competencies are not static. They change over time and in response to specific situations and emerging trends. During the tenure of a leader, demands may change, as they did for me as a college president, from an internal, institutional focus to the need for more attention to external constituencies, legislative advocacy, and fundraising. As demands on a leader change and as the leader develops and gains experience in an institution, different leadership competencies come into play. In this chapter, I will discuss some of the most important emerging challenges for colleges and what leadership competencies will be needed to address them. The chapter also addresses how leadership competencies might have to be expanded or changed in response to these emerging trends.

The Economy

Economic cycles have predictable impacts on institutions of higher education, especially public community colleges. However, the severity of the economic downturn that began in December 2007 brought significant, and perhaps lasting, challenges to community colleges and their leaders. While few states escaped the impact of the recession, some areas of the country were affected more than others. Where factories closed or the workforce was reduced, many unemployed and underemployed workers found their way to local community colleges with hopes of being retrained to reenter the workforce. A 2008 Government Accountability Office (GAO) report underscored the links between community colleges as one-stop centers for supporting workforce needs.

In addition to the unemployed and underemployed, younger students who may have chosen to attend universities under better economic conditions instead chose to enroll at their local community colleges to save money. The College Board found over 40 percent of the students surveyed in the summer of 2008 indicated that economic circumstances changed their college choice behavior. One-fifth of this group said they would consider a community college, and one-third indicated they would look at colleges closer to home (College Board, 2008). Student enrollments surged in community colleges across the country, bringing national attention to these institutions (Mullin and Phillippe, 2009). National television newscasts featured community colleges as saviors that sent staff into closing factories to counsel employees and that did whatever they could to accommodate increased enrollment pressure. For example, in early 2009, *NBC Nightly News* featured Blackhawk Technical College in Janesville, Wisconsin, which sent staff into a General Motors assembly plant that was closing to counsel employees about training options at the college. At about the same time, CNN featured several students who had enrolled at Montgomery County

Community College in Pennsylvania in order to prepare them to reenter the workforce. The colleges did all they could to stretch limited resources and facilities to meet the needs of the increased numbers of students, as exemplified by Bunker Hill Community College's "Graveyard Classes," which were featured on Fox News in September 2009. The "Graveyard Classes" began at 11:45 P.M. and were designed both to stretch facilities and to accommodate the unique scheduling needs of students.

At the same time, however, states began to feel the effect of the economic downturn and responded by cutting apportionments to public higher education institutions, especially community colleges. In some states, federal stimulus funds provided by the American Recovery and Reinvestment Act (ARRA) helped to provide needed funding initially, but as those funds were exhausted, states cut funding to the colleges at a time when they were under historically high enrollment pressure. Student tuition costs began to increase dramatically, and many colleges had to cut class sections and essentially turn students away, denying access to higher education and training to significant numbers of students for the first time.

In this environment, leaders are under significant pressure. While all of the competencies remain important, resource management, communication, and advocacy move to the forefront for leaders. All available resources have to be focused on the most mission-critical components of the college. Priorities have to be established, and tough decisions have to be made and explained to stakeholders. Leaders need to use processes that are as inclusive and transparent as possible, while being accountable for financial decisions. At the same time, many colleges are beginning to place greater emphasis on alternative funding mechanisms, especially private fundraising, sponsorships, and grants.

In order to maintain trust, both on campus and externally, during stressful times such as an economic recession, leaders need to ensure that communication channels are open both within the college and to the external community. Budgets, processes, priorities, and expectations have to be clear. Leaders have to be able to listen and empathize with those who were adversely affected by decisions, but the most critical needs of the institution and its students have to come first.

During challenging times, advocacy becomes more important than ever. During the economic downturn, community college leaders are being called upon to make the case for stable funding support with county and state legislators and members of Congress. There is always internal pressure for community college leaders to hunker down and drop memberships in state and national advocacy organizations during difficult financial times to save money, but the money saved in the short run can have detrimental effects over time. In trying times, the voice of community college leaders needs to be stronger than ever, and leaders need to be able to communicate clearly why advocacy is so important for the college and its students.

NEW DIRECTIONS FOR COMMUNITY COLLEGES • DOI: 10.1002/cc

The Student Success Challenge

On July 14, 2009, President Barack Obama unveiled the American Graduation Initiative: Stronger Skills Through Community Colleges (AGI) at Macomb Community College in Michigan. The president's plan was an ambitious one. It sought to have community colleges provide a pivotal role in assuring the future competitiveness and well-being of the country by calling on them to prepare an additional five million graduates and program completers by 2020, an increase of nearly 50 percent over current levels. Although Congress did not fund the President's AGI proposal, his challenge to improve college completion rates has been embraced by foundations, policymakers, associations, and many college leaders.

However, defining and improving the success rates of students are ambitious challenges for the leaders of institutions that attract the most at-risk students and are the least well funded in American higher education. Improving student persistence and success rates, although worthy goals, is not easy work, especially in times of economic recession and retrenchment. However, dedicated college faculty, researchers, and leaders are learning together what structures, practices, and methods can help students to persist, to learn, and to be successful in accomplishing their educational goals. What is being learned or verified by the initiatives now under way to increase student success and to improve student learning is not only impressive but essential to the success of the learning enterprise of the future. College faculty, staff, and administrators are working to create a culture of evidence on campuses, basing plans and decisions on data and developing and evaluating strategies to increase student retention and completion while maintaining high quality (Brock and others, 2007)—a daunting goal requiring an unprecedented level of operational effort and transparency. This difficult balancing act, preserving the access and inclusion that are cornerstones of the community college mission while implementing informed practices that ensure greater success for students, will test the strength and resolve of these institutions and their leaders.

The shift to a focus on student learning rather than on delivering instruction can also be threatening to the constituencies of a college. Institutions are now being asked to accept responsibility for learning outcomes and for improving them. Institutional leaders will have to develop structures and processes that document student learning outcomes and allow for more flexibility and creativity to improve them. Decisions will have to become more data informed as the institution moves toward a culture of improvement and documentation. Barriers to student success will have to be identified and removed.

The leadership competencies most important for focusing an institution on improvements in student learning outcomes, success, and completion are organizational strategy, collaboration, communication, and resource management. Leaders need to create cultures of improvement based on evidence throughout the organization, consistently using data-informed planning and decision making. In order to improve outcomes, the college community, and in particular the faculty, will have to collaborate to develop and evaluate strategies intended to improve outcomes. The leader will have to be a persistent champion, communicating the rationale for change clearly and courageously. Resources, of course, will have to be realigned to support new priorities that are focused on improving student success.

Accountability

For some time, pressure has been building for institutions of higher education both to improve outcomes for students and to provide greater accountability to the public and other stakeholders. This renewed accountability movement was given sharper focus by the discussions and recommendations of Education Secretary Margaret Spellings's Commission on the Future of Higher Education, which issued its final report in 2006. The Commission, reflecting the views of a growing number of policymakers, painted a critical picture of American higher education as being arrogant, unconcerned about escalating costs, and unwilling to change. While the recommendations of the Commission did not result in any significant policy changes, the attention given to higher education accountability has yielded a number of new regulations and more accountability through regional accreditors. Even though public regard for community colleges has improved significantly in recent years, the institutions are often swept into the same federal and state regulations that are designed for other segments of higher education.

Certainly, the multiple missions of community colleges complicate how institutional performance is measured. Students enter a community college for myriad reasons. Some enroll to prepare for a career; others attend for a single course to upgrade a specific job skill, perhaps to earn a promotion; others seek a baccalaureate by completing their lower-division courses at a community college and then transferring to a four-year college or university; and still others enter community colleges for personal enrichment alone. The varied needs and individual goals of community college students, which represent appropriate and vital aspects of the community college mission, are difficult to measure in meaningful ways. Nonetheless, community college leaders are being called upon to be more accountable for everything from efficient use of resources to improving graduation and transfer rates. The Voluntary Framework of Accountability that is being developed by the American Association of Community Colleges will provide needed guidance on accountability measures that are most appropriate for community colleges (AACC, 2011a).

Communication, resource management, and professionalism are key competencies that come into play as leaders meet demands for increased accountability. Even if the news is bad, leaders must be open and honest in their communications. Of course, leaders can use their communication skills to put things into perspective and to explain how the college is responding to current challenges. Resources must be managed appropriately, and financial audits must be done to ensure that the college is following appropriate legal and ethical requirements. Similar attention should be paid to human resources and to college facilities. Professionalism is a competency that always comes into play, but it is never more important than when a leader is being held accountable for the effective and efficient operation of the college. Questions about expense accounts, for example, have caused serious problems for far too many leaders.

Globalization

Students in community colleges today must be prepared to compete in a global economy and society. Thomas Friedman (2005) described this concept well as today's "flat world": Manufacturing and service jobs, once performed in local communities, have been shifted to other countries, such as China and India; when European economies struggle or the U.S. Congress debates whether to default on debt, stock markets around the world react. Our economy is now intertwined with other nations, and our students will be, or perhaps already are, working in that environment.

If community colleges are to serve their communities well, they must prepare their students for the culture in which they will live and work. The communities and workplaces in today's America are much more interdependent with those in other countries than ever before. In many cases, community colleges present the first and perhaps only opportunity for students to become globally competent. Understanding how to work with others who differ in language and culture is a necessary job skill, even for those who never intend to travel abroad or leave their local communities. Moreover, if the United States is to remain competitive, its leaders and future leaders, many of whom will come through community colleges, will need to know and respect other cultures, understand the culture of international negotiations, and know how to cultivate partnerships across national borders.

America today is largely a country of immigrants. Approximately 25 percent of Americans identify themselves as being something other than "white," and nearly 12 percent are foreign-born. Yet, many of our citizens are insular, ignorant of world geography, untrained in foreign languages, and insensitive to cultural differences. Beyond our borders, people in other countries have a distorted view of Americans, shaped by our foreign policy, our movies, our popular music, and our video games. If the emerging global society is to be a healthy one, we need American students to learn about other cultures and languages, and we need people from other countries to have a more accurate understanding of American culture and values.

Global education is at least as important to our national security as protecting our borders and is important in shaping a more peaceful world. Being the world's only unchallenged superpower is not enough to protect our own citizens from terrorism or to bring peace to the world's trouble spots. Cultural awareness increases from educating international students in our community colleges, as well as educating U.S.-born students about the world. These future leaders will shape the future of the world.

Yet the value of international education is not often understood. Leaders, in particular, need to draw on both communication and advocacy competencies to clearly explain why global education must be an institutional priority. Programs to recruit international students to campus and to send local students to study abroad are valuable. Faculty sabbatical leaves to other countries can bring significant new perspectives to both their students and their colleagues. Partnerships with institutions in other countries can bring benefits in new understandings to both partners. Leaders need to be able to communicate clearly the value of these programs, to support them appropriately, and to advocate for them when necessary.

Skills Gap

When I graduated from high school in northeastern Ohio with a dream of going to college but with no money, my father got me a job at the rubber parts factory where he worked. It was a tough job, working third shift on the press line, moving rubber molds that easily weighed more than I did. I came home every morning after eight hours of hot, demanding, physical labor with the outlines of salt from sweat on my clothes, but I worked in the rubber factory every summer for the four years that it took to make my way through college with a baccalaureate in chemistry, and I am thankful for the opportunity it provided for me to pursue my dream of a college education.

The world was a different place in 1962 when I started college. America emerged from World War II as the leading economic and manufacturing power in the world. Europe was still recovering from the ravages of war, and Japan had not yet emerged as a significant economic power. China and a recently independent India were still isolated and underdeveloped countries. But, by the 1960s, we were engaged in a stubborn Cold War with the Soviet Union, and Russia beat us into space in 1957 with the launch of *Sputnik*. Business and government leaders responded to the challenges of that time by improving higher education programs and increasing access to it.

In the early 1960s, manufacturing jobs were primarily low-skilled. About 36 percent of the U.S. civilian labor force had less than a high school education (U.S. Bureau of the Census, 1964). Although community colleges, which today are the largest provider of higher education and training, were founded in 1901, there were none in northeastern Ohio when I graduated from high school.

The list of world changes since 1962 could fill several volumes, but one thing is certain: We face a much more significant challenge for economic viability as a nation than we did when *Sputnik* was launched. Today's manufacturing jobs are not at all like they were in 1962; they require less brawn and significantly higher-level skills that can be acquired only by education beyond high school.

While America has the highest-educated population in the 55–64 age cohort (Adelman, 2009), our younger people are comparatively less educated (Organization for Economic Cooperation and Development [OECD], 2011). The challenge we face today, as the "Baby Boom" generation retires, is that only 35 percent of Americans aged 25–34 have two or more years of postsecondary education (OECD, 2011). Even more problematic is that minorities, new immigrants, and children from low-income families have much less access to education and training than do their wealthier and more advantaged counterparts. By some estimates, we will have a net deficit of 20 million skilled workers in America by 2025 (Carnevale and Rose, 2011). It is clear that America will need all of its people to be prepared to participate in the economy if it is to remain a strong nation that provides a secure and high quality of life for its people into the future.

Solutions will not come easily, just as they didn't when we met the challenge of *Sputnik* by putting a man on the moon in 1969. Finding the right answers to today's problems will require leaders to rely on collaboration and communication competencies. Community college leaders will need to form strong partnerships with the leaders of business, other educational institutions, and government.

Among the many assets that community colleges and their leaders bring to the table are their responsiveness to the needs of local businesses and communities; extensive partnerships with business and industry; accountability for the services they deliver; and a pragmatic, low-frills approach that is highly cost efficient. Community colleges can customize programs to meet the needs of local businesses, often offering classes at the business site or at a corporate campus. In short, America's community colleges are the key resource for closing the growing skills gap that threatens America's ability to compete globally and to sustain our standard of living.

Mentoring

One leadership responsibility that is all too often overlooked is succession planning or helping to prepare the next generation of community college leaders. Although it is never listed on a leader's job description, mentoring future leaders can be one of the most important and most rewarding leadership responsibilities. Today's leaders also have a unique opportunity to help diversify the ranks of community college leaders of the future.

As institutions with the most diverse student body in higher education, community colleges have a special commitment to diversity and inclusiveness at all levels of their organizations. Community colleges are the gateway to postsecondary education for many minority, low-income, and first-generation postsecondary education students. Undergraduate female enrollment surpassed that of males in 1978, and females have been the majority ever since (Snyder and Dillow, 2011). In addition, the majority of Native American and Hispanic undergraduate students in this country study at these colleges. The desire to provide leadership for community colleges that mirrors the students they serve is both genuine and mission driven.

Cultivating a diverse leadership corps is difficult for most industries and institutions, especially given the lingering educational inequities that face our country. However, the current rapid and profound turnover of personnel at community colleges presents a unique opportunity to bring greater diversity and new energy into their leadership. The challenge facing the colleges and their leaders is to find ways to inspire and prepare a diverse group of candidates with the qualifications to be successful.

Efforts to recruit and prepare a diverse college leadership have been daunting and, in some cases, disappointing. Despite an increase in representation of minority community college presidents in recent years, there is a continued disparity between the ratio of minority students and minority presidents. Minority students currently comprise 32 percent of the community college population, while only 19 percent of presidents are minority (AACC, 2011b). Gender gaps remain as well. Only 29 percent of presidents are women (ACE, 2007), whereas 57 percent of the study body are women (Snyder and Dillow, 2011).

In July 2008, the AACC and the Association of Community College Trustees (ACCT) signed the AACC/ACCT Joint Statement on Leadership and Diversity. The statement is derived from a "National Call to Action" from the AACC Commission on Diversity, Inclusion, and Equity, a group that comprises college presidents, along with representatives from AACC's Affiliated Councils that support leadership development programs, many of which receive support from both AACC and ACCT to enhance diversity in leadership on a national scale. The two national associations have pledged to work together to diversify the ranks of community college leadership.

However, national associations will not have the impact that committed individual college leaders can have when they support and mentor leaders for the future. Two leadership competencies touch on mentoring: organizational strategy and resource management. However, they do not directly address the competencies required of leaders to develop and mentor the next generation of diverse leaders. The competencies related to mentoring should be added to the list for community college leaders.

Conclusion

The six AACC leadership competencies that were developed in 2003 and 2004 are broad enough to cover most situations that leaders will experience.

However, there are situations in which one or more of the competencies emerge as the most important. As situations change and as new challenges emerge, leaders will have to adapt, and the competencies may have to be expanded.

The characteristic that seems to define leadership excellence today is the ability to instill a strong sense of purpose in all of the college's people. At excellent colleges, faculty and staff share a commitment to the student-learning mission and values of the college, and they are not afraid to try something new to meet their objectives. They are proud of their traditions but are not constrained by past practice.

An important contribution today's college leaders can make is instilling a common sense of purpose and commitment to develop and nurture a culture that rewards risk and innovation while allowing for failure. Success is not possible in an environment in which the college's people are afraid to risk failure. Resistance to change and fear of uncertainty are barriers that must be overcome if a college is to be ready for opportunity and success in an environment of constrained resources. Flexible, caring, and competent leadership is essential to the future success of community colleges.

References

Adelman, C. *The Spaces Between Numbers: Getting International Data on Higher Education Straight.* Washington, D.C.: Institute for Higher Education Policy, November 2009.

American Association of Community Colleges. *Competencies for Community College Leaders.* Washington, D.C.: American Association of Community Colleges, 2005.

American Association of Community Colleges. *Voluntary Framework of Accountability.* Washington, D.C.: American Association of Community Colleges, 2011a. Retrieved May 28, 2012, from www.aacc.nche.edu/Resources/aaccprograms/vfa/Pages/default.aspx

American Association of Community Colleges. *Community College Trends and Statistics.* Washington, D.C.: American Association of Community Colleges, 2011b. Retrieved May 28, 2012, from www.aacc.nche.edu/AboutCC/Trends/Pages/default.aspx

American Council on Education. 2007. *The American College President: 2007 Edition.* Washington, D.C.: American Council on Education.

Brock, T., and others. *Building a Culture of Evidence for Community College Student Success: Early Progress in the Achieving the Dream Initiative.* New York: MDRC and the Community College Research Center, May 2007.

Carnevale, A. P., and Rose, S. J. *The Undereducated American.* Washington, D.C.: Georgetown University Center on Education and the Workforce, 2011.

College Board. *Student Poll,* 2008, 7(1). http://professionals.collegeboard.com/data-reports-research/trends/studentpoll/economy.

Friedman, T. *The World Is Flat: A Brief History of the Twenty-First Century.* New York: Farrar, Straus, and Giroux, 2005.

Government Accountability Office. *Workforce Development: Community Colleges and One-Stop Centers Collaborate to Meet 21st Century Workforce Needs.* Washington, D.C.: Government Accountability Office, 2008. Report number GAO-08-547.

Mullin, C. M., and Phillippe, K. *Community College Enrollment Surge: An Analysis of Estimated Fall 2009 Headcount Enrollments at Community Colleges.* Washington, D.C.: AACC Policy Brief 2009-01PBL, December 2009.

Organization for Economic Cooperation and Development. *Education at a Glance 2011: OECD Indicators*. Paris, France: OECD, 2011.

Shults, C. *The Critical Impact of Impending Retirements on Community College Leadership*. Washington, D.C.: AACC Leadership Series, No. 1, 2001.

Snyder, T. D., and Dillow, S. A. *Digest of Education Statistics: 2010* (NCES 2011-015). Washington, D.C.: U.S. Department of Education, Institute of Education Sciences, National Center for Education Statistics, 2011.

U.S. Bureau of the Census. *Statistical Abstract of the United States: 1964* (85th ed.). Washington, D.C.: U.S. Bureau of the Census, 1964. See Table 147. Available at www2.census.gov/prod2/statcomp/documents/1964-03.pdf

GEORGE R. BOGGS *is president and CEO emeritus of the American Association of Community Colleges and superintendent/president emeritus of Palomar College.*

NEW DIRECTIONS FOR COMMUNITY COLLEGES • DOI: 10.1002/cc

10

This chapter describes competencies that leaders need to develop to leverage improved outcomes for their institutions. Abundance, an organizational state achieved through leveraging, develops against a backdrop of context and ideologies that must be addressed to effect change.

Leaders, Leveraging, and Abundance: Competencies for the Future

Richard L. Alfred

Leadership, as it is practiced today in community colleges, has taken three brilliant ideas to excess and made them into guiding ideologies. The first is *growth*, a means for gauging organizational legitimacy and success that has eclipsed other means. The second is *complexity*, which has gained acceptance as a structural necessity for managing mission sprawl. The third is *effectiveness*, which has become an end in itself rather than a tool for enhancing performance.

Each of these ideas began as a solution to a pressing problem—how to create more value for more people. Over time, institutions and leaders have clung to this philosophy, but the makeup of the problem has changed. Resources and capacity are no longer adequate to support growth. This mismatch has caused problems of such urgency that leaders and stakeholders alike are beginning to ask questions about the community college business model. Are community colleges for everyone? What is the future of the open door? Should the mission be altered to accommodate resources? What is the basis of organizational success in a changing landscape? Triggered by conditions largely beyond institutional control, the "do more with less" business model is under scrutiny as inherently unworkable. Also under scrutiny is the efficiency of our colleges, the benefits they deliver to constituencies, and the proficiency of leaders.

It's not that the business model is broken or ineffective; generally speaking, community colleges remain the most efficient of organizations

NEW DIRECTIONS FOR COMMUNITY COLLEGES, no. 159, Fall 2012 © 2012 Wiley Periodicals, Inc.
Published online in Wiley Online Library (wileyonlinelibrary.com) • DOI: 10.1002/cc.20031

for moving people between schooling and jobs. But keeping them on track will depend on our ability to develop leaders with future-focused skills. This task will not be easy. It will require rethinking *runaway ideologies* such as growth and complexity that are of signal importance in our colleges today and identifying *evolutionary ideologies* that will be important tomorrow. Among these new ideologies are *abundance* and *leveraging*—the road to effective leadership will run through them.

The objective of this chapter is to question and rethink foundational principles for leadership in today's community colleges. The chapter begins by examining the changing context for leadership. Forces outside of colleges that demand new skills and competencies are described along with runaway ideologies that shackle leaders by limiting their creativity. Among the skill sets that future leaders will need are an understanding of abundance and a capability for leveraging. Abundance, a state achieved by an institution when its resources are leveraged to a level beyond reasonable expectation, will be a hallmark of high-performing institutions in a postrecessionary economy. Leveraging, the achievement of increasingly positive outcomes with increasingly meager resources, will be a capability that leaders must have to get the most out of institutions with austere resources.

No chapter on leadership would be complete without a list of desirable attributes in leaders. Generally, I do not subscribe to lists of this type; value can be found in almost any attribute if circumstances are right. Toward the close of the chapter, however, I depart from this practice and include my own list of attributes. Why? Because the basis for abundance is rooted in a select group of attributes. The chapter closes with a description of these competencies, where leaders who possess them might be found, and what institutions can do to develop them from within.

Changing Context for Leadership

Prior to the onset of the recession in 2007, the future for community colleges was challenging but at least comprehensible. Now it is a whirlwind of contradictory forces of growth and reduction, access and completion, and demand and decline. Most colleges are encountering opportunities for growth in a market loaded with learners needing more to find their way in the new economy. Counterbalancing these opportunities, however, is uncertainty about the resources colleges will have to support growth and their capacity to absorb more learners. These forces will have a significant effect on how colleges operate in the future.

The New Normal.   Substantive change in the landscape for community colleges can be traced back to the onset of the recession and the election of Barack Obama as president. In 2012, the nation is five years and counting into a recession that has profoundly disrupted every facet of American life. Mobility ground to a sixty-year low in 2010 as unemployment, plunging home values, and declining confidence in the economy forced people to delay major life decisions. The decline in home prices between 2005 and 2009 wiped out a vast amount of wealth and sent consumer spending spiraling downward.

The economy showed signs of rebounding in the first quarter of 2011, only to be stymied by slow job growth and delayed passage of debt ceiling legislation. Volatile financial markets, lingering high unemployment, a widening European debt crisis, and eroding consumer confidence combined to create a recovery that looked more like a recession with the potential for relapse into a crisis. The impact of the Great Recession continues, with a slow-moving recovery that could last for years. The crash of the housing market, high credit card debit, and uncertainty about job security have curbed consumer confidence. A nation long defined by exuberance and a belief that tomorrow will be better has turned gloomy about the future. This "new normal" is something heretofore not manifested in the American psyche.

Dynamic of Contradiction. In every cloud there is a silver lining. Opportunistic investors have long used economic downturns as buying opportunities. Businesses have used the urgency that accompanies slumps to mobilize innovation and renewal. Community colleges have experienced dramatic enrollment gains in periods of economic recession. The current recession is no exception (National Student Clearinghouse Research Center, 2011). Enrollment of traditional-age students in community colleges grew significantly between 2006 and 2009, moving from 42 percent to 45 percent of all first-time students (National Center for Education Statistics [NCES], 2009). Yet this upward trend reversed in 2010. Growth can be attributed to students who in better economic times might have chosen to attend other (and costlier) types of institutions, those who would have joined the workforce after graduating from high school, and those returning to college to retool after becoming unemployed. Decline can be attributed to capacity strain at community colleges and early signs of economic recovery.

Opposing forces of growth and reduction can be likened to accelerators and decelerators. Accelerators facilitate movement by encouraging change, whereas decelerators impede movement by constricting the resources available to institutions. Contradiction is experienced as colleges working with lean resources must find ways to serve learners wanting more and better service at reasonable cost. In effect, decelerators become accelerators when leaders must find creative solutions to adversity (Alfred, 2011).

If the economy moves into a sustained recovery, a scenario driven by forces of deceleration is unlikely. In normal times, people return to a pattern of consumption marked by increased spending during a recovery. The taxes they pay replenish state treasuries, and some of this money finds its way into community college operating budgets. In the "new normal," however, states will change how they do business. New revenue policies and appropriations criteria will be adopted as a hedge against future year down-turns, and colleges will see less money in their budgets.

Summary.   For community colleges, the implication of simultaneous conditions of growth and reduction will be change or die. While coping with the effects of deceleration fueled by a lingering recession and dimin-ished resources, they will simultaneously be coping with forces of accelera-tion fueled by burgeoning learner demand and intensifying calls for accountability. Learners will want more and better service, and policymak-ers will want evidence of better results. For institutions and leaders this will mean innovation—finding new and better ways of delivering service, creating efficiencies and cost economies, and improving outcomes. It will also mean doing things that were heretofore considered unpalatable: chang-ing the business model, procuring significant private sources of funding, redesigning organizational structure, collaborating with competitors, reen-gineering culture, streamlining systems and processes, and learning how to change through substitution.

Runaway Ideologies

The concept of "runaway" ideologies and the structure of the analysis to follow build on the work of Meyer and Kirby (2012). Using the example of the peacock and constructs from evolutionary biology, Meyer and Kirby describe how the tails of peacocks have become ever more flamboyant over time due to one simple fact: peahens exhibit a preference for long-tailed peacocks. A larger tail is a marker of a healthy male that will produce healthy offspring. Consequently, well-feathered males are more likely to pass along this trait. Over many generations, the tails of peacocks have grown larger, but the peacock population has dwindled to the point where human intervention has been necessary to save the species. A larger tail is heavy and more easily seen, thereby making the owner easier prey for enemies. Evolutionary theorists describe this phenomenon as "runaway selection"—a form of biological suicide.

In the case of community colleges, what organizational ideologies might they have adopted that would produce early success but possibly later failure? Put another way: Could there be a mismatch between ideolo-gies of growth, complexity, and effectiveness in today's landscape and orga-nizational success in tomorrow's landscape?

Consider how runaway ideologies might work in community colleges. For instance, a process of redesigning curricula to produce higher student completion rates may result in a streamlined curriculum in which learners are able to finish more quickly, but with skill sets that do not position them effectively for long-term job success. The problem is exacerbated when stu-dents press for course requirements narrowly focused on job skills, rather than for general education courses that equip them with soft skills neces-sary for long-term job success. As job requirements change, graduates are left unprepared. In most cases, misalignments are easy to spot and don't persist for long. The more insidious problems arise when an organizational ideology is valid and leads to early success only to become obsolete as conditions change. This notion of an ideology's becoming obsolete, even counterproductive, over time brings us to growth.

The Obsession With Growth.   For years, among the most frequently asked questions in community colleges has been "What's our enrollment compared to last year?" rather than queries about student retention and completion rates, operating costs, and student outcomes in work and further education. The roots of a focus on growth harken back to fifty years ago when community colleges were established at a rate of one per week and enrollment growth was the fast lane to legitimacy for fledgling institutions. Rapid growth made a statement about institutional vitality and put community colleges on the map. The cost of growth was cheap—sections could easily be added to enroll more students, temporary space could be found to offer more courses and services, and lower-cost part-time instructors could be hired to teach classes. Furthermore, there was upside protection for growth through enrollment-driven state aid formulas.

Growth was not the overall objective; rather it was part of a mission to put postsecondary education access within everyone's reach. But the opportunity to build identity and visibility through growth was attractive, and over time it became an ideology. Leaders working with resources needed a credo to guide decision making, and growth filled the bill quite nicely. Thus was born a runaway ideology that to this day drives the commitment to growth as a way of demonstrating institutional (and leader) success.

The recession has only intensified the need to perpetuate growth and encouraged attention to efficiency to get the most out of capacity. Enormous weight continues to be given to the "more" associated with growth, but comparatively little to the "better" associated with other indicators of performance. Student completion has only recently become a policy issue for community colleges, and value added is just beginning to come into focus. Performance assessment is beginning to change, but noticeably absent are indicators that gauge the intangible side of what institutions do, particularly their effect on people. This runaway ideology will not be curbed until other success criteria counterbalance the obsession with growth. A challenge for community college leaders today and those who will lead tomorrow is identifying success criteria that have enough weight to supplant growth as the barometer of institutional success.

The Surrender to Complexity.   Complexity is a correlate of growth. The easiest and quickest way to accommodate growth when resources are tight is to increase workload and expect more from people. For the most part, however, growth is accommodated through change in infrastructure—adding management divisions and layers, systems and processes, and people and positions. These additions lead to more complexity in organizations.

Complexity results in problems that were not part of a smaller and simpler organization. For example, communication and decision making must now move through layers and processes where none previously existed. The ubiquitous nature of these changes results in staff's accommodating change rather than questioning it. Thus, the effect of complexity is to enable the institution to accommodate growth, but in so doing to contribute to lowered morale and satisfaction. The result is an institution working against itself as allegiance shifts from the institution to the work unit. By separating individuals into units that may not interact, work units—commonly known as "silos"—foster impersonal work environments. Contrast this with the experience of personnel on a small satellite campus distanced from other campuses and the central office of a large community college district. Everyone on campus is known, communication is more apt to be face to face, and silos are mitigated by compact size.

To portray complexity as an ideology is not to say that it must be eliminated—that is all but impossible. In a growth-oriented enterprise the way to manage complexity is not to embrace it but to question the underlying structures and assumptions guiding practice. The challenge for community college leaders today and tomorrow is not one of working with complexity, but of finding and creating simplicity.

The Means–Ends Inversion of Effectiveness.   In organizations it is important to distinguish between the means or process of doing something and its end or outcome goal. An illustration of a fictional case study highlights this tension. Inward Community College is a large institution in a suburban community with a lucrative tax base. Since its establishment in 1964, Inward has maintained a steady course in pursuit of its mission of preparing students for transfer, responding to business and industry needs, and providing programs and services to the community. The college has benefited from strong community support, increased enrollments, and taxpayer approval for funding.

Inward has invested significant resources in the physical plant, retrofitted facilities to stay abreast of technology, hired credentialed faculty and staff, forged linkages with employers and K–12 school districts, and committed itself to a culture of evidence by designing and implementing a comprehensive effectiveness model. The focus of effectiveness, however, is not on continuous improvement—it is on the accountability mandates of external agencies. Though reams of data exist, they do not serve a useful purpose.

The milieu of bliss unraveled in 2011, when Inward suffered a significant enrollment loss and unprecedented decline in local tax revenue caused by declining housing values. Tuition increased by 5 percent to offset lost revenue, and Inward found itself in a horse race for market share with regional four-year colleges. Here the impact of using data for reporting purposes rather than internal improvement became evident. Inward was not able to mount the improvement initiatives necessary to stave off competition from rivals. Beyond its utility for fulfilling the effectiveness mandates of external agencies, effectiveness had no real purpose at Inward. For its competitors, effectiveness was a means to an end of continuous improvement. Inward's approach to effectiveness is a classic example of what might be labeled convoluted ideology. By gathering data and failing to use it for continuous improvement, Inward converted effectiveness into an end in itself.

There are three important lessons implicit in the experience of Inward. First, leaders will need to understand the importance of means–ends alignment and resist the temptation to substitute means for ends. Second, leaders will need to understand the changing basis of competition and the speed at which rivals move. Rivals are moving faster and setting the bar higher with each passing year and cannot be taken for granted. Ideology becomes convoluted when leaders develop a false sense of security from advantage that worked in the past but not in the present. Finally, leaders will need to understand the growing importance of strategy and of differentiation. An institution without a clear strategy that distinguishes it from rivals is headed for trouble. Cost and convenience—the mainstays of community college strategy for decades—will not be sufficient in the future to maintain advantage. By implication this leads to a question that every leader will need to ask and answer: What will be the source of advantage in the future, and how can effectiveness information be used to locate and establish advantage?

These ideologies prompt questions about the emphases that command leader attention and commitment and how effectively these emphases will serve institutions in the future. We know that countervailing forces of growth, resource decline, and accountability are changing the playing field for community colleges. Will prevailing ideologies of growth, complexity, and effectiveness be sufficient to propel community colleges to high performance in the future? Emerging ideologies of *abundance* and *leveraging* provide an alternative.

Abundance and Leveraging

Abundance and scarcity are competing mind-sets in virtually all organizations. How these mind-sets manifest themselves in community colleges have much to do with the ease or difficulty leaders experience in managing an institution. Described simply, some individuals live in a world of scarcity—a world in which resources and opportunities are limited and must be acquired and protected. The scarcity mind-set is a zero-sum game in which one wins at the expense of another. The fear of loss is a driving motive. Losing what one has, losing out on possibilities for getting more, getting less than what one wanted or expected—these are the ingredients of scarcity.

Others live in a world of abundance. Their underlying view is that resources and opportunities are unlimited. To the individual subscribing to abundance, opportunities and challenges must be embraced and pursued. The worst thing one can do is become attached to the status quo because possibilities abound. The abundance mentality involves a win-win mindset—there is plenty for all, and we can achieve more together than apart. Abundance and scarcity serve as endpoints on a continuum in which leaders may have a variety of perspectives based on their location on the continuum.

For faculty, this continuum might be evidenced by instructors who view their position as one of entitlement due to longevity, whereas instructors holding a different position might embrace change and opportunities to bring innovative teaching strategies into classroom teaching. Both instructors have a place in the institution, but they are working with different value systems—one of scarcity and the other of abundance. What will the contribution of each be to student success? In the management arena, the increasingly common saga of presidents in neighboring institutions working to reverse an enrollment dip following several years of unprecedented gains reveals differences in outlook and approach. One president is focusing on a short-term marketing strategy to recoup lost enrollment, while the other is developing a long-term strategy to bring new markets to the college. Both strategies are important. Which is likely, however, to be most effective over the long run?

Leaders in an era of rising demand and reduced resources need to become adept at doing more with less. They will need to generate new sources of revenue to support growth, increase the capacity and productivity of staff, win the war for talent with fast-moving rivals, build cultures that embrace innovation and change, and create networks that enable institutions to pursue opportunity. They will be challenged to develop new organizational designs to get in front of change, and they will need to think differently about organizational success. A tool to achieve these outcomes is *leveraging*—an institution's capacity to achieve superior performance by optimally using its resources.

The principle underlying leveraging is simple: leaders who want to grow institutions with limited resources will need to use current resources more effectively. The key to leveraging, however, is motivating people to effort beyond a reasonable level of expectation. Leveraging, therefore, is not about adding resources—people, money, and technology—but doing more with what an institution already has. It is the basis of *abundance* (creating more), and its polar opposite is *scarcity* (coping with less). Leaders with a capability for leveraging value strength and achievement (positive deviance) in contrast to identifying and solving problems (negative deviance). There are distinct competencies that contribute to a capability for leveraging, which can be developed in leaders. They are identified below in the context of landscape changes that all community colleges are experiencing.

Competencies for Leveraging

For more than four decades, there has been consensus about the kinds of experience community college professionals must have coming into positions of leadership, the personal attributes that give one the appearance of a leader, and the places and positions in which leaders are groomed and formed. Yet change is so rapid today that one leader cannot hope to keep abreast of all developments, much less be responsible for the innovation needed to remain at the forefront of the market. In today's community college, leaders relying on authority alone are not going to be around long.

Colleges require leaders with the intellect and skills to tackle the ideological issues described earlier—growth and complexity, effectiveness and organizational success, and abundance and scarcity. A list of traits alone will not address all these challenges. There are overarching attributes, however, shared by leaders who have this capability for flexible leadership (Alfred, Shults, Jaquette, & Strickland, 2009).

Visioning and Optimization. Effective leaders generate visions for the institution, which involve creating a compelling image of the future and a college's place in the future—what it could be and, more important, what it should be. Leaders skilled at visioning are able to get staff excited about the future. They use stories and metaphors to paint a vivid picture of what a college could be, even if they don't have a clear plan for getting there.

Inventiveness. Leaders need creativity to transform a vision into reality. Even the most compelling vision will lose its power if it floats unconnected above the everyday reality of organizational life. Inventive leaders have the ability to relate vision to what people are actually doing and to give it legs through the eyes and actions of staff.

Relating and Inclusiveness. Leaders generate support for initiatives through earnest and meaningful interactions with staff. Listening with the intent of understanding thoughts and feelings and celebrating success are part of trust building. Integral to the relationship between leaders and staff is something that can best be called an "inclusion factor." Effective leaders do not let size and complexity get in the way of involving staff in decision making.

Simplicity. Conversations with leaders in abundant institutions reveal a commitment to simplicity that is expressed in two basic ways: (1) don't overload the system; and (2) help people understand what is going on by making systems, processes, and communication simple. Leaders in these institutions invoke transparent decision making. They relate the contribution of individuals to institutional performance by working to identify what is important in performance and restricting measurement to mainstream indicators.

Identifying and Developing Talent. Colleges operating in a knowledge economy have little hope of achieving high performance unless leaders initiate and sustain efforts to acquire, train, and retain the best talent. Effective leaders are compulsive talent scouts. They look for talent in unusual places both inside and outside of the institution, they do not permit stereotypical qualities to dictate what they look for in leadership, and they work nonstop to identify and develop talent. Much of what will go into developing successful leaders in the future will involve "fit"— matching of individual, context, and culture.

Creating and Maintaining a Sense of Urgency.   Effective leaders know that change begins with an uncompromising look at an institution's circumstances, its resources, and its performance. Creating urgency allows for critical introspection and moves staff out of their comfort zone. These leaders are engineers of motivation and use this to impel instructors and staff to move beyond yesterday's successes.

Collectively these attributes are the building blocks of abundance. By focusing on the ability of leaders to envision a desired organizational future state, to motivate and inspire staff, and to achieve and maintain peak performance, they enable an institution to leverage its resources. They stand in stark contrast to ideologies of growth and complexity, which drive leader behavior and actions in colleges today.

Leading for Abundance

Finding leaders is increasingly difficult today. Qualified candidates are no longer in abundant supply in the usual places and the war for talent is fierce. Finding individuals with leadership potential is becoming, or will become, the name of the game, but this game will be played in unconventional places with people who defy conventional stereotypes of leadership. For this reason, it is worth rethinking our image of the community college leader and how and where a person will acquire the attributes to become one. We may find that it's through experiences not usually associated with leader development and in places other than community college campuses.

Invisible to Visible.   For one reason or another, many talented individuals inside the ranks of community colleges haven't been viewed as potential leaders. Often this has been because of explicit limitations—for example, access to tools such as social networks, fast-track training programs, stretch assignments, and capable mentors who prepare individuals for positions of influence. More subtle, however, is the influence of what Linda Hill at Harvard University (Harvard Business Review Editorial Staff, 2008) has labeled "stylistic" limitations—attributes of personality that don't fit the conventional image of a leader. We observe this in people who are overlooked for top leadership positions because they don't exhibit the take-charge, direction-setting behavior we often associate with leadership.

The increasing size and complexity of community colleges demands a more inclusive, collaborative style of leadership. This requires leaders who, among other things, are comfortable with sharing power, able to see extraordinary potential in ordinary people, and capable of making decisions with a balance of idealism and pragmatism (*Harvard Business Review* Editorial Staff, 2008).

Developing Leaders From Within.   Leaders are in abundant supply if we are able to suspend preconceptions about the way leaders look and act that blind us to individuals with leadership potential. For tomorrow's leaders, we'll need to look for individuals with a capacity to embrace risk, to inspire a team, to motivate others to optimum performance, and to plant seeds that become others' ideas. Individuals who like people, possess attributes of transparency and authenticity, and have a passion for innovation are likely candidates for leadership. In addition to looking inside for leaders, there are personnel outside college walls who are prepared to lead by virtue of experience with austere resources, customer sensitivity, and high performance in service organizations—in particular, developing professionals in hospitals and health organizations, small-scale entrepreneurial businesses, nonprofit organizations, and social services.

Leading From Behind.   Leading from behind can be likened to an experienced coach removing herself from the bench and watching her team play from a distance. The best players set the pace that others follow, not realizing that all along they are being directed from behind by coaching. This exemplifies tomorrow's community college leader: someone who knows how to create a context or culture in which others are willing to lead. The coaching metaphor also hints at the ability of a team to lead on the basis of its own initiative rather than waiting for a command. In Hill's view, this capability is more likely to be developed when leaders conceive of their role as creating the opportunity for collective leadership, in contrast to merely setting direction.

Leading from behind requires a shift in emphasis in what is expected from leaders and how they view their role. Institutional direction is not always clear in a rapidly shifting landscape. And complexity adds a new dimension to the functioning of community colleges that makes the leader as expert practically impossible. Let's use the example of visioning to see how leading-from-behind might work in a community college. Visioning begins with the president describing the purpose of the process, the themes it might incorporate, and the campus and community stakeholders who could be key contributors. The process unfolds with campus and community groups coming together in listening sessions to create ideas about the future. These ideas are charted and examined by the leadership team and become a network of ideas for formulating a vision that were not available to the team at the beginning of the process. The resulting vision is a product of collective thought—of leading in front upon the initiative of the president and from behind throughout the process.

Parting Advice

Developing the competencies needed to lead tomorrow's colleges requires experience with challenging situations that defy solution. Lead-from-behind skills are particularly important, and one way to develop them is through experience outside of institutional boundaries in collaborative settings where the effort of many is required to achieve a goal (*Harvard Business Review* Editorial Staff, 2008). Learning to work with a diverse group of peers on a team that does not have a designated leader differs in important ways from the early work experience of a college staffer reporting to a line administrator. When individuals work with others who are different from themselves in a setting that is unfamiliar they open themselves to new learning and they also have the opportunity to self-select as leaders. These are the leaders who are invisible today, but visible tomorrow.

Tapping invisible leaders within the organization will help widen the leadership pipeline and may have surprising results. The future of leadership in community colleges will depend to a significant extent on the ability of institutions to identify, not overlook, extraordinary potential for leadership that resides in ordinary people.

References

Alfred, R. L. "The Future of Institutional Effectiveness," in R. B. Head (ed.), *Institutional Effectiveness*. New Directions for Community Colleges, no. 153. San Francisco: Jossey-Bass, 2011.

Alfred, R. L., Shults, C., Jaquette, O., and Strickland, S. *Community Colleges on the Horizon: Challenge, Choice or Abundance*. Lanham, Md.: Rowman and Littlefield, 2009.

Harvard Business Review Editorial Staff. "Where Will We Find Tomorrow's Leaders? A Conversation with Linda Hill," *Harvard Business Review*, Jan.–Feb. 2008, pp. 1–7.

Meyer, C., and Kirby, J. "Runaway Capitalism." *Harvard Business Review*, Jan.–Feb. 2012, pp. 66–75.

National Center for Education Statistics. *Digest of Education Statistics*, 2009. Retrieved May 28, 2012, from nces.ed.gov/pubs2009/2009020.pdf]

National Student Clearinghouse Research Center. *Community College Enrollment Trends: Before, During, and After the Great Recession*. Herdon, Va., 2011. Retrieved May 28, 2012, from www.studentclearinghouse.info/signature/1/NSC_Signature_Report_1.pdf

RICHARD L. ALFRED *is emeritus professor of higher education at the University of Michigan and founding director of the Center for Community College Development.*

INDEX

CC155   **Marginalized Students**
         Elizabeth M. Cox, Jesse S. Watson
         This volume is a continuation of the dialogue begun with Vigil Laden's
         (2004) edited volume *New Directions for Community Colleges: Serving
         Minority Populations*. We build from that work and push boundaries by
         expanding the definition of diversity beyond race and ethnicity to include
         other populations that are not part of the mainstream on campus. The
         authors provide a thoughtful overview of their respective populations
         and provide recommendations for policies and practices that help bring
         students and faculty from the fringe through the development of inclusive
         campus environments. The chapters address philosophical ideals, reviews
         of contemporary literature, and results of current research that will benefit
         those working with marginalized groups, including college presidents,
         administrators, policy makers, faculty, and university leaders, as well as
         community leaders, activists, and other educational providers.
         ISBN: 978-11181-51082

CC154   **Technology Management**
         Tod Treat
         Community colleges have been repeatedly recognized for their focus on
         meeting local needs, responding and adapting very quickly as needs change.
         The institutional alignment close to industry, high level of accountability,
         and rapid response to local needs all contribute to a dynamic environment in
         which the institution's strategy related to technology management takes on
         critical dimensions, particularly the need to collaborate across institutional
         lines, such as academic services, student services, human resources, and
         financial services.
             Community college leaders are seeking ways to better leverage technology
         for business solutions, institutional research, student and organizational
         learning, and communications. Decisions such as who to include in decision
         making, how to balance maintenance and innovation, and what technologies
         to adopt have a deep impact on institutions, reaching far beyond the
         technology itself.
             The purpose of this volume of *New Directions for Community Colleges* is to
         explore technology management from a variety of vantage points. Authors
         represent community college leadership, chief information officers, faculty,
         researchers, and scholars. Their insights provide strong rationale for greater
         care in planning, budgeting, and utilizing technology, recognizing the
         challenges of rapid technological change.
         ISBN: 978-11181-29449

CC153   **Institutional Effectiveness**
         Ronald B. Head
         Institutional effectiveness lies at the heart of accreditation and accountability,
         as regional accrediting agencies, state legislatures, and even the federal
         government have increasingly asked colleges to demonstrate effectiveness
         in all aspects of their operations. Despite the attention that both external
         agencies and community colleges pay to institutional effectiveness, little
         has been written about it in the literature of education. This issue of *New
         Directions for Community Colleges* helps correct this lack of attention by
         exploring a number of aspects of institutional effectiveness as it is practiced
         in the American community college. Institutional effectiveness is not only
         defined, and its origins and history traced, but the process as it has evolved
         in community colleges is described in terms useful to community college
         practitioners. A number of other topics are also explored:

         • How institutional effectiveness drives accreditation (and vice versa)
         • How the accountability movement has influenced and shaped
           institutional effectiveness on community college campuses

- What role traditional offices of institutional research play in the practice of institutional effectiveness at community colleges
- The importance of measuring student success (and how to do so)
- How various stakeholders perceive and influence institutional effectiveness on campuses and influence it
- Speculation about the future of institutional effectiveness in American community colleges

This volume should prove to be an indispensable resource for community college leaders, faculty, administrators, researchers, scholars, and, indeed, anyone else interested in the state of the American community college. ISBN: 978-11180-84137

CC152   Hiring the Next Generation of Faculty
Brent D. Cejda, John P. Murray
Previous research indicates that community college faculty retire at or near the traditional age of sixty-five. With an aging faculty, enrollments that are reaching unprecedented levels, and the federal government calling for the community college to take an even greater role in workforce training, community colleges will need to both replace significant portions of their faculty and hire additional faculty lines between now and 2020. This next hiring wave has implications for community colleges, the diverse student populations who attend these institutions, and society in general.

The first chapter in this volume of *New Directions for Community Colleges* presents an overview of the faculty personnel challenges facing community colleges; the next three discuss the socialization and professional development of new faculty. Authors stress the importance of understanding differences among the types of community colleges and the importance of gender and racial/ethnic diversity among the faculty of the institutions who educate the majority of undergraduate females and students of color. The volume concludes with chapters on legal aspects related to the faculty employment and the experiences of presidents and senior instructional administrators, giving valuable guidance to those actively involved in the hiring process. At the heart of this volume is the continued commitment to the community college ideal of providing educational access and, through quality instruction, facilitating student learning and success. ISBN: 978-11180-24850

CC151   Contemplative Teaching and Learning
Keith Kroll
Higher education has historically done well in fostering teaching and learning with respect to critical reasoning and quantitative analysis—what might be described as higher-order thinking skills. But in our culture today, which can best be described as one of distraction, we also need an education—a kind of thinking, of being, of knowing—that fosters teaching and learning that develops contemplative methods and practice. This kind of learning teaches students to be reflective, to be mindful, and to pay attention. The contemplative theories and practices described in this volume, some of them ancient—for example, mindfulness meditation is thousands of years old—offer a new direction for community college teaching and learning.
ISBN: 978-04709-38553

CC150   Online Education
Regina L. Garza Mitchell
Online courses and programs have grown tremendously since the start of the century, with community colleges at the forefront. Two-year colleges now serve more than half of all online students, and they are poised for continued growth as more adults seek education and retraining. Despite the acceptance,

and even expectation, of online services and programs in education, colleges must address existing issues before expanding these. Organizational changes caused by greater reliance on technology for teaching and learning are still not fully understood, and colleges continue to react to change rather than positioning themselves to take advantage of it. The chapters in this volume use personal narratives and research to discuss how online education continues to lead to organizational, professional, and personal change. This volume of *New Directions for Community Colleges* highlights existing issues and provides strategies for addressing them as the demand for online education continues to grow.
ISBN: 978-04708-89695

CC149   **Leadership in an Era of Change**
Desna L. Wallin
Leadership is about change. In unstable times, effective leaders must not only be able to cope with the environment, they must also be able to shape it. Leaders in today's community colleges must fit that mold.

Change leadership can be said to embody four essential characteristics that might be called the four "A's." First, change leadership *anticipates*; it is visionary and forward-looking and avoids reactionary thinking. Second, change leadership constantly *analyzes* both the internal and external environment to gather reliable data upon which to make decisions; it engages in strategic and tactical planning to make the most of the moment. Third, change leadership *acts*; with a vision and a plan, with accurate and current data, action is collaborative and inclusive. It builds on the strengths of team members and is accountable to stakeholders. Finally, change leadership *affirms*; it is not enough to have a vision, a plan, and action. Once action is implemented, attention is given to reflection, to review, and to sustaining change.

This volume focuses on change leadership at all levels. The authors bring unique perspectives–they are strong, recognized scholars in leadership studies as well as practitioners actively engaged in community college leadership. Both empirical studies and best practices are included to further our knowledge and understanding of effective leadership in the context of change
ISBN: 978-04706-37777

CC148   **Contemporary Issues in Institutional Ethics**
Clifford P. Harbour, Patricia L. Farrell
Community colleges exist within an increasingly complex environment characterized by constant change and a range of conflicting academic, community, political, and financial responsibilities. Campus leaders, faculty, staff, and governing board members are often called on to make decisions that balance interests and concerns framed by these considerations. Often these decisions have an ethical component. College personnel may be able to call on a rich literature that addresses the relevant academic, community, political, and financial dimensions of specific problems. However, there is a limited literature on the ethical dimensions of broad issues that span the institution. The purpose of this volume is to examine the ethical dimensions of various institutional issues, policies, and practices at the community college. Accordingly, the volume focuses on topics that have an important ethical component and transcend specific program areas, campus services, and leadership positions. This emphasis on institutional ethics (and not the professional ethical responsibilities of specific individuals) makes the volume more relevant to a wider audience.
ISBN: 978-04705-92625

Common Errors in English Usage

Paul Brians

Washington State University

WILLIAM, JAMES & CO.

Dedication

For my wife, Paula Elliot. Her sharp
editorial eye, sense of style and support
have helped make this book what it is.

Publishers	Bill Hoffman (william_hoffman@wmjasco.com)
	Jim Leisy (james_leisy@wmjasco.com)
Production Editors	Tom Sumner
	Stephanie Welch
Cover	Ian Shadburne
Marketing	Christine Collier
Order Processing	Krista Brown

Printed in the U.S.A.

Names of all products herein are used for identification purposes only
and are trademarks and/or registered trademarks of their respective
owners. William, James & Co. makes no claim of ownership or
corporate association with the products or companies that own them.

The illustrations used in this book are from the Dover Pictorial
Archive Series, published by Dover Publications, selected by
Jim Harter.

Rights and Permissions
William, James & Co.
8536 SW St. Helens Drive, Suite D
Wilsonville, Oregon 97070

Library of Congress Cataloging-in-Publication data
available from the publisher.

Contents

Introduction

Prescription vs. description

The concept of errors in English usage is a fuzzy one. Language experts like to distinguish between two opposed approaches to the subject: theoretically prescriptionists work from rigid rules and traditions and seek to impose their views of correctness on the writing and speaking public, while descriptionists simply note the prevailing patterns of writers and speakers and report their results without in any way judging them.

But in fact it is not so easy to distinguish between these two approaches to usage: all prescriptionists rely heavily on usage patterns to develop their prescriptions and are willing to make exceptions to general "rules"; and even the most laissez-faire descriptionist will admit that "hte" is a typographical error for "the," that "Heineken remover" is based on a mishearing of "Heimlich maneuver," and that "perverbial" is not just a variant spelling of "proverbial"—it's a mistake.

Reserving judgment

Many teachers of composition feel that covering a paper with red ink just discourages and paralyzes students (in fact, I've found a standard pencil arouses much less anxiety than a red pen). The dominant philosophy of teaching students to write argues that only abundant practice can lead to improved writing. Errors naturally diminish as students read and write more.

This is very true. No list of errors—no matter how diligently memorized—can make you into a fine writer. Nothing beats lots of reading and writing. But the sad truth is that few students read or write much these days, and most of it is done in the anarchic setting of e-mail and chat rooms, where "correctness" is scorned. It is not uncommon for students to make it all the way through school without having their writing thoroughly scrutinized and critiqued until they encounter disaster in the form of a picky professor, editor, or boss. Many businesses consider standard English usage a prime requirement for employment in responsible positions. Would-be schoolteachers are particularly harshly judged if their English is sub-par.

Linguistic discrimination

Much of the tension surrounding debates about usage has to do with concern for various groups—minorities and immigrants in particular—who often suffer discrimination as a result of their deviations from dominant language patterns. Prescriptionism is viewed by many language experts as the equivalent of imperialist tyranny, or to use the jargon of the moment, linguistic hegemony.

It's true that the dominant patterns in English can exclude some very lively and creative language, and that a good deal of wonderful poetry, fiction, and drama has been written in nonstandard dialects. But in almost every case writers who are able to effectively wield the dialect they grew up speaking have also mastered standard English. To take only one of many examples, Langston Hughes brilliantly played the lively Harlem dialect of his character Jesse B. Semple against his own persona's rather formal diction in a long series of classic columns for the *Chicago Defender*.

If you have no access to standard English, a dialect can trap you. If you apply for an executive position by saying "I heared t'other day you done got some jobs open," chances are good you'll be directed to try farther down the corporate hierarchy. It may be deplorable, but the fact is that our language is judged all the time by employers, friends, and potential dates. When some teachers evade the issue by declaring all dialects equal, they set their students up for bitter disappointment in the world outside school. By all means celebrate the variety of Englishes abounding in the world today—but everyone deserves to know what sorts of usage variations may cause them trouble.

Errors, confusions, and non-errors

Errors in usage are a lot like errors in table manners. There are tiny deviations from standard practice few people will notice or care about, like using your salad fork to eat a steak, or using "decimate" to mean "destroy." Saying "I got my dandruff up" rather than "my dander" is more like trying to stab chunks of sweet-and-sour pork with the sharpened end of a chopstick—likely to raise eyebrows. But it's the equivalent of falling face-first into the mashed potatoes when some poor soul refers to a man as "circusized."

An English usage guide is like that really close friend who dares to tell you that there's some spinach stuck between your teeth.

And then there are people who insist you should never drink white wine with red meat; they're like those who heap contempt on split infinitives. Humor them if you must, but most of us feel they're dead wrong. Many linguistic bugaboos of this sort are included in this book so you can be reassured that not all the people who condemn your usage know what they're talking about.

Standard and nonstandard English

Entries are not simply divided into "correct" and "erroneous." The label "standard English" is frequently applied to patterns that sophisticated writers and speakers tend to use. This definition is to some extent circular: we consider them sophisticated partly because they use that kind of English. But standard English is what counts; it's what your own usage may be compared with. It's up to you to decide whether, after learning the dominant pattern, you want to blend in or use a different wording that appeals to you more. I had to rack my brains for a long time to understand the distinction some people make between "which" and "that," but I finally decided that I didn't give a fig about what they thought and generally ignore the distinction in my own writing. Guidelines for usage don't have to be regarded as iron chains dragging you down. You can still choose your own style.

When a usage is labeled as belonging to a dialect, it may be regional, racial, or national. Rather than stigmatize any particular group, I don't try to label these dialectical variations beyond indicating that they differ from standard usage. If you're "down to home," by all means greet your brother-in-law with "Look what the cat drug in!" But in writing your college admissions essay you'd be wiser to use "dragged" as in, "Although I love opera now, I was dragged to my first one protesting loudly."

By no means the majority of the usages discussed in this book are dialectical, however. It also covers technical and business jargon, pretentious but mistaken coinages created by highly educated speakers, and usages that are common but offensive to certain communities.

A special problem is the differences between standard American usage and standard United Kingdom usage, which is also largely followed in Canada, Australia, and some other countries. This particular usage guide is aimed primarily at Americans, but often notes when patterns are different elsewhere.

Who says?

Because of current trends in English studies, the folks you find patrolling the usage beat are not likely to be trained linguists these days; and I'm no exception. I have a Ph.D. in comparative literature, not in English composition. But I love good writing and encourage it in my students. I first got the idea of writing about usage while studying the mangled language on restaurant menus, and you'll find several examples of that sort of thing in this book.

Common Errors in English Usage does not merely enshrine my personal preferences, however. I've consulted dictionaries and other usage manuals and consulted with colleagues more expert than myself. Web search engines have been a very handy tool for confirming the extent to which many errors have spread. Unlike the editors of some distinguished usage guides, I don't have a formal board of consultants; but I do have something that functions rather like one. This project began in 1997 as a Web site called "Common Errors in English" (**http://www.wsu.edu/~brians/errors**), and since then it's earned many positive reviews, received numerous awards, and attracted well over a million visitors, thousands of whom have written to me with thanks or suggestions.

The Web site contains a list of "More Errors," many of which are too bizarre to be included here, but too entertaining to be omitted there. The Web site is also where you'll find an e-mail link if you want to write me.

If you think having a teacher criticize your writing is hard to bear, imagine being open to constant carping by the pickiest people in existence. Though I don't always agree with my correspondents, I've learned a lot from them. They've tipped me off to common errors that have escaped the notice of other usage guide authors and sometimes argued me out of my own prejudices against usages that turned out to be more standard than I had thought.

This book is thus the result of an ongoing conversation among people from all over the world and all walks of life who care about the language, and I owe those contributors a profound debt. Although "Common Errors in English" is not particularly aimed at non-native speakers, many correspondents struggling to learn English have found its explanations of the differences between seemingly similar words and phrases helpful.

You may find certain words or phrases criticized here listed in dictionaries. Note carefully labels like *dial.* (dialectical), *nonstandard,* and *obsolete* before assuming that the dictionary is endorsing them. The primary job of a dictionary is to track how people actually use language. Dictionaries differ among themselves on how much guidance to usage they provide; but the goal of a usage guide like this is substantially different: to protect you against patterns regarded as nonstandard by substantial numbers of well-educated people.

What's different about this usage guide?

Common Errors in English Usage is unusual in a number of other ways besides having originated on the World Wide Web.

Because it concentrates on the most common errors, it's much shorter—and not incidentally, cheaper—than most, though I include some oddities that I consider especially interesting or which are simply pet peeves of mine.

This guide makes no pretense to exhaustively exploring complex topics, limiting itself to pointing out the most commonly encountered problems and giving hints for avoiding them, using a minimum of technical terminology. This is the equivalent of a first-aid manual, not of the *Physician's Desk Reference.*

It avoids discussing most common misspellings, leaving the correction of such slips to your spelling checker, concentrating instead on linguistic confusions your computer won't catch.

It discusses many casual, slangy forms that are beneath the notice of some of the more high-toned usage guides.

It incorporates up-to-date comments on words and phrases from the world of the Internet and from other technologies.

It provides illustrative examples written in the sort of English familiar to most people likely to use this book. When writing a book about common errors, it would be pointless to select learned examples a general audience would not relate to.

It also places the primary discussion of words and phrases alphabetically under their erroneous forms, so you don't need to know the correct forms to look them up. A cross-reference is given at the expected location to guide you if you do know the correct form.

It's written in a chatty, informal tone designed to take the edge off what could otherwise be an unpleasant barrage of criticism. It makes abundant use of the first- and second-person voice to create the effect of an informal chat rather than a pompous lecture.

And from time to time, it tries to entertain. People often write to tell me that they laugh as well as groan as they make their way through what I've written. I hope you find this book fun to read as well as informative.

—*P.B.*

Common Errors
in English Usage

abject

"Abject" is always negative—it means "hopeless," not "extreme." You can't experience "abject joy" unless you're being deliberately paradoxical.

about

"This isn't about you." What a great rebuke! But conservatives sniff at this sort of abstract use of "about," as in "I'm all about good taste" or "successful truffle-making is about temperature control"; so it's better to avoid it in very formal English.

absorbtion/absorption

Although it's "absorbed" and "absorbing," the correct spelling of the noun is "absorption."

accede/exceed

If you drive too fast, you exceed the speed limit. "Accede" is a much rarer word meaning "give in, agree."

accent marks

In what follows, "accent mark" will be used in a loose sense to include all diacritical marks that guide pronunciation. Operating systems and programs differ in how they produce accent marks, but it's worth learning how yours works. Writing them in by hand afterwards looks amateurish.

Words adopted from foreign languages sometimes carry their accent marks with them, as in "fiancé," "protégé," and "cliché." As words become more at home in English, they tend to shed the marks: "café" is often spelled "cafe." Unfortunately, "résumé" seems to be losing its marks one at a time (*see under* "vitae/vita").

Many computer users have not learned their systems well enough to understand how to produce the desired accent and often insert an apostrophe ['] or foot mark ['] after the accented letter instead: "cafe'." This is both ugly and incorrect. The same error is commonly seen on storefront signs.

So far we've used examples containing *acute* (right-leaning) accent marks. French and Italian (but not Spanish) words often contain *grave* (left-leaning) accent marks; in Italian it's a *caffè*. It is important not to substitute one kind of accent for the other.

The *diaeresis* over a letter signifies that it is to be pronounced as a separate syllable: "Noël" and "naïve" are sometimes spelled with a diaeresis, for instance. The *umlaut*, which looks identical, modifies the sound of a vowel, as in German *Fräulein*, where the accent mark changes the "ow" sound of *Frau* (woman) to "froy" (girl). Rock groups like "Blue Öyster Cult" scatter umlauts about nonsensically to create an exotic look.

Spanish words not completely assimilated into English like *piñata* and *niño* retain the *tilde*, which tells you that an "N" is to be pronounced with a "Y" sound after it.

In English-language publications accent marks are often discarded, but the acute and grave accents are the ones most often retained.

accept/except

If you offer me Godiva chocolates I will gladly accept them—except for the candied violet ones. Just remember that the "X" in "except" excludes things—they tend to stand out, be different. In contrast, just look at those two cozy "C's" snuggling up together. Very accepting. And be careful; when typing "except" it often comes out "expect."

access/get access to

"Access" is one of many nouns that's been turned into a verb in recent years. Conservatives object to phrases like, "You can access your account online." Substitute "use," "reach," or "get access to" if you want to please them.

accessory

There's an "ack" sound at the beginning of this word, though some mispronounce it as if the two "C's" were to be sounded the same as the two "SS's."

accidently/accidentally

You can remember this one by remembering how to spell "accidental." There are quite a few words with "-ally" suffixes (like "incidentally"), which are not to be confused with words that have "-ly" suffixes (like "independently"). "Incidental" is a word, but "independental" is not.

according to/per

See "per/according to."

acronyms and apostrophes

One unusual modern use of the apostrophe is in plural acronyms, like "ICBM's," "NGO's," and "CD's." Since this pattern violates the rule that apostrophes are not used before an "S" indicating a plural, many people object to it. It is also perfectly legitimate to write "CDs," etc. Likewise for "50s." But the use of apostrophes with initialisms like "learn your ABC's" and "mind your P's and Q's" is now so universal as to be acceptable in almost any context.

Note that "acronym" was used originally only to label pronounceable abbreviations like "NATO," but is now generally applied to all sorts of initialisms. Be aware that some people consider this extended definition of "acronym" to be an error.

See also "apostrophes."

acrosst/accrossed/across

In some dialects, "acrosst" is a common misspelling of "across." Also, the chicken may have *crossed* the road, but did so by walking *across* it.

actual fact/actually
"In actual fact" is an unnecessarily complicated way of saying "actually."

adapt/adopt
You can adopt a child or a custom or a law; in these cases you are making the object of the adoption your own, accepting it. If you adapt something, however, you are changing it.

add/ad
"Advertisement" is abbreviated "ad," not "add."

added bonus
See "redundancies."

adieu/ado
See "without further adieu/without further ado."

administer/minister
You can minister to someone by administering first aid. Note how the "ad" in "administer" resembles "aid" in order to remember the correct form of the latter phrase. "Minister" as a verb always requires "to" following it.

adopt/adapt
See "adapt/adopt."

adultry/adultery
"Adultery" is often misspelled "adultry," as if it were something every adult should *try*. This spelling error is likely to get you snickered at. The term does not refer to all sorts of illicit sex: at least one of the partners involved has to be married for the relationship to be adulterous.

advance/advanced
When you hear about something in advance, earlier than other people, you get *advance* notice or information. "Advanced" means

"complex, sophisticated" and doesn't necessarily have anything to do with the revealing of secrets.

adverse/averse

The word "adverse" turns up most frequently in the phrase "adverse circumstances," meaning difficult circumstances, circumstances which act as an adversary; but people often confuse this word with "averse," a much rarer word, meaning having a strong feeling against, or aversion toward.

advice/advise

"Advice" is the noun, "advise" the verb. When Miss Manners advises people, she gives them advice.

adviser/advisor

"Adviser" and "advisor" are equally fine spellings. There is no distinction between them.

affect/effect

There are four distinct words here. When "affect" is accented on the final syllable (a-FECT), it is a verb meaning "have an influence on": "The million-dollar donation from the industrialist did not affect my vote against the Clean Air Act." A much rarer meaning is indicated when the word is accented on the first syllable (AFF-ect), meaning "emotion." In this case the word is used mostly by psychiatrists and social scientists—people who normally know how to spell it. The real problem arises when people confuse the first spelling with the second: "effect." This too can be two different words. The more common one is a noun: "When I left the stove on, the *effect* was that the house filled with smoke." When you *affect* a situation, you have an *effect* on it. The less common is a verb meaning "to create": "I'm trying to *effect* a change in the way we purchase widgets." No wonder people are confused. Note especially that the proper expression is not "take affect" but "take effect"—become effective. Hey, nobody ever said English was logical: just memorize it and get on with your life.

affluence/effluence

Wealth brings affluence; sewage is effluence.

agreeance/agreement
When you agree with someone you are in agreement.

ahold/hold
In formal English you just "get hold" of something or somebody.

ain't/am not/isn't/aren't
"Ain't" has a long and vital history as a substitute for "isn't," "aren't," and so on. It was originally formed from a contraction of "am not" and is still commonly used in that sense. Even though it has been universally condemned as the classic "mistake" in English, everyone uses it occasionally as part of a joking phrase or to convey a down-to-earth quality. But if you always use it instead of the more "proper" contractions you're sure to be branded as uneducated.

all
Put this word where it belongs in the sentence. In negative statements, don't write, "All the pictures didn't show her dimples" when you mean, "The pictures didn't all show her dimples."

all goes well/augurs well
Some folks who don't understand the word "augur" (to foretell based on omens) try to make sense of the common phrase "augurs well" by mangling it into "all goes well." "Augurs well" is synonymous with "bodes well."

all of the sudden/all of a sudden
Use "a," not "the," in this phrase.

all ready/already
"All ready" is a phrase meaning "completely prepared," as in, "As soon as I put my coat on, I'll be all ready." "Already," however, is an adverb used to describe something that has happened before a certain time, as in, "What do you mean you'd rather stay home? I've already got my coat on."

all right/alright
See "alright/all right."

all the farther/as far as
In some American dialects it is not uncommon to hear sentences such as "Abilene is all the farther the rustlers got before the posse caught up with them." The strangely constructed expression "all the farther" should be replaced with the much more straightforward "as far as."

all together/altogether
See "altogether/all together."

alleged
Journalists write that a person is *alleged* to have committed a crime to avoid labeling the person a criminal before a trial or confession has definitively established guilt (though it's redundant and senseless to refer to "an alleged suspect"). It's mainly a device for avoiding libel lawsuits. After the trial, it's safe to call the convicted murderer a murderer. And it insults the victim to speak of an "alleged robbery" unless there is real doubt that the crime actually took place.

allegory
See "parallel/symbol."

alliterate/illiterate
Pairs of words with the same initial sound *alliterate*, like "wild and wooly." Those who can't read are *illiterate*.

alls/all
"Alls I know is . . ." may result from anticipating the "S" in "is," but the standard expression is "All I know is. . . ."

allude/elude
You can allude (refer) to your daughter's membership in the honor society when boasting about her, but a criminal tries to elude (escape) captivity. There is no such word as "illude."

allude/refer

To allude to something is to refer to it indirectly, by suggestion. If you are being direct and unambiguous, you are referring to the subject rather than alluding to it.

allusion/illusion

An allusion is a reference, something you allude to: "Her allusion to flowers reminded me that Valentine's Day was coming." In that English paper, don't write "literary illusions" when you mean "allusions." A mirage, hallucination, or a magic trick is an illusion. (Doesn't being fooled just make you *ill*?)

almost

Like "only," "almost" must come immediately before the word or phrase it modifies: "She almost gave a million dollars to the museum" means something quite different from, "She gave almost a million dollars to the museum." Right? So you shouldn't write, "There was almost a riotous reaction when the will was read" when what you mean is, "There was an almost riotous reaction."

almost always/most always

See "most always/almost always."

alot/a lot

Perhaps this common spelling error began because there does exist in English a word spelled "allot" which is a verb meaning to apportion or grant. The correct form, with "a" and "lot" separated by a space, is not often encountered in print because formal writers usually use other expressions such as "a great deal," "often," etc. If you can't remember the rule, just remind yourself that just as you wouldn't write "alittle" you shouldn't write "alot."

already/all ready

See "all ready/already."

alright/all right

The correct form of this phrase has become so rare in the popular press that many readers have probably never noticed that it is actually two words. But if you want to avoid irritating traditionalists you'd better tell them that you feel "all right" rather than "alright."

altar/alter

An altar is that platform at the front of a church or in a temple; to alter something is to change it.

alterior/ulterior

When you have a concealed reason for doing something, it's an *ulterior* motive.

alternate/alternative

Although U.K. authorities disapprove, in U.S. usage, "alternate" is frequently an adjective, substituted for the older "alternative": "an alternate route." "Alternate" can also be a noun; a substitute delegate is, for instance, called an "alternate." But when you're speaking of "every other" as in "our club meets on alternate Tuesdays," you can't substitute "alternative."

altogether/all together

"Altogether" is an adverb meaning "completely," "entirely." For example: "When he first saw the examination questions, he was altogether baffled." "All together," in contrast, is a phrase meaning "in a group." For example: "The wedding guests were gathered all together in the garden." Undressed people are said in informal speech to be "in the altogether" (perhaps a shortening of the phrase "altogether naked").

alumnus/alumni

We used to have "alumnus" (male singular), "alumni" (male plural), "alumna" (female singular), and "alumnae" (female plural); but the latter two are now popular only among older female graduates, with the first two terms becoming unisex. However, it is still important to distinguish between one alumnus and a stadium full of alumni. Never say, "I am an alumni," if you don't want to cast discredit on your school. Many avoid the whole problem by resorting to the informal abbreviation "alum."

Alzheimer's disease
See "old-timer's disease/Alzheimer's disease."

AM/PM
"AM" stands for the Latin phrase *Ante Meridiem*—which means "before noon"—and "PM" stands for *Post Meridiem*: "after noon." Although digital clocks routinely label noon "12:00 PM" you should avoid this expression not only because it is incorrect, but because many people will imagine you are talking about midnight instead. The same goes for "12:00 AM." Just say or write "noon" or "midnight" when you mean those precise times.

It is now rare to see periods placed after these abbreviations: "A.M.," but in formal writing it is still preferable to capitalize them, though the lower-case "am" and "pm" are now so popular they are not likely to get you into trouble.

Occasionally computer programs encourage you to write "AM" and "PM" without a space before them, but others will misread your data if you omit the space. The nonstandard habit of omitting the space is spreading rapidly, and should be avoided in formal writing.

am not/isn't/aren't/ain't
See "ain't/am not/isn't/aren't."

amature/amateur
Most of the words we've borrowed from the French that have retained their "-eur" endings are pretty sophisticated, like "restaurateur" (notice, no "n") and "auteur" (in film criticism), but "amateur" attracts amateurish spelling.

ambiguous/ambivalent
Even though the prefix "ambi-" means "both," "ambiguous" has come to mean "unclear, undefined," while "ambivalent" means "torn between two opposing feelings or views." If your attitude cannot be defined into two polarized alternatives, then you're ambiguous, not ambivalent.

ambivalent/indifferent

If you feel pulled in two directions about some issue, you're ambivalent about it; but if you have no particular feelings about it, you're indifferent.

American

Many Canadians and Latin Americans are understandably irritated when U.S. citizens refer to themselves simply as "Americans." Canadians (and only Canadians) use the term "North American" to include themselves in a two-member group with their neighbor to the south, though geographers usually include Mexico in North America. When addressing an international audience composed largely of people from the Americas, it is wise to consider their sensitivities.

However, it is pointless to try to ban this usage in all contexts. Outside of the Americas, "American" is universally understood to refer to things relating to the U.S. There is no good substitute. Brazilians, Argentineans, and Canadians all have unique terms to refer to themselves. None of them refer routinely to themselves as "Americans" outside of contexts like the "Organization of American States." Frank Lloyd Wright promoted "Usonian," but it never caught on. For better or worse, "American" is standard English for "citizen or resident of the United States of America."

amongst/among

Although "amongst" has not aged nearly as badly as "whilst," it is still less common in standard speech than "among."

amoral/immoral

"Amoral" is a rather technical word meaning "unrelated to morality." When you mean to denounce someone's behavior, call it "immoral."

amount/number

This is a vast subject. I will try to limit the number of words I expend on it so as not to use up too great an amount of space. The confusion between the two categories of words relating to amount and number is so pervasive that those of us who still distinguish between them constitute an endangered species; but if you want to avoid our ire, learn the difference. Amount words relate to quantities of things that are measured in bulk; number words to things that can be counted.

In the second sentence above, it would have been improper to write "the amount of words" because words are discrete entities that can be counted, or numbered.

Here is a handy chart to distinguish the two categories of words:

amount	number
quantity	number
little	few
less	fewer
much	many

You can eat fewer cookies, but you drink less milk. If you ate too many cookies, people would probably think you've had too much dessert. If the thing being measured is being considered in countable units, then use number words. Even a substance that is considered in bulk can also be measured by number of units. For instance, you shouldn't drink too much wine, but you should also avoid drinking too many glasses of wine. Note that here you are counting glasses. They can be numbered.

The most common mistake of this kind is to refer to an "amount" of people instead of a "number" of people. Just to confuse things, "more" can be used either way: you can eat more cookies and drink more milk.

amuse/bemuse
See "'bemuse/amuse."

analog/analogue
See "'lite' spelling."

analogy
See "parallel/symbol."

anchors away/anchors aweigh
Anchors are "weighed" by being gathered up on chains. The correct expression is "anchors aweigh."

and also/and, also
"And also" is redundant; say just "and" or "also."

and plus
See "redundancies."

anecdote/antidote
A humorist relates "anecdotes." The doctor prescribes "antidotes" for children who have swallowed poison. Laughter may be the best medicine, but that's no reason to confuse these two with each other.

angel/angle
People who want to write about winged beings from Heaven often miscall them "angles." A triangle has three angles. The Heavenly Host is made of angels. Just remember the adjectival form: "angelic." If you pronounce it aloud you'll be reminded that the "E" comes before the "L."

annihilate
See "decimate/annihilate, slaughter, etc."

anticlimatic/anticlimactic
This word has to do with climaxes, not climate, so the word is "anticlimactic."

antidote/anecdote
See "anecdote/antidote."

antisocial/asocial
See "asocial/antisocial."

anxious/eager
Most people use "anxious" interchangeably with "eager," but its original meaning had to do with worrying, being full of anxiety. Perfectly correct phrases like "anxious to please" obscure the nervous tension implicit in this word and lead people to say less correct things like, "I'm anxious for Christmas morning to come so I can open my

presents." Traditionalists frown on anxiety-free anxiousness. Say instead you are eager for or looking forward to a happy event.

any
Instead of saying, "He was the worst of any of the dancers," say, "He was the worst of the dancers."

anymore/any more
In the first place, the traditional (though now uncommon) spelling is as two words: "any more" as in "We do not sell bananas any more." In the second place, it should not be used at the beginning of a sentence as a synonym for "nowadays." In certain dialects of English it is common to utter phrases like, "Anymore you have to grow your own if you want really ripe tomatoes," but this is guaranteed to jolt listeners who aren't used to it. Even if they can't quite figure out what's wrong, they'll feel that your speech is vaguely clunky and awkward. "Any more" always needs to be used as part of an expression of negation except in questions like, "Do you have any more bananas?" Now you won't make that mistake any more, will you?

anytime/any time
Though it is often compressed into a single word by analogy with "anywhere" and similar words, "any time" is traditionally a two-word phrase.

anyways/anyway
"Anyways" at the beginning of a sentence usually indicates that the speaker has resumed a narrative thread: "Anyways, I told Matilda that guy was a lazy bum before she ever married him." It also occurs at the end of phrases and sentences, meaning "in any case": "He wasn't all that good-looking anyways." A slightly less rustic quality can be imparted to these sentences by substituting the more formal "anyway." Neither expression is a good idea in formal written English. The two-word phrase "any way" has many legitimate uses, however: "Is there any way to prevent the impending disaster?"

apart/a part

Paradoxically, the one-word form implies separation while the two-word form implies union. Feuding roommates decide to live *apart*. Their time together may be *a part* of their lives they will remember with some bitterness.

apostrophes

First let's all join in a hearty curse of the grammarians who inserted the wretched apostrophe into possessives in the first place. It was all a mistake. Our ancestors used to write "Johns hat" meaning "the hat of John" without the slightest ambiguity. However, sometime in the Renaissance certain scholars decided that the simple "s" of possession must have been formed out of a contraction of the more "proper" "John his hat." Since in English we mark contractions with an apostrophe, they did so, and we were stuck with the stupid "John's hat." Their error can be a handy reminder though: if you're not sure whether a noun ending in "s" should be followed by an apostrophe, ask yourself whether you could plausibly substitute "his" or "her" for the "s."

The exception to this pattern is personal pronouns indicating possession like "his," "hers," and "its." *For more on this point, see* "its/it's."

Get this straight once and for all: when the "s" is added to a word simply to make it a plural, no apostrophe is used (except in expressions where letters or numerals are treated like words, like "mind your P's and Q's" and "learn your ABC's").

Apostrophes are also used to indicate omitted letters in real contractions: "do not" becomes "don't."

Why can't we all agree to do away with the wretched apostrophe? Because its two uses—contraction and possession—have people so thoroughly confused that they are always putting in apostrophes where they don't belong, in simple plurals ("cucumber's for sale") and family names when they are referred to collectively ("the Smith's").

The practice of putting improper apostrophes in family names on signs in front yards is an endless source of confusion. "The Brown's" is just plain wrong. (If you wanted to suggest "the Browns' residence" you would have to write "Browns'," with the apostrophe *after* the "S," which is there to indicate a plural number, not as an indication of possession.) If you simply want to indicate that a family named Brown lives here, the sign out front should read simply "The Browns." When a name ends in an "S" you need to add an "ES" to make it plural: "the Adamses."

No apostrophes for simple plural names or names ending in "S," OK? I get irritated when people address me as "Mr. Brian's." What about when plural names are used to indicate possession? "The Browns' cat" is standard (the second "S" is "understood"), though some prefer "the Browns's cat." The pattern is the same with names ending in "S": "the Adamses' cat" or—theoretically—"the Adamses's cat," though that would be mighty awkward.

It is not uncommon to see the "S" wrongly apostrophized even in verbs, as in the mistaken "He complain's a lot."

See also "acronyms and apostrophes" and "'50s."

appraise/apprise

When you estimate the value of something, you appraise it. When you inform people of a situation, you apprise them of it.

apropos/appropriate

"Apropos" (anglicized from the French phrase *à propos*) means relevant, connected with what has gone before; it should not be used as an all-purpose substitute for "appropriate." It would be inappropriate, for example, to say, "Your tuxedo was perfectly apropos for the opera gala."

aren't/ain't/am not/isn't

See "ain't/am not/isn't/aren't."

artic/arctic

Although some brand names have incorporated this popular error, remember that the Arctic Circle is an arc. By the way, Ralph Vaughan Williams called his suite drawn from the score of the film *Scott of the Antarctic* the *Sinfonia Antartica*, but that's Italian, not English.

artical/article
The correct spelling is "article."

as far as/all the farther
See "all the farther/as far as."

as far as/as far as . . . is concerned
Originally people used to say things like "As far as music is concerned, I especially love Baroque opera." Recently they have begun to drop the "is concerned" part of the phrase. Perhaps this shift was influenced by confusion with a similar phrase, "as for." "As for money, I don't have any," is fine; "As far as money, I don't have any," is clumsy.

as follow/as follows
"My birthday requests are as follows." This standard phrase doesn't change number when the items to follow grow from one to many. It's never correct to say "as follow."

as if/like
See "like/as if."

as of yet/yet
"As of yet" is a windy and pretentious substitute for plain old English "yet" or "as yet," an unjustified extension of the pattern in sentences like "as of Friday the 27th of May."

as per/in accordance with
"Enclosed is the shipment of #2 toggle bolts as per your order of June 14" writes the businessman, unaware that not only is the "as" redundant, he is sounding very old-fashioned and pretentious. The meaning is "in accordance with," or "in response to the request made"; but it is better to avoid these cumbersome substitutes altogether: "Enclosed is the shipment of bolts you ordered June 14."

ashfault/asphalt
"Ashfault" is a common misspelling of "asphalt."

Asian/Asiatic/Oriental
See "Oriental/Asiatic/Asian."

asocial/antisocial
Someone who doesn't enjoy socializing at parties might be described as either "asocial" or "antisocial"; but "asocial" is too mild a term to describe someone who commits an antisocial act like planting a bomb. "Asocial" suggests indifference to or separation from society, whereas "antisocial" more often suggests active hostility toward society.

aspect/respect
When used to refer to different elements of or perspectives on a thing or idea, these words are closely related, but not interchangeable. It's "in all respects," not "in all aspects." Similarly, one can say "in some respects" but not "in some aspects." One says "in this respect," not "in this aspect. " One looks at all "aspects" of an issue, not at all "respects."

assumably/presumably
The correct word is "presumably."

assure/ensure/insure
To "assure" a person of something is to make him or her confident of it. According to Associated Press style, to "ensure" that something happens is to make certain that it does, and to "insure" is to issue an insurance policy. Other authorities, however, consider "ensure" and "insure" interchangeable. To please conservatives, make the distinction. However, it is worth noting that in older usage these spellings were not clearly distinguished.

European "life assurance" companies take the position that all policy-holders are mortal and someone will definitely collect, thus assuring heirs of some income. American companies tend to go with "insurance" for coverage of life as well as of fire, theft, etc.

asterick/asterisk

Some people not only spell this word without its second "S," they say it that way too. It comes from Greek *asteriskos*: "little star." Tisk, tisk, remember the "-isk"; "asterick" is icky.

at home/to home

See "to home/at home."

athiest/atheist

An atheist is the opposite of a theist. *Theos* is Greek for "god." Make sure the "TH" is followed immediately by an "E."

athlete

Tired of people stereotyping you as a dummy just because you're a jock? One way to impress them is to pronounce "athlete" properly, with just two syllables, as "ATH-leet" instead of using the common mispronunciation "ATH-uh-leet."

ATM machine/ATM

"ATM" means "Automated Teller Machine," so if you say "ATM machine" you are really saying "Automated Teller Machine machine."

augur/auger

An "augur" was an ancient Roman prophet, and as a verb the word means "foretell"—"their love augurs well for a successful marriage." Don't mix this word up with "auger," a tool for boring holes.

    See also "all goes well/augurs well."

aural/oral

"Aural" has to do with things you hear, "oral" with things you say, or relating to your mouth.

averse/adverse

See "adverse/averse."

avocation/vocation

Your "avocation" is just your hobby; don't mix it up with your job: your "vocation."

awhile/a while

When "awhile" is spelled as a single word, it is an adverb meaning "for a time" ("stay awhile"); but when "while" is the object of a prepositional phrase, like "Lend me your monkey wrench for a while," the "while" must be separated from the "a." (But if the preposition "for" were lacking in this sentence, "awhile" could be used in this way: "Lend me your monkey wrench awhile.")

ax/ask

The dialectical pronunciation of "ask" as "ax" suggests to most people that the speaker has a substandard education and is to be avoided in formal speaking situations.

axel/axle

The center of a wheel is its axle. An axel is a tricky jump in figure skating named after Axel Paulson.

---

backslash/slash

This is a slash: /. Because the top of it leans forward, it is sometimes called a "forward slash."

This is a backslash: \. Notice the way it leans back, distinguishing it from the regular slash.

Slashes are often used to indicate directories and subdirectories in computer systems such as Unix and in World Wide Web addresses. Unfortunately, many people, assuming "backslash" is some sort of technical term for the regular slash, use the term incorrectly, which risks confusing those who know enough to distinguish between the two but not enough to realize that web addresses never contain backslashes. Newer browsers will silently correct this error, but older ones may not.

backward/backwards

As an adverb, either word will do: "put the shirt on backward" or "put the shirt on backwards." However, as an adjective, only "backward" will do: "a backward glance." When in doubt, use "backward."

bad/badly

"I feel bad" is standard English, as in "This t-shirt smells bad" (not "badly"). "I feel badly" is an incorrect hyper-correction by people who think they know better than the masses. People who are happy can correctly say they feel good, but if they say they feel well, we know they mean to say they're healthy. However, you may impress your beloved more if you say "I need you really badly" rather than the less correct "I need you real bad."

baited breath/bated breath

Although the odor of the chocolate truffle you just ate may be irresistible bait to your beloved, the proper expression is "bated breath." "Bated" here means "held, abated." You do something with "bated breath" when you're so tense you're holding your breath.

barb wire/bob wire/barbed wire

In some parts of the country this prickly stuff is commonly called "barb wire" or even "bob wire." When writing for a general audience, stick with the standard "barbed wire."

bare/bear

There are actually three words here. The simple one is the big growly creature (unless you prefer the Winnie-the-Pooh type). Hardly anyone past the age of 10 gets that one wrong. The problem is the other two. Stevedores bear burdens on their backs and mothers bear children. Both mean "carry" (in the case of mothers, the meaning has been extended from carrying the child during pregnancy to actually giving birth). But strippers bare their bodies—sometimes bare-naked. The confusion between this latter verb and "bear" creates many unintentionally amusing sentences; so if you want to entertain your readers while convincing them that you are a dolt, by all means mix them up.

21

"Bear with me," the standard expression, is a request for forbearance or patience. "Bare with me" would be an invitation to undress. "Bare" has an adjectival form: "The pioneers stripped the forest bare."

No one wondered what she had said; it was, "Bear with me."

based around/based on
"Based around" has become a common but illogical substitute for the traditional expression "based on."

basicly/basically
There are "-ly" words and "-ally" words, and you basically just have to memorize which is which. But "basically" is very much overused and is often better avoided in favor of such expressions as "essentially," "fundamentally," or "at heart."

bated breath/baited breath
See "baited breath/bated breath."

bazaar/bizarre
A "bazaar" is a market where miscellaneous goods are sold. "Bizarre," in contrast, is an adjective meaning "strange, weird." Let all those "A's" in "bazaar" remind you that this is a Persian word denoting traditional markets.

bear/bare
See "bare/bear."

beaurocracy/bureaucracy
The French *bureaucrats* from whom we get this word worked at their *bureaus* (desks, spelled *bureaux* in French) in what came to be known as *bureaucracies*.

because/due to the fact that
See "due to the fact that/because."

because/since
See "since/because."

beckon call/beck and call
This is a fine example of what linguists call "popular etymology." People don't understand the origins of a word or expression and make one up based on what seems logical to them. "Beck" is just an old, shortened version of "beckon." If you are at people's beck and call it means they can summon you whenever they want: either by gesture (beck) or speech (call).

beginning a sentence with a conjunction
See "conjunction, beginning a sentence with a."

beginning of time
Stephen Hawking writes about the beginning of time, but few other people do. People who write "from the beginning of time" or "since time began" are usually being lazy. Their grasp of history is vague, so they resort to these broad, sweeping phrases. Almost never is this

usage literally accurate: people have not fallen in love since time began, for instance, because people arrived relatively late on the scene in the cosmic scheme of things. When I visited Ferrara several years ago I was interested to see that the whole population of the old city seemed to use bicycles for transportation, cars being banned from the central area. I asked how long this had been the custom and was told "We've ridden bicycles for centuries." Since the bicycle was invented only in the 1890s, I strongly doubted this (no, Leonardo da Vinci did not invent the bicycle—he just drew a picture of what one might look like—and some people think that picture is a modern forgery). If you really don't know the appropriate period from which your subject dates, you could substitute a less silly but still vague phrase such as "for many years," or "for centuries"; but it's better simply to avoid historical statements if you don't know your history.

begs the question

An argument that improperly assumes as true the very point the speaker is trying to argue for is said in formal logic to "beg the question." Here is an example of a question-begging argument: "This painting is trash because it is obviously worthless." The speaker is simply asserting the worthlessness of the work, not presenting any evidence to demonstrate that this is in fact the case. Since we never use "begs" with this odd meaning ("to improperly take for granted") in any other phrase, many people mistakenly suppose the phrase implies something quite different: that the argument demands that a question about it be asked—*raises* the question. If you're not comfortable with formal terms of logic, it's best to stay away from this phrase, or risk embarrassing yourself.

behaviors/behavior

"Behavior" has always referred to patterns of action, including multiple actions, and did not have separate singular and plural forms until social scientists created them. Unless you are writing in psychology, sociology, anthropology, or a related field, it is better to avoid the use of "behaviors" in your writing.

See also "peoples."

bemuse/amuse

When you bemuse someone, you confuse them, and not necessarily in an entertaining way. Don't confuse this word with "amuse."

It was an act that left the audience both bemused and amused.

beside/besides

"Besides" can mean "in addition to" as in "besides the puppy chow, Spot scarfed up the filet mignon I was going to serve for dinner." "Beside," in contrast, usually means "next to." "I sat beside Cheryl all evening, but she kept talking to Jerry instead." Using "beside" for "besides" won't usually get you in trouble, but using "besides" when you mean "next to" will.

better

When Chuck says, "I better get my research started; the paper's due tomorrow," he means "I *had* better," abbreviated in speech to "I'd better." The same pattern is followed for "he'd better," "she'd better," and "they'd better."

between

"Between 1939 to 1945" is obviously incorrect to most people—it should be "between 1939 and 1945"—but the error is not so obvious when it is written thus: "between 1939–1949." In this case, the "between" should be dropped altogether. Also incorrect are expressions like "there were between 15 to 20 people at the party." This should read "between 15 and 20 people."

25

Some people argue that "between" should only be used with two items, "among" with more. The "-tween" in "between" is clearly linked to the number two; but, as the *Oxford English Dictionary* notes, "In all senses, between has, from its earliest appearance, been extended to more than two." We're talking about Anglo-Saxon here—early. Pedants have labored to enforce "among" when there are three or more objects under discussion, but largely in vain. Even the pickiest speaker does not naturally say, "A treaty has been negotiated among England, France, and Germany."

between you and I/between you and me

"Between you and me" is preferred in standard English.

See also "me/I/myself."

beyond the pail/beyond the pale

In medieval Ireland, the area around Dublin was within the limit of English law, everything outside being considered as wild, dangerous territory. The boundary was marked by a fence called the "Pale" (compare with "palisade"). The expression "beyond the pale" came to mean "bizarre, beyond proper limits"; but people who don't understand the phrase often alter the last word to "pail."

bias/biased

A person who is influenced by a bias is *biased*. The expression is not "they're bias," but "they're biased." Also, many people say someone is "biased toward" something or someone when they mean biased *against*. To have a bias toward something is to be biased in its favor.

See also "prejudice/prejudiced."

Bible

Whether you are referring to the Jewish Bible (the Torah plus the Prophets and the Writings), the Protestant Bible (the Jewish Bible plus the New Testament), or the Catholic Bible (which contains everything in the Jewish and Protestant Bibles plus several other books and passages mostly written in Greek in its Old Testament), the word "Bible" must be capitalized. Even when used generically, as in, "The *Qur'an* is the Bible of the Muslims," the word is usually capitalized. Just remember that it is the title of a book, and book titles are normally capitalized. An oddity in English usage is, however, that "Bible" and the names of the various parts of the Bible are not italicized or placed between quotation marks. "Biblical" may be capitalized or not, as you choose (or as your editor chooses).

Those who wish to be sensitive to the Jewish authorship of the Jewish Bible may wish to use "Hebrew Bible" and "Christian Scriptures" instead of the traditionally Christian nomenclature: "Old Testament" and "New Testament." Modern Jewish scholars sometimes use the Hebrew acronym "Tanakh" to refer to their Bible, but this term is not generally understood by others.

biweekly/semiweekly

Technically, a biweekly meeting occurs every two weeks and a semiweekly one occurs twice a week; but so few people get this straight that your club is liable to disintegrate unless you avoid these words in the newsletter and stick with "every other week" or "twice weekly." The same is true of "bimonthly" and" semimonthly," though "biennial" and "semiannual" are less often confused with each other.

bizarre/bazaar

See "bazaar/bizarre."

blatant

The classic meaning of "blatant" is "noisily conspicuous," but it has long been extended to any objectionable obviousness. A person engaging in blatant behavior is usually behaving in a highly objectionable manner, being brazen. Unfortunately, many people nowadays think that "blatant" simply means "obvious" and use it in a positive sense, as in "Kim wrote a blatantly brilliant paper." Use "blatant" or "blatantly" only when you think the people you are talking about should be ashamed of themselves.

boatload/buttload

See "buttload/boatload."

bob wire

See "barb wire/bob wire/barbed wire."

bonafied/bona fide

Bona fide is a Latin phrase meaning "in good faith," most often used to mean "genuine" today. It is often misspelled as if it were the past tense of an imaginary verb: "bonify."

bored of/bored with

It's "bored with."

born out of/born of

Write "My love of dance was born of my viewing old Ginger Rogers-Fred Astaire movies," not "born out of." The latter expression is probably substituted because of confusion with the expression "borne out" as in "My concerns about having another office party were borne out when Mr. Peabody spilled his beer into the fax machine." The only correct (if antiquated) use of "born out of" is in the phrase "born out of wedlock."

borrow/loan

In some dialects it is common to substitute "borrow" for "loan" or "lend," as in "Borrow me that hammer of yours, will you, Jeb?" In standard English the person providing an item can loan it; but the person receiving it borrows it.

See also "lend/loan."

both/each

There are times when it is important to use "each" instead of "both." Few people will be confused if you say, "I gave both of the boys a baseball glove," meaning "I gave both of the boys baseball gloves" because it is unlikely that two boys would be expected to share one glove; but you risk confusion if you say, "I gave both of the boys $50." It is possible to construe this sentence as meaning that the boys shared the same $50 gift. "I gave each of the boys $50" is clearer.

boughten/bought

"Bought" is the past tense of "buy," not "boughten." "Store-bought," a colloquial expression for "not home-made," is already not formal

English; but it is not improved by being turned into "store-boughten."

bound/heading
See "heading/bound."

bourgeois
In the original French, a *bourgeois* was merely a free inhabitant of a *bourg*, or town. Through a natural evolution it became the label for members of the property-owning class, then of the middle class. As an adjective it is used with contempt by bohemians and Marxists to label conservatives whose views are not sufficiently revolutionary. The class made up of bourgeois (which is both the singular and the plural form) is the bourgeoisie. Shaky spellers are prone to leave out the "E" from the middle because "eoi" is not a natural combination in English; but these words have remarkably enough retained their French pronunciation: "boorzh-WAH" and "boorzh-WAH-zee." The feminine form, *bourgeoise*, is rarely encountered in English.

bouyant/buoyant
Buoys are buoyant. In the older pronunciation of "buoy" as "bwoy" this unusual spelling made more sense. Now that the pronunciation has shifted to "boy" we have to keep reminding ourselves that the "U" comes before the "O."

bran new/brand new
The scarecrow in *The Wizard of Oz* (the book), was given "bran-new" brains composed literally of bran; but for everyone else the expression should be "brand new."

brand names
Popular usage frequently converts brand names into generic ones, with the generic name falling into disuse. Few people call gelatin dessert mix anything other than "Jell-O," which helps to explain why it's hard to find Nabisco's Royal Gelatin on the grocery shelves. All facial tissues are "Kleenex" to the masses, all photocopies "Xeroxes." Such commercial fame is, however, a two-edged sword: sales may be

lost as well as gained from such over-familiarity. Few people care whether their "Frisbee" is the genuine Wham-O brand original or an imitation. Some of these terms lack staying power: "Hoover" used to be synonymous with "vacuum cleaner," and the brand name was even transmuted into a verb: "to hoover" (these uses are still common in the U.K.). Most of the time this sort of thing is fairly harmless, but if you are a motel operator offering a different brand of whirlpool bath in your rooms, better not call it a "Jacuzzi."

brang/brung/brought

In some dialects the past tense of "bring" is "brang" and "brung" is the past participle; but in standard English both are "brought."

breach/breech

Substitute a "K" for the "CH" in "breach" to remind you that the word has to do with breakage: you can breach (break through) a dam or breach (violate the terms of) a contract. As a noun, a breach is something broken off or open, as in a breach in a military line during combat.

"Breech," however, refers to rear ends, as in "breeches" (slang spelling "britches"). Thus "breech cloth," "breech birth," or "breech-loading gun."

"Once more into the breach, dear friends," means "let's fill up the gap in the line of battle," not "let's reach into our pants again."

breath/breathe

When you need to breathe, you take a breath. "Breathe" is the verb, "breath" the noun.

bring/take

When you are viewing the movement of something from the point of arrival, use "bring." "When you come to the potluck, please bring a green salad." Viewing things from the point of departure, you should use "take": "When you go to the potluck, take a bottle of wine."

brought/brung/brang

See "brang/brung/brought."

build off of/build on
You build on your earlier achievements, you don't build off of them.

bumrush/bum's rush
A 1987 recording by the rap group Public Enemy popularized the slang term "bumrush" as a verb meaning "to crash into a show hoping to see it for free," evidently by analogy with an earlier usage in which it meant "a police raid." In the hip-hop world to be "bumrushed" (also spelled as two words) has evolved a secondary meaning, "to get beaten up by a group of lowlifes, or 'bums'." However, older people are likely to take all of these as mistakes for the traditional expression "bum's rush," as in "Give that guy the bum's rush," i.e., throw him out unceremoniously, treating him like an unwanted bum. It was traditionally the bum being rushed, whereas in the newer expressions the bums are doing the rushing. It's good to be aware of your audience when you use slang expressions like this, to avoid baffling listeners.

buoyant/bouyant
See "buoyant/bouyant."

burn/burned
See "-ed/-t."

butt naked/buck naked
The standard expression is "buck naked," and the contemporary "butt naked" is an error that will get you laughed at in some circles. However, it might be just as well if the new form were to triumph. Originally a "buck" was a dandy, a pretentious, overdressed show-off of a man. Condescendingly applied in the U.S. to Native Americans and black slaves, it quickly acquired negative connotations. To the historically aware speaker, "buck naked" conjures up stereotypical images of naked "savages" or—worse—slaves laboring naked on plantations. Consider using the alternative expression "stark naked."

buttload/boatload
The original expression (meaning "a lot"), both more polite and more logical, is "boatload."

by/'bye/buy

These are probably confused with each other more often through haste than through actual ignorance, but "by" is the common preposition in phrases like "you should know by now." It can also serve a number of other functions, but the main point here is not to confuse "by" with the other two spellings: "'bye" is an abbreviated form of "goodbye" (preferably with an apostrophe before it to indicate the missing syllable), and "buy" is the verb meaning "purchase." "Buy" can also be a noun, as in "that was a great buy." The term for the position of a competitor who advances to the next level of a tournament without playing is a "bye." All others are "by."

by accident/on accident
See "on accident/by accident."

by in large/by and large
The expression is "by and large." Some also write erroneously "by enlarge."

⚜

cache/cachet
"Cache" comes from the French verb *cacher*, meaning "to hide," and in English is pronounced exactly like the word "cash." But reporters speaking of a cache (hidden horde) of weapons or drugs often mispronounce it to sound like *cachet*—"ca-SHAY"—a word with a very different meaning: originally a seal affixed to a document, now a quality attributed to anything with authority or prestige. Rolex watches have *cachet*.

Caesar/Ceasar
See "Ceasar/Caesar."

callous/callused
Calling someone "callous" is a way of metaphorically suggesting a lack of feeling similar to that caused by calluses on the skin; but if you are

speaking literally of the tough build-up on a person's hand or foot, the word you need is "callused."

calm, cool, and collective/calm, cool, and collected

Unless you're living in an unusually tranquil commune, you wouldn't be "calm, cool, and collective." The last word in this traditional phrase is "collected," in the sense of such phrases as "let me sit down a minute and collect my thoughts." If you leave out "cool" the last word still has to be "collected."

calls for/predicts

Glendower:	I can call spirits from the vasty deep.
Hotspur:	Why, so can I, or so can any man;
	But will they come when you do call for them?

—Shakespeare: *Henry IV, Part 1*

Newspeople constantly joke that the weather service is to blame for the weather, so we shouldn't be surprised when they tell us that the forecast "calls for" rain when what they mean is that it "predicts" rain. Remember, wherever you live, the weather is uncalled for.

Calvary/cavalry

"Calvary," always capitalized, is the hill on which Jesus was crucified. It means "hill of skulls." Soldiers mounted on horseback are cavalry.

cannot/can not

These two spellings are largely interchangeable, but by far the most common is "cannot"; and you should probably use it except when you want to be emphatic: "No, you can *not* wash the dog in the Maytag."

See also "may/might."

canon/cannon

"Canon" used to be such a rare word that there was no temptation to confuse it with "cannon": a large piece of artillery. The debate over the literary canon (a list of officially-approved works) and the popularity of Pachelbel's *Canon* (an imitative musical form commonly called a round) have changed all that—confusion is rampant. Just remember that the big gun is a "cannon." All the rest are "canons." Note that there are metaphorical uses of "cannon" for objects shaped like large guns, such as a horse's "cannon bone."

capital/capitol

A "capitol" is always a building. Cities and all other uses are spelled with an "A" in the last syllable. Would it help to remember that Congress with an "O" meets in the Capitol with another "O"?

capitalization

Proper nouns (names of people and places: "Frederick," "Paris") and proper adjectives ("French," "Biblical") must be capitalized. Many people used to casual e-mail patterns have begun to omit capitals throughout their writing, even at the beginning of sentences when writing in more formal contexts. Unless your correspondent is someone that you know prefers the all-lower-case approach, to be taken seriously you should take the trouble to hit that Shift key when necessary. Particularly watch out for this sloppy habit in writing timed examinations. A teacher who has devoted 20 years to the study of Chinese art flinches when she sees her cherished subject demoted to "chinese."

caramel/Carmel

Take Highway 1 south from Monterey to reach the charming seaside town of Carmel, of which Clint Eastwood was formerly mayor. Dissolve sugar in a little water and cook it down until the sugar turns brown to create caramel. A nationwide chain uses the illiterate spelling "Karmelkorn™," which helps to perpetuate the confusion between these two words.

carat/caret/carrot/karat

"Carrots" are those crunchy orange vegetables Bugs Bunny is so fond of, but this spelling gets misused for less familiar words which are pronounced the same but have very different meanings. Precious stones like diamonds are weighed in carats. The same word is used to express the proportion of pure gold in an alloy, though in this usage it is sometimes spelled "karat" (hence the abbreviation "20K gold"). A caret is a proofreader's mark showing where something needs to be inserted, shaped like a tiny pitched roof. It looks rather like a French circumflex, but is usually distinct from it on modern computer keyboards. Carets are extensively used in computer programming. Just remember, if you can't eat it, it's not a carrot.

card shark/cardsharp
Although he may behave like a shark, the slick, cheating card player is a "cardsharp."

A cardsharp may also be a sharp dresser.

care less
See "could care less/could not care less."

caret/carrot/karat/carat
See "carat/caret/carrot/karat."

caring

Most people are comfortable referring to "caring parents," but speaking of a "caring environment" is jargon, not acceptable in formal English. The environment may contain caring people, but it does not itself do the caring.

Carmel/caramel

See "caramel/Carmel."

carrot/karat/carat/caret

See "carat/caret/carrot/karat."

carrot on a stick/the carrot or the stick

Authoritative dictionaries agree—the expression refers to offering to reward a stubborn mule or donkey with a carrot or threatening to beat it with a stick and not to a carrot being dangled from a stick. For me, the clincher is that no one actually cites the form of the "original expression." In what imaginable context would it possibly be witty or memorable to say that someone or something had been motivated by a carrot on a stick? Why not an apple on a stick, or a bag of oats? Boring, right? Not something likely to pass into popular usage. This saying belongs to the same general family as "You can draw more flies with honey than with vinegar." It is never used except when such contrast is implied.

case and point/case in point

The example before us is a "case in point," not "case and point."

catalog/catalogue

See "'lite' spelling."

catch-22/catch

People familiar with Joseph Heller's novel are irritated when they see "catch-22" used to label any simple hitch or problem rather than this sort of circular dilemma: you can't get published until you have an agent, and you can't get an agent until you've been published. "There's a catch" will do fine for most other situations.

catholic religion
See "religion."

cavalry/Calvary
See "Calvary/cavalry."

CD-ROM disc/CD-ROM disk/CD-ROM
"CD-ROM" stands for "compact disc, read-only memory," so adding another "disc" or "disk" is redundant. The same goes for "DVD" (from "Digital Video Disc" or "Digital Versatile Disc"—there are non-video versions). Don't say "give me that DVD disk," just "give me that DVD."

Ceasar/Caesar
Did you know that the German *Kaiser* is derived from the Latin *Caesar*? The Germans kept the authentic hard "K" sound of the initial letter in the Latin word. We're stuck with our illogical pronunciation, so we have to memorize the correct spelling. (The Russians messed up the pronunciation as thoroughly as the English, with their *Czar*.) Thousands of menus are littered with "Ceasar salads" throughout America—named after the restaurateur Caesar Cardini, not the emperor (but they both spelled their names the same way). Julius Caesar's family name was "Julius"; he made the name "Caesar" famous all by himself.

celibate/chaste
Believe it or not, you can be celibate without being chaste, and chaste without being celibate. A celibate person is merely unmarried, usually (but not always) because of a vow of celibacy. The traditional assumption is that such a person is not having sex with anyone, which leads many to confuse the word with "chaste," denoting someone who does not have illicit sex. A woman could have wild sex twice a day with her lawful husband and technically still be chaste, though the word is more often used to imply a general abstemiousness from sex and sexuality. You can always amuse your readers by misspelling the latter word as "chased."

Celtic

Because the Boston Celtics basketball team pronounces its name as if it began with an "S," Americans are prone to use this pronunciation of the word as it applies to the Bretons, Cornish, Welsh, Irish, and Scots; but the dominant pronunciation among sophisticated U.S. speakers is "KEL-tik." Just remember: "Celts in kilts."

Interestingly, the Scots themselves often use the "S" pronunciation, notably in referring to the soccer team: "Glasgow Celtic."

cement/concrete

People in the building trades distinguish cement (the gray powder that comes in bags) from concrete (the combination of cement, water, sand, and gravel which becomes hard enough in your driveway to drive your car on). In contexts where technical precision matters, it's probably better to speak of a "concrete sidewalk" rather than of a "cement sidewalk."

center around/center on/revolve around

Two perfectly good expressions—"center on" and "revolve around"—get conflated in this nonsensical neologism. When a speaker says his address will "center around the topic of" whatever, my interest level plummets.

center of attraction/center of attention

"Center of attraction" makes perfect sense, but the standard phrase is "center of attention."

cents

On a sign displaying a cost of 29 cents for something, the price can be written as ".29," as "$.29," or as "29¢," but don't combine the two forms. ".29¢" makes no sense, and "$.29¢" is worse.

century names

See "eighteen hundreds/nineteenth century."

chai tea/chai

Chai is simply the word for "tea" in Hindi and several other Asian languages. Indians often brew their tea with lots of milk and spices (called *masala*—they call this drink *masala chai*); and that's what most people in the West know as "chai." Since everyone likely to be attracted by the word "chai" already knows it's a tea-based drink, it's both redundant and pointless to call the product "chai tea."

chaise longue
When English speakers want to be elegant they commonly resort to French, often mangling it in the process. The *entrée*, the dish served before the *plat*, usurped the latter's position as main dish. And how in the world did French *lingerie* (originally meaning linen goods of all sorts, later narrowed to underwear only), pronounced—roughly— "LANZH-uh-ree" come to be English "LAWNZH-uh-ray"? *Quelle horreur! Chaise longue* (literally "long chair"), pronounced— roughly—"SHEZZ lohng" with a hard "G" on the end, became in English "SHAYZ long." Many speakers, however, confuse French *chaise* with English "chase" and French *longue* with English "lounge" (understandable since the article in question is a sort of couch or lounge), resulting in the mispronunciation "chase lounge." We may imagine the French as chasing each other around their lounges, but a *chaise* is just a chair.

champ at the bit/chomp at the bit
See "chomp at the bit/champ at the bit."

chaste
See "celibate/chaste."

cheap at half the price/cheap at twice the price
"Cheap at half the price" implies the price is too high. The only logical version of this common phrase is "cheap at twice the price."

cheat/gyp
See "gyp/cheat."

chemicals
Markets offering "organic" produce claim it has been raised "without chemicals." News stories fret about "chemicals in our water supply." This common error in usage indicates quite clearly the lamentable

level of scientific literacy in our population. Everything on earth save a few stray subatomic particles and various kinds of energy (and—if you believe in it—pure spirit) is composed of chemicals. Pure water consists of the chemical dihydrogen oxide. Vitamins and minerals are chemicals. In the broadest sense, even simple elements like nitrogen can be called chemicals. Writers who use this term sloppily contribute to the obfuscation of public debate over such serious issues as pollution and malnutrition.

"Guaranteed not to be free of chemicals!"

Chicano/Latino/Hispanic

"Chicano" means "Mexican-American," and not all the people denoted by this term like it. When speaking of people from various other Spanish-speaking countries, "Chicano" is an error for "Latino" or "Hispanic." Only "Hispanic" can include people with a Spanish as well as with a Latin American heritage; and only "Latino" could logically include Portuguese-speaking Brazilians, though that is rarely done.

chick/chic

Something fashionable can be labeled with the French adjective *chic*, but it is definitely not *chic* to spell the word "chick" or "sheek."

chomp at the bit/champ at the bit

"Champ at the bit" is the only common use of this old word meaning "gnash," and it conjures up a restless horse chewing on its bit, eager to get underway. Its unfamiliarity makes some people mistakenly substitute the slangy "chomp."

chunk/chuck

In casual conversation, you may get by with saying, "Chuck [throw] me that monkey wrench, will you?" But you will mark yourself as illiterate beyond mere casualness by saying instead, "Chunk me that wrench." This is a fairly common substitution in some dialects of American English.

Church/church

Catholics routinely refer to their church as the Church, with a capital "C." This irritates the members of other churches, but is standard usage. When "Church" stands by itself (that is, not as part of a name like "First Methodist Church"), capitalize it only to mean "Roman Catholic Church."

See also "religion."

cite/site/sight

You cite the author in an endnote; you visit a Web site or the site of the crime, and you sight your beloved running toward you in slow motion on the beach (a sight for sore eyes!).

cleanup/clean up

"Cleanup" is usually a noun: "the cleanup of the toxic waste site will cost billions of dollars." "Clean" is a verb in the phrase "clean up": "You can go to the mall after you clean up your room."

cliché/clichéd

One often hears young people say, "That movie was so cliché!" "Cliché" is a noun, meaning an over-familiar phrase or image. A work containing clichés is clichéd.

click/clique

Students lamenting the division of their schools into snobbish factions often misspell "clique" as "click." In the original French, *clique* was synonymous with *claque*—an organized group of supporters at a theatrical event who tried to prompt positive audience response by clapping enthusiastically.

climax/crescendo

See "crescendo/climax."

close/clothes

Because the "TH" in "clothes" is seldom pronounced distinctly, it is often misspelled "close." Just remember the "TH" in "clothing," where it is obvious. Clothes are made of cloth. Rags can also be cloths (without an "E").

close proximity/close/in proximity to

A redundancy: "in proximity to" means "close to."

coarse/course

"Coarse" is always an adjective meaning "rough, crude." Unfortunately, this spelling is often mistakenly used for a quite different word, "course," which can be either a verb or a noun (with several different meanings).

coincidentally/ironically

See "ironically/coincidentally."

collaborate/corroborate

People who work together on a project collaborate (share their labor); people who support your testimony as a witness corroborate (strengthen by confirming) it.

Colombia/Columbia

Although both are named after Columbus, the U.S. capital is the District of Columbia, whereas the South American country is Colombia.

colons/semicolons

Colons have a host of uses, mostly to connect what precedes them with what follows them. Think of the two dots of a colon as if they were stretched out to form an equal sign, so that you get cases like this: "He provided all the ingredients: sugar, flour, butter, and vanilla." There are a few exceptions to this pattern, however. One unusual use of colons is in between the chapter and verses of a Biblical citation, for instance, "Matthew 6:5." In bibliographic citation a colon separates the city from the publisher: "New York: New Directions, 1979." It also separates minutes from hours in times of day when given in figures: "8:35."

It is incorrect to substitute a semicolon in any of these cases. Think of the semicolon as erecting a little barrier with that dug-in comma under the dot; semicolons always imply separation rather than connection. A sentence made up of two distinct parts whose separation needs to be emphasized may do so with a semicolon: "Mary moved to Seattle; she was sick of getting sunburned in Los Angeles." When a compound sentence contains commas within one or more of its clauses, you have to escalate to a semicolon to separate the clauses themselves: "It was a mild, deliciously warm spring day; and Mary decided to walk to the fair." The other main use of semicolons is to separate one series of items from another—a series within a series, if you will: "The issues discussed by the board of directors were many: the loud, acrimonious complaints of the stockholders; the abrupt, devastating departure of the director; and the startling, humiliating discovery that he had absconded with half the company's assets." Any time the phrases that make up a series contain commas—for whatever reason—they need to be separated by semicolons.

Many people are so terrified of making the wrong choice that they try to avoid colons and semicolons altogether, but I'm afraid this just can't be done. Formal writing requires their use, and it's necessary to learn the correct patterns.

Columbia/Colombia
See "Colombia/Columbia."

commas

What follows is not a comprehensive guide to the many uses of commas, but a quick tour of the most common errors involving them.

The first thing to note is that the comma often marks a brief pause in the flow of a sentence, and it helpfully marks off one phrase from another. If you write "I plan to see Shirley and Fred will go shopping while we visit" your reader is naturally going to think the announced visit will be to both Shirley and Fred until the second half surprises them into realizing that Fred is not involved in this visit at all. A simple comma makes everything clear: "I plan to see Shirley, and Fred will go shopping while we visit." People who read and write little have trouble with commas if they deal with English primarily as a spoken language, where emphasis and rhythm mark out phrases. It takes a conscious effort to translate the rhythm of a sentence into writing using punctuation.

Not many people other than creative writers have the occasion to write dialogue, but it is surprising how few understand that introductory words and phrases have to be separated from the main body of speech in direct address: "Well, what did you think of that?" "Good evening, Mr. Nightingale."

Commas often help set off interrupting matter within sentences. The proper term for this sort of word or phrase is "parenthetical." There are three ways to handle parenthetical matter. For asides sharply interrupting the flow of the sentence (think of your own examples) use parenthesis marks. For many other kinds of fairly strong interjections, dashes—if you know how to type them properly—work best. Milder interruptions, like this, are nicely set off with commas. Many writers don't realize that they are setting off a phrase, so they begin with the first comma but omit the second, which should conclude the parenthetical matter. Check for this sort of thing in your proofreading.

A standard use for commas is in separating the items in a series: "cats, dogs, and gerbils." Authorities differ as to whether that final comma before the "and" is required. Follow the style recommended by your teacher, editor, or boss when you have to please them; but if you are on your own, I suggest you use the final comma. It often removes ambiguities.

A different kind of series has to do with a string of adjectives modifying a single noun: "He was a tall, strong, handsome, but stupid man." But when the adjectives modify each other instead of the noun, then no comma is used: "He was wearing a garish bright green tie." A simple test: if you could logically insert "and" between the adjectives in a series like this, you need commas.

English teachers refer to sentences where clauses requiring some stronger punctuation are instead lightly pasted together with a comma as "comma splices." Here's an example: "He brought her a dozen roses, he had forgotten she was allergic to them." In this sentence the reader needs to be brought up sharply and reoriented mid-sentence with a semicolon; a comma is too weak to do the trick. Here's a worse example of a comma splice: "It was a beautiful day outside, she remembered just in time to grab the coffee mug." There is no obvious logical connection between the two parts of this sentence. They don't belong in the same sentence at all. The comma should be a period, with the rest being turned into a separate sentence.

Some writers insert commas seemingly at random: "The unabridged dictionary, was used mainly to press flowers." When you're not certain a comma is required, read your sentence aloud. If it doesn't seem natural to insert a slight pause or hesitation at the point marked by the comma, it should probably be omitted.

See also "colons/semicolons" *and* "hyphens & dashes."

compare and contrast/compare

Hey kids, here's a chance to catch your English teacher in a redundancy! To compare two things is to note their similarities and their differences. There's no need to add "and contrast."

compare to/compare with

These are sometimes interchangeable, but when you are stressing similarities between the items compared, the most common word is "to": "She compared his home-made wine to toxic waste." If you are examining both similarities and differences, use "with": "The teacher compared Steve's exam with Robert's to see whether they had cheated."

45

complement/compliment

Originally these two spellings were used interchangeably, but they have come to be distinguished from each other in modern times. Most of the time the word people intend is "compliment": nice things said about someone ("She paid me the compliment of admiring the way I shined my shoes."). "Complement," much less common, has a number of meanings associated with matching or completing. Complements supplement each other, each adding something the others lack, so we can say that "Alice's love for entertaining and Mike's love for washing dishes *complement* each other." Remember, if you're not making nice to someone, the word is "complement."

complementary/complimentary

When paying someone a compliment like "I love what you've done with the kitchen!" you're being complimentary. A free bonus item is also a complimentary gift. But colors that go well with each other are complementary.

a completely different/a whole 'nother

See "a whole 'nother/a completely different."

comprised of/composed of

Although "comprise" is used primarily to mean "to include," it is also often stretched to mean "is made up of"—a meaning that some critics object to. The most conservative route is to avoid using "of" after any form of "comprise" and substitute "is composed of" in sentences like this: "Jimmy's paper on Marxism was composed entirely of sentences copied off the Marx Brothers home page."

comptroller

Although it is less and less often heard, the traditional pronunciation of "comptroller" is identical with "controller." The *Oxford English Dictionary*, indeed, considers "comptroller" to have begun as a misspelling of "controller"—back in the 16th century.

concensus/consensus

You might suppose that this word had to do with taking a census of the participants in a discussion, but it doesn't. It is a good old Latin word that has to do with arriving at a common sense of the meeting, and the fourth letter is an "S."

concerted effort

One cannot make a "concerted effort" all by one's self. To work "in concert" is to work together with others. The prefix "con-" means "with." One can, however, make a concentrated effort.

concrete/cement

See "cement/concrete."

conflicted/conflicting feelings

Phrases like "conflicted feelings" or "I feel conflicted" are considered jargon by many and out of place in formal writing. Use "I have conflicting feelings" instead, or write "I feel ambivalent."

Confusionism/Confucianism

This spelling error isn't exactly an English error, but it's very common among my students. Confucius is the founder of Confucianism. His name is not spelled "Confucious," and his philosophy is not called "Confusionism." When you spot the confusion in the latter term, change it quickly to "Confucianism."

congradulations/congratulations

I fear that all too many people are being "congradulated" for *grad*uating from high school who don't know that this word should be spelled "congratulations." Try a search for this misspelling on your favorite Web search engine and be prepared to be astonished.

conjunction, beginning a sentence with a

It offends those who wish to confine English usage in a logical straitjacket that writers often begin sentences with "and" or "but." True, one should be aware that many such sentences would be improved by becoming clauses in compound sentences; but there are many effective and traditional uses for beginning sentences thus. One example is the reply to a previous assertion in a dialogue: "But, my dear Watson, the criminal obviously wore expensive boots or he would not have taken such pains to scrape them clean." Make it a rule to consider whether your conjunction would repose more naturally within the previous sentence or would lose in useful emphasis by being demoted from its position at the head of a new sentence.

connaisseur/connoisseur

Some complain that English "connoisseur" is a misspelling of French *connaisseur*; but when we borrowed this word from the French in the 18th century, it was spelled *connoisseur*. Is it our fault the French later decided to shift the spelling of many "OI" words to the more phonetically accurate "AI"? Of those Francophone purists who insist we should follow their example I say, let 'em eat *bifteck*.

consensus/concensus

See "concensus/consensus."

continual/continuous

"Continuous" refers to actions that are uninterrupted: "My upstairs neighbor played his stereo continuously from 6:00 P.M. to 3:30 A.M." Continual actions, however, need not be uninterrupted, only repeated: "My father continually urges me to get a job."

contrasts/contrasts with

"With" must not be omitted in sentences like this: "Julia's enthusiasm for rugby contrasts with Cheryl's devotion to chess."

conversate/converse

"Conversate" is what is called a "back-formation" based on the noun "conversation." But the verb for this sort of thing is "converse."

convince/persuade

Some people like to distinguish between these two words by insisting that you persuade people until you have convinced them; but "persuade" as a synonym for "convince" goes back at least to the 16th century. It can mean both to attempt to convince and to succeed. It is no longer common to say things like "I am persuaded that you are an illiterate fool," but even this usage is not in itself wrong.

copy and paste/cut and paste
See "cut and paste/copy and paste."

copywrite/copyright
You can copyright writing, but you can also copyright a photograph or song. The word has to do with securing *rights*.

core/corps/corpse
Apples have cores. A corps is an organization, like the Peace Corps. A corpse is a dead body, a carcass.

corroborate/collaborate
See "collaborate/corroborate."

cortage/cortege
"Cortage" is a common misspelling of "cortege."

could care less/could not care less
Clichés are especially prone to scrambling because they become meaningless through overuse. In this case an expression that originally meant "it would be impossible for me to care less than I do because I do not care at all" is rendered senseless by being transformed into the now-common "I could care less." Think about it: if you could care less, that means you care some. The original already drips sarcasm, so it's pointless to argue that the newer version is ironic. People who misuse this phrase are just being careless.

could of, should of, would of/
could have, should have, would have
This is one of those errors typically made by a person more familiar with the spoken than the written form of English. A sentence like "I would have gone if anyone had given me free tickets" is normally spoken in a slurred way so that the two words "would have" are not distinctly separated, but blended together into what is properly rendered "would've." Seeing that "V" tips you off right away that

"would've" is a contraction of "would have." But many people hear "would of" and that's how they write it. Wrong.

Note that "must of" is similarly an error for "must have."

See also "verb tense."

council/counsel/consul

The first two words are pronounced the same but have distinct meanings. An official group that deliberates, like the Council on Foreign Relations, is a "council"; all the rest are "counsels": your lawyer, advice, etc. A consul is a local representative of a foreign government.

countries/states

See "states/countries."

coupe de gras/coup de grace

A *coupe de gras* (pronounced "coop duh grah") would be a cup of fat; what is intended is the French fencing term *coup de grace* (pronounced "coo duh grahss"), the final blow that puts the defeated victim out of his misery.

couple/couple of

Instead of "She went with a couple sleazy guys before she met me," write "a couple *of* guys" if you are trying to sound a bit more formal. Leaving the "of" out is a casual, slangy pattern.

course/coarse

See "coarse/course."

credible/credulous

"Credible" means "believable" or "trustworthy." It is also used in a more abstract sense, meaning something like "worthy": "She made a credible lyric soprano." Don't confuse "credible" with "credulous," a much rarer word that means "gullible." "He was incredulous" means "he didn't believe it," whereas "he was incredible" means "he was wonderful" (but use the latter expression only in casual speech).

See also "incredible."

50

crescendo/climax

When something is growing louder or more intense, it is going through a crescendo (from an Italian word meaning "growing"). Traditionalists object to its use when you mean "climax." A crescendo of cheers by an enthusiastic audience grows until it reaches a climax, or peak. "Crescendo" as a verb is common, but also disapproved by many authorities. Instead of "the orchestra crescendos," write "the orchestra plays a crescendo."

criteria/criterion

There are several words with Latin or Greek roots whose plural forms ending in "A" are constantly mistaken for singular ones. You can have one criterion or many criteria. Don't confuse them.

See also "data/datum" and "media/medium."

criticism

Beginning literature or art history students are often surprised to learn that in such contexts "criticism" can be a neutral term meaning simply "evaluating a work of literature or art." A critical article about *The Color Purple* can be entirely positive about Alice Walker's novel. Movie critics write about films they like as well as about films they dislike: writing of both kinds is called "criticism."

critique/criticize

A critique is a detailed evaluation of something. The formal way to request one is "give me your critique," though people often say informally "critique this"—meaning "evaluate it thoroughly." But "critique" as a verb is not synonymous with "criticize" and should not be routinely substituted for it. "Josh critiqued my backhand" means Josh evaluated your tennis technique but not necessarily that he found it lacking. "Josh criticized my backhand" means that he had a low opinion of it.

You can write criticism on a subject, but you don't criticize *on* something, you just criticize it.

crucifiction/crucifixion

One might suppose that this common misspelling was a product of skepticism were it not for the fact that it most often occurs in the

51

writings of believers. The word should make clear that Jesus was affixed to the cross, not imply that his killing is regarded as a fiction.

currant/current

"Current" is an adjective having to do with the present time. It can also be a noun naming a thing that, like time, flows: electrical current and currents of public opinion. "Currant" refers only to little fruits.

currently/presently

See "presently/currently."

cut and dry

Many people mishear the standard expression meaning "set," "not open to change," as "cut and dry." Although this form is listed in the *Oxford English Dictionary*, it is definitely less common in sophisticated writing. The dominant modern usage is "cut and dried." When used to modify a noun, it must be hyphenated: "cut-and-dried plan."

cut and paste/copy and paste

Because "cut and paste" is a familiar phrase, many people say it when they mean "copy and paste" in a computer context. This can lead to disastrous results if followed literally by an inexpert person. If you mean to tell someone to duplicate something rather than move it, say "copy." And when you are moving bits of computer information from one place to another, the safest sequence is often to copy the original, paste the copy elsewhere, and only then delete (cut) the original.

cut the muster/cut the mustard

Some people insist that the original phrase is "cut the muster" rather than the seemingly nonsensical "cut the mustard." This etymology seems plausible at first. Its proponents often trace it to the American Civil War. We do have the analogous expression "to pass muster," which probably first suggested this alternative; but although the origins of "cut the mustard" are somewhat obscure, the latter is definitely the form used in all sorts of writing throughout the 20th century. No advocate of the rival form has ever documented an authentic instance of its use in a 19th-century context. Common sense would suggest that a person cutting a muster is not someone being selected as fit, but someone eliminating the unfit.

Sometimes even mustard cuts the mustard.

damped/dampened

When the vibration of a wheel is reduced it is damped, but when you drive through a puddle your tire is dampened. "Dampened" always has to do with wetting, if only metaphorically: "The announcement that Bob's parents were staying home after all dampened the spirits of the party-goers." The parents are being a wet blanket.

dashes

See "hyphens & dashes."

data/datum

There are several words with Latin or Greek roots whose plural forms ending in "A" are constantly mistaken for singular ones. "Datum" is

53

so rare now in English that people may assume "data" has no singular form. Many American usage communities, however, use "data" as a singular and some have even gone so far as to invent "datums" as a new plural. This is a case where you need to know the patterns of your context. An engineer or scientist used to writing "the data is" may well find that the editors of a journal or publishing house insist on changing this phrase to "the data are." Usage is so evenly split in this case that there is no automatic way of determining which is right; but writers addressing an international audience of nonspecialists would probably be safer treating "data" as plural.

See also "criteria/criterion" and "media/medium."

deaf/hearing-impaired
See "hearing-impaired/deaf."

decade names
See "'50s."

decimate/annihilate, slaughter, etc.
This comes under the heading of the truly picky. Despite the fact that most dictionaries have caved in, some of us still remember that when the Romans killed one out of every 10 (*decem*) soldiers in a rebellious group as an example to the others, they decimated them. People sensitive to the roots of words are uncomfortably reminded of that 10 percent figure when they see the word used instead to mean "annihilate," "obliterate," etc. You can usually get away with using "decimate" to mean "drastically reduce in numbers," but you're taking a bigger risk when you use it to mean "utterly wipe out."

deep-seeded/deep-seated
Those who pine for the oral cultures of Ye Olden Dayes can rejoice as we enter an era where many people are unfamiliar with common expressions in print and know them only by hearsay.* The result is

---

* The notion that English should be spelled as it is pronounced is widespread, but history is against the reformers in most cases. Pronunciation is often a poor guide to spelling. The veneration of certain political movements for the teaching of reading through phonics is nicely caricatured by a t-shirt slogan I've seen: "Hukt awn fonix."

mistakes like "deep-seeded." The expression has nothing to do with a feeling being planted deep within one, but instead refers to its being seated firmly within one's breast: "My aversion to anchovies is deep-seated." Compounding their error, most people who misuse this phrase leave the hyphen out. Tennis players may be seeded, but not feelings.

defence/defense

If you are writing for a British publication, use "defence," but the American "defense" has the advantages of greater antiquity, similarity to the words from which it was derived, and consistency with words like "defensible."

definate/definite

Any vowel in an unstressed position can sometimes have the sound linguists call a *schwa*: "uh." The result is that many people tend to guess when they hear this sound, but "definite" is definitely the right spelling. Also common are various misspellings of "definitely," including the bizarre "defiantly."

defuse/diffuse

You defuse a dangerous situation by treating it like a bomb and removing its fuse; to diffuse, in contrast, is to spread something out: "Bob's cheap cologne diffused throughout the room, wrecking the wine-tasting."

degrade/denigrate/downgrade

See "downgrade/degrade/denigrate."

deities/dieties

See "dieties/deities."

deja vu

In French *déjà vu* means literally "already seen" and usually refers to something excessively familiar. However, the phrase—sans accent marks—was introduced into English mainly as a psychological term indicating the sensation one experiences when feeling that something has been experienced before when this is in fact not the case. If you feel strongly that you have been previously in a place where you know you have never before been, you are experiencing a sensation of deja vu. English usage is rapidly sliding back toward the French meaning, confusing listeners who expect the phrase to refer to a false sensation rather than a factual familiarity, as in "Congress is in session and talking about campaign finance reform, creating a sense of deja vu." In this relatively new sense, the phrase has the same associations as the colloquial "same old, same old" (increasingly often misspelled "sameo, sameo" by illiterates). A common misspelling by those who know a little French is "deja vous."

Baseball player Yogi Berra famously mangled this expression in his redundant statement, "It's like deja vu all over again." Over the ensuing decades clever writers would allude to this blunder in their prose by repeating the phrase "deja vu all over again," assuming that their readers would catch the allusion and share a chuckle with them. Unfortunately, recently the phrase has been worn to a frazzle and become all but substituted for the original, so that not only has it become a very tired joke indeed—a whole generation has grown up thinking that Berra's malapropism is the correct form of the expression. Give it a rest, folks!

Democrat Party/Democratic Party
Certain Republican members of Congress have played the childish game in recent years of referring to the opposition as the "Democrat Party," hoping to imply that Democrats are not truly democratic. They succeed only in making themselves sound ignorant, and so will you if you imitate them. The name is "Democratic Party."

depends/depends on
In casual speech, we say, "It depends who plays the best defense," but in writing follow "depends" with "on."

depreciate/deprecate
To depreciate something is to actually make it worse, whereas to deprecate something is simply to speak or think of it in a manner that demonstrates your low opinion of it.

See also "downgrade/degrade/denigrate."

desert/dessert

Perhaps these two words are confused partly because "dessert" is one of the few words in English with a double "S" pronounced like "Z" ("brassiere" is another). That impoverished stretch of sand called a "desert" can only afford one "S." In contrast, that rich gooey extra thing at the end of the meal called a "dessert" indulges in two of them. The word in the phrase "he got his just deserts" is confusingly pronounced just like "desserts."

device/devise

"Device" is a noun. A can-opener is a device. "Devise" is a verb. You can devise a plan for opening a can with a sharp rock instead. Only in law is "devise" properly used as a noun, meaning something deeded in a will.

diaeresis

See "accent marks."

dialate/dilate

The influence of "dial" causes many people to mispronounce and misspell "dilate" by adding an extra syllable.

dialogue/discuss

"Dialogue" as a verb in sentences like "The Math Department will dialogue with the Dean about funding" is commonly used jargon in business and education settings, but abhorred by traditionalists. Say "have a dialogue" or "discuss" instead.

did/done

See "done/did."

dieties/deities

This one is always good for a laugh. The gods are deities, after the Latin *deus*, meaning "god."

differ/vary

"Vary" can mean "differ," but saying "our opinions vary" makes it sound as if they were changing all the time when what you really mean is "our opinions differ." Pay attention to context when choosing one of these words.

different than/different from/different to
Americans say "Scuba-diving is different from snorkeling," the British sometimes say "different to" and those who don't know any better say "different than."

diffuse/defuse
See "defuse/diffuse."

dilate/dialate
See "dialate/dilate."

dilemma/difficulty
A dilemma is a difficult *choice*, not just any difficulty or problem. Whether to invite your son's mother to his high school graduation when your current wife hates her is a dilemma. Cleaning up after a hurricane is just a problem, though a difficult one.

dire straights/dire straits
When you are threading your way through troubles as if you were traversing a dangerously narrow passage, you are in "dire straits." The expression and the band by that name are often transformed by those who don't understand the word "strait" into "dire straights."

    See also "straightjacket/straitjacket."

disburse/disperse
You *disburse* money by taking it out of your purse (French *bourse*) and distributing it. If you refuse to hand out any money, the eager mob of beggars before you may *disperse* (scatter).

disc/disk
"Compact disc" is spelled with a "C" because that's how its inventors decided it should be rendered; but a computer disk is spelled with a "K" (unless it's a CD-ROM, of course). The *New York Times* insisted for many years on the spelling "compact disk" in its editorial pages,

often incongruously next to ads containing the patented spelling "disc"; but now even it has given in.

discreet/discrete

The more common word is "discreet," meaning "prudent, circumspect": "When arranging the party for Agnes, be sure to be discreet; we want her to be surprised." "Discrete" means "separate, distinct": "He arranged the guest list into two discrete groups: meat-eaters and vegetarians." Note how the "T" separates the two "E's" in "discrete."

discuss/dialogue

See "dialogue/discuss."

discussed/disgust

"Discussed" is the past tense of the verb "discuss." Don't substitute for it the noun "disgust" in such sentences as "The couple's wedding plans were thoroughly discussed."

disinterested/uninterested

A bored person is uninterested. Do not confuse this word with the much rarer "disinterested," which means "objective, neutral."

"Perhaps I should state it more exactly: I'm not disinterested; I'm uninterested."

disk/disc
See "disc/disk."

disk/drive
See "drive/disk."

disperse/disburse
See "disburse/disperse."

disrespect
The hip-hop subculture has revived the use of "disrespect" as a verb. In the meaning "to have or show disrespect," this usage has been long established, if unusual. However, the new street meaning of the term, ordinarily abbreviated to "dis," is slightly but significantly different: to act disrespectfully, or—more frequently—insultingly toward someone. In some neighborhoods "dissing" is defined as merely failing to show sufficient terror in the face of intimidation. In those neighborhoods, it is wise to know how the term is used; but an applicant for a job who complains about having been "disrespected" elsewhere is likely to incur further disrespect . . . and no job. Street slang has its uses, but this is one instance that has not become generally accepted.

diswraught/distraught
"Diswraught" is a common misspelling of "distraught."

dived/dove
See "dove/dived."

do to/due to
This expression, meaning "because of," is often misspelled "do to." Some authorities urge substituting "because" in formal writing; but it's not likely to get you into trouble.

doctorial/doctoral
"Doctoral" is occasionally misspelled—and often mispronounced—"doctorial."

documentated/documented
The proper form is "documented."

doesn't/don't
See "don't/doesn't"

doggy dog world/dog-eat-dog world
The punning name of the popular rap star Snoop Doggy Dogg did a lot to spread this misspelling. The original image is of a cannibalistically competitive world in which people turn on each other, like dogs eating other dogs.

dolly/handcart
A dolly is a flat platform with wheels on it, often used to make heavy objects mobile or by an auto mechanic lying on one under a car body. Many people mistakenly use this word to designate the vertically oriented, two-wheeled device with upright handles and horizontal lip. This latter device is more properly called a "handcart" or "hand truck."

dominate/dominant
The verb is "dominate"; the adjective is "dominant." The dominant chimpanzee tends to dominate the others.

done/did
The past participle of "do" is "done," so it's not "they have did what they promised not to do" but "they have *done*. . . ." But without a helping verb, the word is "did." Nonstandard: "I done good on the test." Standard: "I did well on the test."

done/finished
Some claim "dinner is done; people are finished." I pronounce this an antiquated distinction rarely observed in modern speech. Nobody really supposes the speaker is saying he or she has been roasted to a turn. In older usage people said, "I have done," to indicate they had completed an action. "I am done" is not really so very different.

don't/doesn't

In formal English, "don't" is not used in the third person singular. "I don't like avocado ice cream" is correct, and so is "they don't have their passports yet" and "they don't have the sense to come in out of the rain"; but "he don't have no money," though common in certain dialects, is nonstandard on two counts: it should be "he doesn't" and "any money." The same is true of other forms: "she don't" and "it don't" should be "she doesn't" and "it doesn't."

double negatives

It is not true, as some assert, that double negatives are always wrong; but the pattern in formal speech and writing is that two negatives equal a mild positive: "He is a not untalented guitarist" means he has some talent. In informal speech, however, double negatives are intended as negatives: "He ain't got no talent" means he is a lousy musician. People are rarely confused about the meaning of either pattern, but you do need to take your audience into account when deciding which pattern to follow.

One of the funniest uses of the literary double negative is Douglas Adams' description of a machine dispensing "a substance almost, but not quite, entirely unlike tea."

doubt that/doubt whether/doubt if

If you really doubt that something is true (suspect that it's false), use "doubt that": "I doubt that Fred has really lost 25 pounds." If you want to express genuine uncertainty, use "whether": "I doubt whether we'll see the comet if the clouds don't clear soon." "Doubt if" can be substituted for "doubt whether," though it's considered somewhat more casual, but don't use it when you mean "doubt that."

doubtlessly/doubtless

Leave off the unnecessary "-ly" in "doubtless."

dove/dived

Although "dove" is a common form of the past tense of "dive," a few authorities consider "dived" preferable in formal writing.

down the pipe/down the pike

People in the northeastern U.S. know that a pike is a highway, but others who don't understand the term mistakenly substitute the seemingly logical "pipe."

downfall/drawback

A downfall is something that causes a person's destruction, either literal or figurative: "expensive cars were Fred's downfall: he spent his entire inheritance on them and went bankrupt." A drawback is not nearly so drastic, just a flaw or problem of some kind, and is normally applied to plans and activities, not to people: "Gloria's plan to camp on Mosquito Island had just one drawback: she had forgotten to bring her insect repellent." Also, "downfall" should not be used when the more moderate "decline" is meant; reserve it for ruin, not to designate simple deterioration.

downgrade/degrade/denigrate

Many people use "downgrade" instead of "denigrate" to mean "defame, slander." "Downgrade" is entirely different in meaning. When something is downgraded, it is lowered in grade (usually made worse), not just considered worse. "When the president of the company fled to Rio with $15 million, its bonds were downgraded to junk bond status." "Degrade" is much more flexible in meaning. It can mean to lower in status or rank (like "downgrade") or to corrupt or make contemptible; but it always has to do with actual reduction in value rather than mere insult, like "denigrate." Most of the time when people use "downgrade" they would be better off instead using "insult," "belittle," or "sneer at."

While we're at it, let's distinguish between "deprecate," meaning "disapprove," and "depreciate," which, like "downgrade," is not a mere matter of approval or opinion but signifies an actual lowering of value.

dragged/drug

See "drug/dragged."

drank/drunk

Many verbs in English change form when their past tense is preceded by an auxiliary ("helping") verb: "I ran, I have run." The same is true of "drink." Don't say "I've drank the beer" unless you want people to think you are drunk. An even more common error is "I drunk all the milk." It's "I've drunk the beer" and "I drank all the milk."

drastic

"Drastic" means "severe" and is always negative. Drastic measures are not just extreme, they are likely to have harmful side effects. Don't use this word or "drastically" in a positive or neutral sense. A drastic rise in temperature should be seen as downright dangerous, not just surprisingly large. Often people mean "dramatic" instead.

drawback/downfall
See "downfall/drawback."

dreamt/dreamed
See "-ed/-t."

dribble/drivel

"Dribble" and "drivel" originally meant the same thing: drool. But the two words have become differentiated. When you mean to criticize someone else's speech as stupid or pointless, the word you want is "drivel."

drier/dryer
A clothes *dryer* makes the clothes *drier.*

drive/disk

A hard drive and a hard disk are much the same thing; but when it comes to removable computer media, the drive is the machinery that turns and reads the disk. Be sure not to ask for a drive when all you need is a disk.

drownding/drowning
Before you are drowned, you are "drowning," without the extra "D." Later, you have not "drownded." You've "drowned."

drug/dragged

"Well, look what the cat drug in!" Unless you are trying to render dialectical speech to convey a sense of down-home rusticity, use "dragged" as the past tense of "drag."

drunk/drank

See "drank/drunk."

dual/duel

"Dual" is an adjective describing the two-ness of something—dual carburetors, for instance. A "duel" is a formal battle intended to settle a dispute.

duck tape/duct tape

A commercial firm has named its product "Duck Tape," harkening back to the original name for this adhesive tape (which was green), developed during World War II by Johnson & Johnson to waterproof ammunition cases. The generic term is now usually "duct tape," for its use in connecting ventilation and other ducts (which match its current silver color).

due to/do to

See "do to/due to."

due to the fact that/because

Although "due to" is now a generally acceptable synonym for "because," "due to the fact that" is a clumsy and wordy substitute that should be avoided in formal writing. "Due to" is often misspelled "do to."

duel/dual

See "dual/duel."

dwelt/dwelled

See "-ed/-t."

dyeing/dying

If you are using dye to change your favorite t-shirt from white to blue you are *dyeing* it; but if you don't breathe for so long that your face turns blue, you may be *dying*.

---

e.g./i.e.

When you mean "for example," use "e.g." It is an abbreviation for the Latin phrase *exempli gratia*. When you mean "that is," use "i.e." It is an abbreviation for the Latin phrase *id est*. Either can be used to clarify a preceding statement—the first by example, the second by restating the idea more clearly or expanding upon it. Because these uses are so similar, the two abbreviations are easily confused. If you just stick with good old English "for example" and "that is" you won't give anyone a chance to sneer at you. If you insist on using the abbreviation, perhaps "example given" will remind you to use "e.g.," while "in effect" suggests "i.e."

e-mail

See "email/e-mail."

each

"Each" as a subject is always singular: think of it as equivalent to "every one." The verb whose subject it is must also be singular. Some uses, like "To keep them from fighting, each dog has been given its own bowl," cause no problem. No one is tempted to say "have been given." But when a prepositional phrase with a plural object intervenes between subject and verb, we are likely to be misled into saying things like "Each of the children have to memorize their own locker combinations." The subject is "each," not "children." The tendency to avoid specifying gender by using "their" adds to pressure toward plurality; but the correct version of this sentence is "Each of the children has to memorize his or her own locker combination." One can avoid the entire problem by pluralizing throughout: "All the children have to memorize their own locker combinations" (but see the entry on singular "they" for more on this point). In many uses, however, "each" is not the subject, as in "We each have our own favorite flavor of ice cream," which is correct because "we," not "each," is the subject of the verb "have."

"Each other" cannot be a subject, so the question of verb number does not arise; but the number of the possessive creates a problem for some writers. "They gazed into each other's eyes" is correct and "each others'" is incorrect because "each other" is singular. Reword to "each gazed into the other's eyes" to see the logic behind this rule. "Each other" is always two distinct words separated by a space although it functions grammatically as a sort of compound word.

See also "both/each."

eager/anxious
See "anxious/eager."

Earth/earth/Moon/moon
Soil is lower-case "earth." And in most uses even the planet itself remains humbly in lower-case letters: "peace on earth." But in astronomical contexts, the Earth comes into its own with a proud initial capital, and in science fiction it drops the introductory article and becomes "Earth," just like Mars and Venus. A similar pattern applies to Earth's satellite: "shine on, harvest moon," but "from the Earth to the Moon." Because other planets also have moons, it never loses its article.

ecology/environment
"Ecology" is the study of living things in relationship to their environment. The word can also be used to describe the totality of such relationships; but it should not be substituted for "environment" in statements like "Improperly discarded lead batteries harm the ecology." It's not the relationships that are being harmed, but nature itself: the batteries are harming the environment.

economical/economic
Something is economical if it saves you money; but if you're talking about the effect of some measure on the world's economy, it's an *economic* effect.

ecstatic
Pronounced "eck-STA-tic," not "ess-TA-tic."

ect./etc.
"Etc." is an abbreviation for the Latin phrase *et cetera*, meaning "and others." (*Et* means "and" in French too.) Just say "et cetera" out loud to yourself to remind yourself of the correct order of the "T" and "C." Also to be avoided is the common mispronunciation "excetera." "And etc." is a redundancy.

-ed/-ing
In some dialects it is common to say "my shoes need shined" instead of the standard "my shoes need shining" or "my shoes need to be shined."

-ed/-t
You have *learnt* your lessons only in U.K.-influenced countries; you've *learned* them in the U.S. There are several common verbs that often have "T" endings in Britain which seem a little quaint and poetic in American English, where we prefer "-ed." Other examples: "dreamt/dreamed," "dwelt/dwelled," "leant/leaned," "leapt/leaped," and "spelt/spelled." However, the following alternatives are both common in the U.S.: "burned/burnt" and "kneeled/knelt."

effect/affect
See "affect/effect."

effluence/affluence
See "affluence/effluence."

ei/ie
The familiar rule is that English words are spelled with the "I" before the "E" unless they follow a "C," as in "receive." But it is important to add that words in which the vowel sound is an "A" like "neighbor" and "weigh" are also spelled with the "E" first. And there are a few exceptions like "counterfeit" and "seize."

    See also "neice/niece."

1800s/19th century

"Eighteen hundreds," "sixteen hundreds," and so forth are not exactly errors; the problem is that they are used almost exclusively by people who are nervous about saying "19th century" when, after all, the years in that century begin with the number 18. This should be simple: few people are unclear about the fact that this is the 21st century even though our dates begin with "20." Just be consistent about adding one to the second digit in a year and you've got the number of its century. It took 100 years to get to the year 100, so the next 100 years, which are named "101," "102," etc., were in the second century. This also works B.C. The 400s B.C. are the fifth century B.C. Using phrases like "1800s" is a signal to your readers that you are weak in math and history alike.

either

"Either" often gets misplaced in a sentence: "He either wanted to build a gambling casino or a convent" should be "He wanted to build either a gambling casino or a convent." Put "either" just before the first thing being compared.

either are/either is

As a subject, "either" is singular. It's the opposite of "both" and refers to one at a time: "Either ketchup or mustard is good on a hot dog." But if "either" is modifying a subject in an "either . . . or" phrase, then the number of the verb is determined by the number of the second noun: "Either the puppy or the twins seem to need my attention every other minute."

elapse/lapse

Both these words come from a Latin root meaning "to slip." "Elapse" almost always refers to the passage of time. "Lapse" usually refers to a change of state, as in lapsing from consciousness into unconsciousness. Here are examples of the correct uses of these words you might get in the mail: "Six months have elapsed since your last dental appointment" and "You have allowed your subscription to *Bride Magazine* to lapse." Occasionally "lapse" can be used as a synonym of "elapse" in the sense "to slip away." Substituting one for the other is dangerous, however, if you are a lawyer. Insurance policies and collective bargaining agreements do not elapse when they expire; they lapse.

electorial college/electoral college
It's "electoral."

electrocute/shock
To electrocute is to kill using electricity. If you live to tell the tale, you've been shocked, but not electrocuted. For the same reason, the phrase "electrocuted to death" is a redundancy.

elicit/illicit
The lawyer tries to elicit a description of the attacker from the witness. "Elicit" is always a verb. "Illicit," in contrast, is always an adjective describing something illegal or naughty.

ellipses
Those dots that come in the middle of a quotation to indicate something omitted are called an "ellipsis" (plural "ellipses"): "Tex told Sam to get the . . . cow out of the bunk house." Here Tex's language has been censored, but you are more likely to have a use for ellipses when quoting some source in a paper: "Ishmael remarks at the beginning of *Moby Dick*, 'some years ago . . . I thought I would sail about a little'—a very understated way to begin a novel of high adventure." The three dots stand for a considerable stretch of prose that has been omitted. If the ellipsis falls between sentences, some editorial styles require *four* dots, the first of which is a period: From the same paragraph in *Moby Dick:* "almost all men . . . cherish very nearly the same feelings. . . ." Note that the period in the second ellipsis has to be snug up against the last word quoted, with spaces between the other dots.

Some modern styles do not call for ellipses at the beginning and ending of quoted matter unless not doing so would be genuinely misleading, so check with your teacher or editor if you're uncertain whether to use one in those positions. It is never correct to surround a quoted single word or short phrase with ellipses: "Romeo tells Juliet that by kissing her again his 'sin is purged'" (note, by the way, that I began the quotation after the first word in the phrase "*my* sin is purged" in order to make it work grammatically in the context of the sentence).

When text is typeset, the spaces are often but not always omitted between the dots in an ellipsis. Since modern computer printer output looks much more like typeset writing than old-fashioned typewriting, you may be tempted to omit the spaces; but it is better to include them and let the publisher decide whether they should be eliminated.

An ellipsis that works perfectly well on your computer may "break" when your text is transferred to another computer if it comes at the end of a line, with one or more of the dots wrapping around to the next line. To avoid this, learn how to type "non-breaking spaces" between the dots of ellipses: in Word for Windows it' Control-Shift-Spacebar; on a Mac, it's Option-Spacebar. When writing HTML code to create a Web page, make a non-breaking space with this code: < > (angle brackets are standard HTML quotation marks and are not to be actually typed as part of the code).

elude/allude
See "allude/elude."

email/e-mail
Although "email" is common in casual correspondence, most authorities prefer the form "e-mail."

embaress/embarrass
You can pronounce the last two syllables as two distinct words as a jog to memory, except that then the word may be misspelled "embareass," which isn't right either. You also have to remember the double "R" in "embarrass."

embedded/imbedded
See "imbedded/embedded."

emergent/emergency
The error of considering "emergent" to be the adjectival form of "emergency" is common only in medical writing, but it is becoming widespread. "Emergent" properly means "emerging" and normally

71

refers to events that are just beginning—barely noticeable rather than catastrophic. "Emergency" is an adjective as well as a noun, so rather than writing "emergent care," use the homely "emergency care."

emigrate/immigrate

To "emigrate" is to leave a country. The "E" at the beginning of the word is related to the "E" in other words having to do with going out, such as "exit." "Immigrate," in contrast, looks as if it might have something to do with going in, and indeed it does—it means to move into a new country. The same distinction applies to "emigration" and "immigration." Note the double "M" in the second form. A migrant is someone who continually moves about.

eminent/imminent/immanent

By far the most common of these words is "eminent," meaning "prominent, famous." "Imminent," in phrases like "facing imminent disaster," means "threatening." It comes from Latin *minere*, meaning "to project or overhang." Think of a mine threatening to cave in. Positive events can also be imminent: they just need to be coming soon. The rarest of the three is "immanent," used by philosophers to mean "inherent" and by theologians to mean "present throughout the universe" when referring to God. It comes from Latin *manere*, "remain." Think of God creating *man* in his own image.

empathy/sympathy

If you think you feel just like another person, you are feeling *empathy*. If you just feel sorry for another person, you're feeling *sympathy*.

emphasize on/emphasize

You can place emphasis on something or you can emphasize it, but you can't emphasize *on* it or stress *on* it, though you can *place* stress on it.

end result/end

"End result" is usually a redundancy. Most of the time plain "end" will do fine.

ending a sentence with a preposition

The prohibition against ending a sentence with a prepostion is a fine example of an artificial "rule" that ignores standard usage. The famous witticism usually attributed to Winston Churchill makes the point well: "This is the sort of English up with which I cannot put."

endnotes/footnotes

See "footnotes/endnotes."

endquote/unquote

Some people get upset at the common pattern by which speakers frame a quotation by saying "quote . . . unquote," insisting that the latter word should logically be "endquote"; but illogical as it may be, "unquote" has been used in this way for about a century, and "endquote" is nonstandard.

enormity/enormousness

Originally these two words were synonymous, but "enormity" got whittled down to meaning something monstrous or outrageous. Don't wonder at the "enormity" of the Palace of Versailles unless you wish to express horror at this embodiment of Louis XIV's ego.

enquire/inquire

These are alternative spellings of the same word. "Enquire" is perhaps slightly more common in the U.K., but either is acceptable in the U.S.

ensure/insure/assure

See "assure/ensure/insure."

enthuse

"Enthuse" is a handy word and "state enthusiastically" is not nearly so striking; but unfortunately "enthuse" is not acceptable in the most formal contexts.

entitled/titled

Some people argue that you should say a book is "titled" such-and-such rather than "entitled." But no less a writer than Chaucer is cited by the *Oxford English Dictionary* as having used "entitled" in this sense, the very first meaning of the word listed by the OED. It may be a touch pretentious, but it's not wrong.

envelop/envelope

To wrap something up in a covering is to envelop it (pronounced "en-VELL-up"). The specific wrapping you put around a letter is an envelope (pronounced variously, but with the accent on the first syllable).

envious/jealous

Although these are often treated as synonyms, there is a difference. You are envious of what others have that you lack. Jealousy, on the other hand, involves wanting to hold on to what you *do* have. You can be jealous of your boyfriend's attraction to other women, but you're envious of your boyfriend's CD collection.

enviroment/environment

The second "N" in "environment" is seldom pronounced distinctly, so it's not surprising that it is often omitted in writing. If you know the related word "environs," it may help remind you.

environment/ecology

See "ecology/environment."

epigram/epigraph/epitaph/epithet

An epigram is a pithy saying, usually humorous. Mark Twain was responsible for many striking, mostly cynical epigrams, such as "Always do right. That will gratify some of the people, and astonish the rest." (Unfortunately, he was also responsible for an even more famous one that has been confusing people ever since: "Everyone is a moon, and has a dark side which he never shows to anybody." It's true that the moon keeps one side away from the earth, but—if you don't count the faint glow reflected from the earth—it is not any darker than the side that faces us. In fact, over time, the side facing us is darkened slightly more often because it is occasionally eclipsed by the shadow of the earth.)

An epigraph is a brief quotation used to introduce a piece of writing or the inscription on a statue or building.

An epitaph is the inscription on a tombstone or some other tribute to a dead person.

In literature, an epithet is a term that replaces or is added to the name of a person, like "clear-eyed Athena," in which "clear-eyed" is the epithet. You are more likely to encounter the term in its negative sense, as a term of insult or abuse: "The shoplifter hurled epithets at the guard who had arrested her."

epitomy/epitome

Nothing makes you look quite so foolish as spelling a sophisticated word incorrectly. Taken directly from Latin, where it means "abridgement," "epitome" is now most often used to designate an extremely representative example of the general class: "*Snow White* is the epitome of a Disney cartoon feature." Those who don't misspell this word often mispronounce it, misled by its spelling, as "EP-i-tohm," but the proper pronunciation is "ee-PIT-o-mee." The word means "essence," not "climax," so instead of writing "The market had reached the epitome of frenzied selling at noon," use "peak" or a similar word.

especially/expecially

See "expecially/especially."

espresso/expresso

See "expresso/espresso."

etc.

See "ect./etc."

ethnic

It's misleading to refer to minority groups as "ethnics" since everyone has ethnicity, even a dominant majority.

every (plural vs. singular)

"Every," "everybody," "everyone," and related expressions are normally treated as singular in American English: "Every woman I ask out tells me she already has plans for Saturday night." However, constructions like "everyone brought their own lunch" are widely accepted now because of a desire to avoid specifying "his" or "her."

See also "they/their (singular)."

everyday

"Everyday" is a perfectly good adjective, as in "I'm most comfortable in my everyday clothes." The problem comes when people turn the adverbial phrase "every day" into a single word. It is incorrect to write "I take a shower everyday." It should be "I take a shower every day."

He wore his hat every day, but it was no everyday hat.

everytime/every time

"Every time" is always two separate words.

evidence to/evidence of

You can provide evidence *to* a court, even enough evidence to convict someone; but the standard expression "is evidence of" requires "of" rather than "to" in sentences like this: "Driving through the front entrance of the Burger King is evidence of Todd's inexperience in driving." If you could substitute "evidences" or "evidenced" in your sentence, you need "of."

exacerbated/exasperated
See "exasperated/exacerbated."

exact same/exactly the same
In casual speech we often say things like, "The shirt he gave me was the exact same kind I'd thrown away the week before"; but in formal English the phrase is "exactly the same," as in, "The shirt he gave me was exactly the same kind I'd thrown away the week before.

exacting revenge/extracting revenge
See "extracting revenge/exacting revenge."

exaggerated/over-exaggerated
See "over-exaggerated/exaggerated."

exalt/exult
When you celebrate joyfully, you exult. When you raise something high (even if only in your opinion), you exalt it. Neither word has an "H" in it.

exasperated/exacerbated
When you get fed up, you're exasperated. When you make something worse, it's exacerbated.

excape/escape
The proper spelling is "escape." Say it that way too.

exceed/accede
See "accede/exceed."

except/accept
See "accept/except."

exceptional/exceptionable

If you take exception (object) to something, you find it "exception-able." The more common word is "exceptional," applied to things that are out of the ordinary, usually in a positive way: "These are exceptional Buffalo wings."

exhileration/exhilaration

"Exhilaration" is closely related to "hilarious," whose strongly accented "A" should help remind you of the correct spelling.

expecially/especially

"Expecially" is a common mispronunciation of "especially."

exponential

Something grows exponentially when it repeatedly grows by multiples of some factor in a rapidly accelerating fashion. Don't use the word loosely to refer to ordinary rapid, but steady, growth.

See also "orders of magnitude."

expresses that/says that

"In her letter Jane expresses that she is getting irritated with me for not writing" should be corrected to "In her letter Jane says that. . . ." You can express an idea or a thought, but you can't ever express *that*. In technical terms, "express" is a transitive verb and requires an object.

expresso/espresso

I've read several explanations of the origin of this word: the coffee is made expressly for you upon your order, or the steam is expressed through the grounds, or (as most people suppose—and certainly wrongly) the coffee is made at express speed. One thing is certain: the word is "espresso," not "expresso."

While you're at an American espresso stand, you might muse on the fact that both *biscotti* and *panini* are plural forms, but you're likely to baffle the *barista* if you ask in correct Italian for a *biscotto* or a *panino*.

extracting revenge/exacting revenge
The use of a rare sense of "exact" ("obtain forcibly") confuses people, but the traditional phrase is "exacting revenge"; not the seemingly logical "extracting revenge."

exult/exalt
See "exalt/exult."

---

fabulous
See "incredible."

factoid
The "-oid" ending in English is normally added to a word to indicate that an item is not the real thing. A humanoid is not quite human. Originally "factoid" was an ironic term indicating that the "fact" being offered was not actually factual. However, CNN and other sources have taken to treating the "-oid" as if it were a mere diminutive and using the term to mean "trivial but true fact." As a result, the definition of "factoid" is hopelessly confused and it's probably better to avoid using the term altogether.

fair/fare
When you send your daughter off to camp, you hope she'll *fare* well. That's why you bid her a fond farewell. "Fair" as a verb is a rare word meaning "to smooth a surface to prepare it for being joined to another."

family name/last name
See "last name/family name."

fantastic
See "incredible."

far and few between/few and far between
The common expression "few and far between" is often carelessly flipped.

fare/fair
See "fair/fare."

farther/further
Some authorities (like the Associated Press) insist on "farther" to refer to physical distance and on "further" to refer to an extent of time or degree, but others treat the two words as interchangeable except for insisting on "further" for "in addition" or "moreover." You'll always be safe in making the distinction; some people get really testy about this.

fastly/fast
"Fastly" is an old form that has died out in English. Interest in soccer is growing fast, not "fastly."

fatal/fateful
A "fatal" event is a deadly one; a "fateful" one is determined by fate. If there are no casualties left lying at the scene—whether mangled corpses or failed negotiations—the word you are seeking is "fateful." The latter word also has many positive uses, such as "George fondly remembered that fateful night in which he first met the woman he was to love to his dying day."

faze/phase
"Faze" means to embarrass or disturb, but is almost always used in the negative sense, as in "The fact that the overhead projector bulb was burned out didn't faze her." "Phase" is a noun or verb having to do with an aspect of something. "He's just going through a temperamental phase." "They're going to phase in the new accounting procedures gradually." Unfortunately, *Star Trek* confused matters by calling its ray pistols "phasers." Too bad they aren't "fazers" instead.

fearful/fearsome

To be "fearful" is to be afraid. To be "fearsome" is to cause fear in others. Remember that someone who is fierce is fearsome rather than fearful.

Febuary/February

Few people pronounce the first "R" in "February" distinctly, so it is not surprising that it is often omitted in spelling. This poor month is short on days; don't further impoverish it by robbing it of one of its letters.

feet/foot

See "foot/feet."

fell swoop/foul swoop/fowl swoop

See "foul swoop/fowl swoop/fell swoop."

few/little

See "amount/number."

few and far between/far and few between

See "far and few between/few and far between."

fewer/less

See "amount/number."

fiery/firey

See "firey/fiery."

'50s

There's no requirement for the apostrophe before the "S" in decade names like 50s and 60s, since there are no omitted letters, though it's also acceptable to include one. The term may be written "'50s" since "19" is being omitted, but "50s" is fine too. Writers who wish to have their references to decades clearly understood in the 21st century would be well advised not to omit the first two digits.

Note that you may have to turn off "smart quotes" in your word processor to get a leading apostrophe like the one in "'50s" to curl correctly unless you know how to type the character directly. Or you can just type two apostrophes in a row and delete the first one.

Filipinos/Philippines
See "Philippines/Filipinos."

fill the bill/fit the bill
See "fit the bill/fill the bill."

film/video
See "video/film."

finalize/finish, put into final form
"Finalize" is very popular among bureaucrats, but many people hate it. Avoid it unless you know that everyone in your environment uses it too.

finished/done
See "done/finished."

firey/fiery
It's "fire," so why isn't it "firey?" If you listen closely, you hear that "fire" has two distinct vowel sounds in it: "fi-er." Spelling the adjective "fiery" helps to preserve that double sound.

first annual
Some people get upset when the "first annual" occurrence of some event is announced, arguing that it doesn't become annual until it's been repeated. But "first annual" simply means "the first of what is planned to be an annual series of events"—it's a fine expression.

first come, first serve/first come, first served
It might seem logical to put both verbs in the same form, as in "first come, first serve," but actually the phrase means something like "the first to come will be the first to be served." Early comers do not do the serving; they are served.

first person

Some teachers frown on the first-person voice in student writing, striking out "I," "me," and "myself" whenever they encounter them; but although there are times when it is inappropriate to call attention to yourself, writing something like "public displays of affection are disgusting" is not more modest than "public displays of affection disgust me." The impersonal form arrogantly implies that you are the final authority and that all right-minded people must agree with you. The phrase "the author" substituted for "I" is no longer generally used even in the most formal writing. When you are arguing for a theory or opinion, it is often best to stand squarely behind it by using the first-person voice.

See also "me/I/myself."

fiscal/physical

In budget matters, it's the *fiscal* year, relating to *finances* with an "F." The middle syllable of "physical" is often omitted in pronunciation, making it sound like the unrelated word "fiscal." Sound that unaccented "I" distinctly.

fit the bill/fill the bill

Originally a "bill" was any piece of writing, especially a legal document (we still speak of bills being introduced into Congress in this sense). More narrowly, it also came to mean a list such as a restaurant "bill of fare" (menu) or an advertisement listing attractions in a theatrical variety show such as might be posted on a "billboard." In 19th-century America, when producers found short acts to supplement the main attractions, nicely filling out an evening's entertainment, they were said in a rhyming phrase to "fill the bill." People who associate bills principally with shipping invoices frequently transform this expression, meaning "to meet requirements or desires," into "fit the bill." They are thinking of bills as if they were orders, lists of requirements. It is both more logical and more traditional to say "fill the bill."

flair/flare

"Flair" is conspicuous talent: "She has a flair for organization." "Flare" is either a noun meaning "flame" or a verb meaning to blaze with light or to burst into anger.

83

flak/flack

"Flak" is airman's slang for shells being fired at you in the air, so to catch a lot of flak is to feel in danger of being shot down. However, most civilians these days have never heard of "flak," so they use "flack" instead, which originally meant "salesman" or "huckster." You need to worry about this only if you're around old-time veterans.

flammable/inflammable
See "inflammable/flammable."

flare/flair
See "flair/flare."

flaunt/flout

To flaunt is to show off: you flaunt your new necklace by wearing it to work. "Flout" has a more negative connotation; it means to treat with contempt some rule or standard. The cliché is "to flout convention." Flaunting may be in bad taste because it's ostentatious, but it is not a violation of standards.

flesh out/flush out

To "flesh out" an idea is to give it substance, as a sculptor adds clay flesh to a skeletal armature. To "flush out" a criminal is to drive him or her out into the open. The latter term is derived from bird-hunting, in which one flushes out a covey of quail. If you are trying to develop something further, use "flesh"; but if you are trying to reveal something hitherto concealed, use "flush."

floppy disk/hard disk

Floppy disks are fast disappearing from the computer world, but it's been many years since they were literally floppy. The fact that a 3½" diskette is enclosed in a hard plastic case should not lead you to call it a "hard disk." A hard disk is a high-capacity storage medium like the main disk inside your computer on which your programs, operating system, and data are stored.

flounder/founder

As a verb, "founder" means "to fill with water and sink." It is also used metaphorically of various kinds of equally catastrophic failures. In contrast, to flounder is to thrash about in the water (like a flounder), struggling to stay alive. "Flounder" is also often used metaphorically to indicate various sorts of desperate struggle. If you're sunk, you've foundered. If you're still struggling, you're floundering.

flout/flaunt

See "flaunt/flout."

flush out/flesh out

See "flesh out/flush out."

flustrated/frustrated

You may be flustered when you're frustrated, but there is no such word as "flustrated."

foot/feet

You can use eight-foot boards to side a house, but "foot" is correct only in this sort of adjectival phrase combined with a number (and usually hyphenated). The boards are eight feet (not foot) long. It's always x feet per second and x feet away.

footnotes/endnotes

About the time that computers began to make the creation and printing of footnotes extremely simple and cheap, style manuals began to urge a shift away from them to *endnotes* printed at the ends of chapters or at the end of a book or paper rather than at the foot of the page. I happen to think this was a big mistake; but in any case, if you are using endnotes, don't call them "footnotes."

for/fore/four

The most common member of this trio is the preposition "for," which is not a problem for most people. "Fore" always has to do with the front of something (it's what you shout to warn people when you've sent a golf ball their way). "Four" is just the number "4."

for free/free

Some people object to "for free" because any sentence containing the phrase will read just as well without the "for," but it is standard English.

for one /for one thing

People often say "for one" when they mean "for one thing": "I really want to go to the movie. For one, Kevin Spacey is my favorite actor." (One what?) The only time you should use "for one" by itself to give an example of something is when you have earlier mentioned a class to which the example belongs: "There are a lot of reasons I don't want your old car. For one, there are squirrels living in the upholstery." (One reason.)

for sale/on sale

If you're selling something, it's *for* sale; but if you lower the price, it goes *on* sale.

forbidding/foreboding/formidable

"Foreboding" means "ominous," as in "The sky was a foreboding shade of gray" (i.e., predictive of a storm). The prefix "fore-" with an "E" often indicates futurity, e.g. "forecast," "foreshadowing," and "foreword" (a prefatory bit of writing at the beginning of a book, often misspelled "forword"). A forbidding person or task is hostile or dangerous: "The trek across the desert to the nearest latte stand was forbidding." The two are easily confused because some things, like storms, can be both foreboding and forbidding.

"Formidable," which originally meant "fear-inducing" ("Mike Tyson is a formidable opponent"), has come to be used primarily as a compliment meaning "awe-inducing" ("Gary Kasparov's formidable skills as a chess player were of no avail against Deep Blue").

See also "fearful/fearsome."

forceful/forcible/forced

These words sometimes overlap, but generally "forceful" means "powerful" ("He imposed his forceful personality on the lions"), while "forcible" must be used instead to describe the use of force ("The

86

burglar made a forcible entry into the apartment"). "Forced" is often used for the latter purpose, but some prefer to reserve this word to describe something that is done or decided upon as a result of outside causes without necessarily being violent: "a forced landing," "a forced smile," or "forced labor."

forego/forgo

The "E" in "forego" tells you it has to do with going before. It occurs mainly in the expression "foregone conclusion," a conclusion arrived at in advance. "Forgo" means to abstain from or do without. "After finishing his steak, he decided to forgo the blueberry cheesecake."

foreword/forward/forwards

See "forward/forwards/foreword."

formally/formerly

These two are often mixed up in speech. If you are doing something in a formal manner, you are behaving formally; but if you previously behaved differently, you did so formerly.

former/late

See "late/former."

formidable

See "forbidding/foreboding/formidable."

forsee/foresee

"Foresee" means "to see into the future." There are lots of words with the prefix "fore-" that are future-oriented, including "foresight," "foretell," "forethought," and "foreword," all of which are often misspelled by people who omit the "E."

fortuitous/fortunate

"Fortuitous" events happen by chance; they need not be fortunate events, only random ones: "It was purely fortuitous that the meter reader came along five minutes before I returned to my car." Although fortunate events may be fortuitous, when you mean "lucky," use "fortunate."

forward/forwards/foreword
Although some style books prefer "forward" and "toward" to "forwards" and "towards," none of these forms is really incorrect, though the forms without the final "S" are perhaps a smidgen more formal. The spelling "foreword" applies exclusively to the introductory matter in a book.

foul/fowl
A chicken is a fowl. A poke in the eye is a foul.

foul swoop/fowl swoop/fell swoop
The poetic phrase "in one fell swoop" uses an old meaning of "fell": "evil, terrible." Don't substitute "fowl" unless you're talking about a dive-bombing chicken.

founder/flounder
See "flounder/founder."

four/for/fore
See "for/fore/four."

fragments
See "sentence fragments."

Frankenstein
"Frankenstein" is the name of the scientist who creates the monster in Mary Shelley's novel. The monster itself has no name, but is referred to popularly as "Frankenstein's monster."

frankly
Sentences beginning with this word are properly admissions of something shocking or unflattering to the speaker; but when a public spokesperson for a business or government is speaking, it almost always precedes a self-serving statement. "Frankly, my dear, I don't give a damn" is correct; but "Frankly, I think the American people can make their own decisions about health care" is an abuse of language. The same contortion of meaning is common in related phrases.

When you hear a public figure say, "to be completely honest with you," expect a lie.

free/for free
See "for free/free."

free gift
See "redundancies."

French dip with au jus/French dip
This diner classic consists of sliced roast beef on a more or less firm bun, with a side dish of broth in which to dip it. *Au jus* means "with broth," so adding "with" to "au jus" is redundant. In fancier restaurants, items are listed entirely in French with the English translation underneath:

> *Tête de cochon avec ses tripes farcies*
> Pig's head stuffed with tripe

Mixing the languages is hazardous if you don't know what the original means. "With au jus broth" is also seen from time to time. People generally know what a French dip sandwich is, and they'll see the broth when it comes. Why not just call it a "French dip?"

from . . . to
"From soup to nuts" makes sense because soup was the traditional first course in a formal meal, nuts the last. Similarly "from A to Z" makes sense because these are the first and last letters of the alphabet. But this construction, which identifies the extremes of a spectrum or range, is often improperly used when no such extremes are being identified, as in "She tried everything from penicillin to sulfa drugs." These are not extremes, just examples of different sorts of drugs. Even worse is "He gave his daughter everything from a bicycle to lawn darts to a teddy bear." A range can't have more than two extremes. "He gave his daughter everything from paper dolls to a Cadillac" conveys the notion of a spectrum from very cheap to very expensive and is fine. Often when people are tempted to use "from. . . to" they would be better off using a different expression, as, for example, in

this sentence: "She tried all sorts of medicines, including penicillin and sulfa drugs."

from the beginning of time

Stephen Hawking writes about the beginning of time, but few other people do. People who write "from the beginning of time" or "since time began" are usually being lazy. Their grasp of history is vague, so they resort to these broad, sweeping phrases. Almost never is this usage literally accurate: people have not fallen in love since time began, for instance, because people arrived relatively late on the scene in the cosmic scheme of things. If you really don't know the appropriate period from which your subject dates, you could substitute a less silly but still vague phrase such as "for many years," or "for centuries," but it's better simply to avoid historical statements if you don't know your history.

See also "today's modern society/today."

frustrated/flustrated

See "flustrated/frustrated."

Fujiyama

See "Mount Fujiyama/Fujiyama."

-ful/-fuls

It's one cupful, but two cupfuls, not "two cupsful." The same goes for "spoonfuls" and "glassfuls."

fulsome

Because its most common use is in the phrase "fulsome praise," many people suppose that this word means something like "generous" or "whole-hearted." Actually, it means "disgusting," and "fulsome praise" is disgustingly exaggerated praise.

further/farther

See "farther/further."

g/q

Lower-case "q" is the mirror image of lower-case "g" in many type-
faces, and the two are often confused with each other and the
resulting misspelling missed in proofreading, for instance "quilt"
when "guilt" is intended.

gaff/gaffe

Gaffe is a French word meaning "embarrassing mistake" and should
not be mixed up with "gaff": a large hook.

gamut/gauntlet

To "run a gamut" or "run the gamut" is to go through the whole scale
or spectrum of something. To "run the gauntlet" (also "gantlet") is to
run between two lines of people who are trying to beat you. And
don't confuse "gamut" with "gambit," a play in chess, and by extension, a tricky maneuver of any kind.

Gandhi/Ghandi

See "Ghandi/Gandhi."

gaurd/guard

Too bad the Elizabethan "guard" won out over the earlier, French-
derived spelling "garde," but the word was never spelled "gaurd." The
standard spelling is related to Italian and Spanish "guarda," pronounced "GWAR-da."

gender

Feminists eager to remove references to sexuality from discussions of
females and males that don't involve mating or reproduction revived
an older meaning of "gender," which had come to refer in modern
times chiefly as a synonym for "sex" in phrases such as "Our goal is to
achieve gender equality." Americans, always nervous about sex,
eagerly embraced this usage, which is now standard. In some scholarly
fields, "sex" is used to label biologically determined aspects of
maleness and femaleness (reproduction, etc.), while "gender" refers to
their socially determined aspects (behavior, attitudes, etc.); but in
ordinary speech this distinction is not always maintained. It is
disingenuous to pretend that people who use "gender" in the new

senses are making an error, just as it is disingenuous to maintain that "Ms." means "manuscript" (that's "MS"). Nevertheless, I must admit I was startled to discover that the tag on my new trousers describes not only their size and color, but their "gender."

genre
Often mispronounced "jaundra" and sometimes misspelled that way too. Say "ZHON-ruh."

get access to/access
See "access/get access to."

Ghandi/Gandhi
Mohandas K. Gandhi's name has an "H" after the "D," not after the "G." Note that "Mahatma" ("great soul") is an honorific title, not actually part of his birth name.

gibe/jibe/jive
"Gibe" is a now rare term meaning "to tease." "Jibe" means "to agree," but is usually used negatively, as in "The alibis of the two crooks didn't jibe." The latter word is often confused with "jive," which derives from slang that originally meant to treat in a jazzy manner ("Jivin' the Blues Away") but also came to be associated with deception ("Don't give me any of that jive").

gig/jig
"The jig is up" is an old slang expression meaning "the game is over—we're caught." A musician's job is a gig.

gild/guild
You *gild* an object by covering it with gold; you can join an organization like the Theatre *Guild.*

God/god
When "God" is the name of a god, as in Judaism, Christianity, and Islam, it needs to be capitalized like any other name ("Allah" is just Arabic for "God," and many modern Muslims translate the name

when writing in English). When it is used as a generic term, as in "He looks like a Greek god," it is not capitalized.

If you see the word rendered "G*d" or "G-d," it's not an error, but a Jewish writer reverently following the Orthodox prohibition against spelling out the name of the deity in full.

goes

"So he goes 'I thought your birthday was tomorrow,' and I'm—like— 'Well, duh!'" Perhaps this bizarre pattern developed in analogy to childish phrases such as "the cow goes 'moo'" and "the piggy goes 'oink, oink.'" Is there any young person unaware that the use of "go" to mean "say" drives most adults crazy? Granted, it's deliberate slang rather than an involuntary error; but if you get into the habit of using it all the time, you may embarrass yourself in front of a class by saying something witless like "So then Juliet goes 'A rose by any other name would smell as sweet.'"

gone/went

This is one of those cases in which a common word has a past participle which is not formed by the simple addition of "-ed" and which often trips people up. "I should have went to the business meeting, but the game was tied in the ninth" should be "I should have gone. . . ." The same problem crops up with the two forms of the verb "to do." Say "I should have done my taxes before the IRS called" rather than "I should have did. . . ."

good/well

"Good" is the adjective; "well" is the adverb. You do something well, but you give someone something good. The exception is verbs of sensation in phrases such as "the pie smells good" or "I feel good." Despite the arguments of nigglers, this is standard usage. Saying "the pie smells well" would imply that the pastry in question had a nose. Similarly, "I feel well" is also acceptable, especially when discussing health; but it is not the only correct usage.

got/gotten

In England, the old word "gotten" dropped out of use except in such stock phrases as "ill-gotten" and "gotten up," but in the U.S. it is frequently used as the past participle of "get." Sometimes the two are interchangeable. However, "got" implies current possession, as in "I've got just five dollars to buy my dinner with." "Gotten," in contrast, often implies the process of getting hold of something: "I've gotten five dollars for cleaning out Mrs. Quimby's shed," emphasizing the earning of the money rather than its possession. Phrases that involve some sort of process usually involve "gotten": "My grades have gotten better since I moved out of the fraternity." When you have to leave, you've got to go. If you say you've "gotten to go" you're implying someone gave you permission to go.

government
Be careful to pronounce the first "N" in "government."

graduate/graduate from
In certain dialects (notably that of New York City), it is common to say, "He is going to graduate school in June." rather than the more standard "graduate from." When writing for a national or international audience, use the "from."

grammer/grammar
It's amazing how many people write to thank me for helping them with their "grammer." It's "grammar." The word is often incorrectly used to label patterns of spelling and usage that have nothing to do with the structure of language, the proper subject of grammar in the most conservative sense. Not all bad writing is due to bad grammar.

grateful/greatful
See "greatful/grateful."

gratis/gratuitous
If you do something nice without being paid, you do it "gratis." Technically, such a deed can also be "gratuitous"; but if you do or say something obnoxious and uncalled for, it's always "gratuitous," not "gratis."

greatful/grateful
Your appreciation may be great, but you express gratitude by being grateful.

grievious/grievous
There are just two syllables in "grievous," and it's pronounced "GRIEVE-us."

grisly/grizzly
"Grisly" means "horrible"; a "grizzly" is a bear. "The grizzly left behind the grisly remains of his victim." "Grizzled" means "having gray hairs," not to be confused with "gristly," full of gristle.

ground zero
"Ground zero" refers to the point at the center of the impact of a nuclear bomb, so it is improper to talk about "building from ground zero" as if it were a place of new beginnings. You can start from scratch, or begin at zero, but if you're at ground zero, you're at the end. The metaphorical extension of this term to the site of the destruction of the World Trade Center towers is, however, perfectly legitimate.

group (plural vs. singular)
When the group is being considered as a whole, it can be treated as a single entity: "The group was ready to go on stage." But when the individuality of its members is being emphasized, "group" is plural: "The group were in disagreement about where to go for dinner."

grow
We used to grow our hair long or grow tomatoes in the yard, but now we are being urged to "grow the economy" or "grow your investments." Business and government speakers have extended this usage widely, but it irritates traditionalists. Use "build," "increase," "expand," "develop," or "cause to grow" instead in formal writing.

guild/gild
See "gild/guild."

gyp/cheat
Gypsies complain that "gyp" ("cheat") reflects bias; but the word is so well entrenched and its origin so obscure to most users that there is little hope of eliminating it from standard use any time soon.

---

had ought/ought
Just say, "She ought to come in before she drowns," not "had ought."

hairbrained/harebrained
Although "hairbrained" is common, the original word "harebrained," means "silly as a hare (rabbit)" and is preferred in writing.

handcart/dolly
See "dolly/handcart."

hangar/hanger
You park your plane in a *hangar* but hang up your slacks on a *hanger.*

hanged/hung
Originally these words were pretty much interchangeable, but "hanged" eventually came to be used pretty exclusively to mean "executed by hanging." Does nervousness about the existence of an indelicate adjectival form of the word prompt people to avoid the correct word in such sentences as "Lady Wrothley saw to it that her ancestors' portraits were properly hung"? Nevertheless, "hung" is correct except when capital punishment is being imposed.

hanging indents
Bibliographies are normally written using hanging indents, where the first line extends out to the left-hand margin, but the rest of the entry is indented:

> Hoffman, Andrew Jay. *Inventing Mark Twain: The Lives of Samuel Langhorne.* New York: William Morrow, 1997.

These are extremely easy to create on a word processor, but many people have never mastered the technique. Normally the left-hand margin marker at the top of the page consists of two small arrows. Drag the top one to the right to make a normal indent, the bottom one to create a hanging indent. In most programs, you have to hold down the Shift key while dragging the bottom marker to leave the top part behind. Don't get into the habit of substituting a carriage return and a tab or spaces to create hanging indents because when your work is transferred to a different computer the result may look quite different—and wrong.

harbringer/harbinger
The correct spelling is "harbinger."

hard disk/floppy disk
See "floppy disk/hard disk."

hardly
When Bill says, "I can't hardly bend over with this backache," he means he *can* hardly bend over, and that's what he should say. Similarly, when Jane says, "You can feed the cat without hardly bending over," she means "almost without bending over."

hardly never/hardly ever
The expression is "hardly ever."

hardy/hearty
These two words overlap somewhat, but usually the word you want is "hearty." The standard expressions are "a hearty appetite," "a hearty meal," a "hearty handshake," "a hearty welcome," and "hearty applause." "Hardy" turns up in "hale and hardy," but should not be substituted for "hearty" in the other expressions. "Party hearty" and "party hardy" are both common renderings of a common youth saying, but the first makes more sense.

harebrained/hairbrained
See "hairbrained/harebrained."

he, she/him, her
See "him, her/he, she."

heading/bound
If you're reporting on traffic conditions, it's redundant to say "heading northbound on I-5." It's either "heading north" or "northbound."

healthy/healthful
Many argue "people are healthy, but vegetables are *healthful*." Logic and tradition are on the side of those who make this distinction, but I'm afraid phrases like "part of a healthy breakfast" have become so widespread that they are rarely perceived as erroneous except by the hyper-correct. On a related though slightly different subject, it is interesting to note that in English adjectives connected to sensations in the perceiver of an object or event are often transferred to the object or event itself. In the 19th century it was not uncommon to refer, for instance, to a "grateful shower of rain," and we still say "a gloomy landscape," "a cheerful sight," and "a happy coincidence."

hear/here
If you find yourself writing sentences like "I know I left my wallet hear!" you should note that "hear" has the word "ear" buried in it and let that remind you that it refers only to hearing and is always a verb (except when you are giving the British cheer "Hear! Hear!"). "I left my wallet here" is the correct expression.

heared/heard
In some dialects "heared" is substituted for "heard" in the past tense when spoken aloud. This is not acceptable standard English.

hearing-impaired/deaf
"Hearing-impaired" is not an all-purpose substitute for "deaf" since it strongly implies some residual ability to hear.

heart-rendering/heart-rending
Your heart is "rent" (torn) when you experience something heart-rending, not "rendered."

hearty/hardy
See "hardy/hearty."

heighth/height
"Width" has a "TH" at the end, so why doesn't "height"? In fact it used to, but the standard pronunciation today ends in a plain "T" sound. People who use the obsolete form misspell it as well, so pronunciation is no guide. By the way, this is one of those pesky exceptions to the rule, "I before E except after C," but the vowels are seldom switched, perhaps because we see it printed on so many forms along with "age" and "weight."

help the problem/help solve the problem
People say they want to help the problem of poverty when what they really mean is that they want to help solve the problem of poverty. Poverty flourishes without any extra help, thank you. I guess I know what a "suicide help line" is, but I'd rather it were a "suicide prevention help line." I suppose it's too late to ask people to rename alcoholism support groups as sobriety support groups, but it's a shoddy use of language.

here/hear
See "hear/here."

hero/protagonist
In ordinary usage "hero" has two meanings: "leading character in a story" and "brave, admirable person." In simple tales the two meanings may work together, but in modern literature and film the leading character or "protagonist" (a technical term common in literary criticism) may behave in a very unheroic fashion. Students who express shock that the "hero" of a play or novel behaves despicably reveal their inexperience. In literature classes avoid the word unless you mean to stress a character's heroic qualities. However, if you are discussing the main character in a traditional opera, where values are often simple, you may get by with referring to the male lead as the "hero"—but is Don Giovanni really a *hero*?

heroin/heroine
Heroin is a highly addictive opium derivative; the female main character in a narrative is a heroine.

See also "hero/protagonist."

hesitant/reticent
See "reticent/hesitant."

highly looked upon/highly regarded
Many people, struggling to come up with the phrase "highly regarded," come up with the awkward "highly looked upon" instead, which suggests that the looker is placed in a high position, looking down, when what is meant is that the looker is looking up to someone or something admirable.

hilarious/hysterical
See "hysterical/hilarious."

him, her/he, she
There is a group of personal pronouns to be used as subjects in a sentence, including "he," "she," "I," and "we." Then there is a separate group of object pronouns, including "him," "her," "me," and "us." The problem is that the folks who tend to mix up the two sets often don't find the subject/object distinction clear or helpful and say things like, "Her and me went to the movies."

A simple test is to substitute "us" for "her and me." Would you say, "Us went to the movies"? Obviously not. You'd normally say, "We went to the movies," so when "we" is broken into the two persons involved it becomes "She and I went to the movies."

But you would say, "The murder scene scared us," so it's correct to say, "The murder scene scared her and me."

If you aren't involved, use "they" and "them" as test words instead of "us" and "we." "They won the lottery" becomes "He and she won the lottery," and "the check was mailed to them" becomes "The check was mailed to him and her."

See also "me/I/myself."

himself/hisself
See "hisself/himself."

hippy/hippie
A long-haired '60s flower child was a "hippie." "Hippy" is an adjective describing someone with wide hips. The "IE" is not caused by a "Y" changing to "IE" in the plural as in "puppy" and "puppies." It is rather a dismissive diminutive, invented by older, more sophisticated hipsters looking down on the new kids as mere "hippies." Confusing these two is definitely unhip.

Hispanic/Chicano/Latino
See "Chicano/Latino/Hispanic."

hisself/himself
In some dialects people say "hisself" for "himself," but this is nonstandard.

an historic/a historic
You should use "an" before a word beginning with an "H" only if the "H" is not pronounced: "An honest effort." It's properly "a historic event" though many sophisticated speakers somehow prefer the sound of "an historic," so that version is not likely to get you into any real trouble.

historic/historical
The meaning of "historic" has been narrowed down to "famous in history." One should not call a building, site, district, or event "historical." Sites may be of historical interest if historians are interested in them, but not just because they are old. In America "historic" is grossly overused as a synonym for "older than my father's day."

HIV virus
"HIV" stands for "human immunodeficiency virus," so adding the word "virus" to the acronym creates a redundancy. "HIV" is the name of the organism that is the cause of AIDS, not a name for the disease

itself. A person may be HIV-positive (a test shows the person to be infected with the virus) without having yet developed AIDS (acquired immunodeficiency syndrome). HIV is the cause; AIDS the result.

hoard/horde

A greedily hoarded treasure is a *hoard*. A herd of wildebeests or a mob of people is a *horde*.

hoi polloi

Hoi polloi is Greek for "the common people," but it is often misused to mean "the upper class" (does "hoi" make speakers think of "high" or "hoity-toity"?). Some urge that since "hoi" is the article, "the hoi polloi" is redundant; but the general rule is that articles such as "the" and "a" in foreign language phrases cease to function as such in place names, brands, and catch phrases except for some of the most familiar ones in French and Spanish, where everyone recognizes "la"—for instance—as meaning "the." "The El Niño" is redundant, but "the hoi polloi" is standard English.

hold/ahold

See "ahold/hold."

hold your peace/say your piece

Some folks imagine that since these expressions are opposites, the last word in each should be the same; but in fact they are unrelated expressions. "Hold your peace" means "maintain your silence," and "say your piece" means literally "speak aloud a piece of writing" but is used to express the idea of making a statement.

holistic/wholistic

See "wholistic/holistic "

holocaust

"Holocaust" is a Greek-derived translation of the Hebrew term *olah*, which denotes a sort of ritual sacrifice in which the food offered is completely burnt up rather than being merely dedicated to God and then eaten. It was applied with bitter irony by Jews to the destruction of millions of their number in the Nazi death camps. Although phrases like "nuclear holocaust" and "Cambodian holocaust" have become common, you risk giving serious offense by using the word in less severe circumstances, such as calling a precipitous decline in stock prices a "sell-off holocaust."

home in/hone in
See "hone in/home in."

home page
On the World Wide Web, a "home page" is normally the first page a person entering a site encounters, often functioning as a sort of table of contents for the other pages. People sometimes create special pages within their sites introducing a particular topic, and these are also informally called "home pages" (as in "The Emily Dickinson Home Page"); but it is a sure sign of a Web novice to refer to all Web pages as home pages. Spelling "homepage" as a single word is common on the Web, but distinctly more casual than "home page."

homophobic
Some object to this word, arguing that it literally means "man-fearing," but the "homo" in "homosexual" and in this word does not refer to the Latin word for "man," but is derived from a Greek root meaning "same," while the "-phobic" means literally "having a fear of," but in English has come to mean "hating." "Homophobia" is now an established term for "prejudice against homosexuals."

hone in/home in
You home in on a target (the center of the target is "home"). "Honing" has to do with sharpening knives, not aim.

Hoover
See "brand names."

hopefully
This word has meant "it is to be hoped" for a very long time, and those who insist it can only mean "in a hopeful fashion" display more hopefulness than realism.

horde/hoard
See "hoard/horde."

hors d'oeuvres
If you knew only a little French, you might interpret this phrase as meaning "out of work," but in fact it means little snack foods served before or outside of (*hors*) the main dishes of a meal (the *oeuvres*). English speakers have trouble mastering the sounds in this phrase, but it is normally rendered "or-DERVES," in a rough approximation of the original. Mangled spellings like "hors' dourves" are not uncommon. Actually, many modern food writers have decided we needn't try to wrap our tongues around this peculiar foreign phrase and now prefer "starters."

hot water heater
See "redundancies."

how come/why
"How come?" is a common question in casual speech, but in formal contexts use "why?"

howsomever/however
"Howsomever" is a dialectical substitute for "however," to be avoided in formal English.

hyphenation
The *Chicago Manual of Style* contains a huge chart listing various sorts of phrases that are or are not to be hyphenated. Consult such a reference source for a thorough-going account of this matter, but you may be able to get by with a few basic rules. An adverb/adjective combination in which the adverb ends in "-ly" is never hyphenated: "His necktie reflected his generally grotesque taste." Other sorts of adverbs are followed by a hyphen when combined with an adjective: "His long-suffering wife finally snapped and fed it through the office shredder." The point here is that "long" modifies "suffering," not "wife." When both words modify the same noun, they are not hyphenated. A "light-green suitcase" is pale in color, but a "light green

suitcase" is not heavy. In the latter example "light" and "green" both modify "suitcase," so no hyphen is used.

Adjectives combined with nouns having an "-ed" suffix are hyphenated: "Frank was a hot-headed cop."

A phrase composed of a noun and a present participle ("-ing" word) must be hyphenated: "The antenna had been climbed by thrill-seeking teenagers who didn't realize the top of it was electrified."

Hyphenate ages when they are adjective phrases involving a unit of measurement: "Her 10-year-old car is beginning to give her trouble." A girl can be a "10-year-old" ("child" is implied). But there are no hyphens in such an adjectival phrase as "Her car is 10 years old." In fact, hyphens are generally omitted when such phrases follow the noun they modify except in phrases involving "all" or "self" such as "all-knowing" or "self-confident." Fractions are almost always hyphenated when they are adjectives: "He is one-quarter Irish and three-quarters Nigerian." But when the numerator is already hyphenated, the fraction itself is not, as in "ninety-nine and forty-four one hundredths." Fractions treated as nouns are not hyphenated: "He ate one quarter of the turkey."

These are the main cases in which people are prone to misuse hyphens. If you can master them, you will have eliminated the vast majority of such mistakes in your writing. Some styles call for spaces around dashes (a practice of which I strongly disapprove), but it is never proper to surround hyphens with spaces, though in the following sort of pattern you may need to *follow* a hyphen with a space: "Follow standard pre- and post-operative procedures."

hyphens & dashes

Dashes are longer than hyphens, but since some browsers do not reliably interpret the code for dashes, they are usually rendered on the Web as they were on old-fashioned typewriters, as double hyphens (like this: --). Dashes tend to separate elements, and hyphens to link them. Few people would substitute a dash for a hyphen in an expression like "a quick-witted scoundrel," but the opposite is common. In a sentence like "Astrud—unlike Inger—enjoyed vacations in Spain rather than England," one often sees hyphens incorrectly substituted for dashes.

When you are typing for photocopying or direct printing, it is a good idea to learn how to type a true dash instead of the double hyphen. In old-fashioned styles, dashes (but never hyphens) are surrounded by spaces — like this. With modern computer output, which emulates professional printing, this makes little sense. Skip the spaces unless your editor or teacher insists on them.

There are actually two kinds of dashes. The most common is the "em dash" (theoretically the width of a letter "M"—but this is often not the case). To connect numbers, it is traditional to use an "en dash" which is somewhat shorter, but not as short as a hyphen: "cocktails 5–7 P.M." All modern computers can produce en dashes, but few people know how to type them (try searching your program's help menu). For most purposes you don't have to worry about them, but if you are preparing material for print, you should learn how to use them.

hypocritical

"Hypocritical" has a narrow, very specific meaning. It describes behavior or speech that is intended to make one look better or more pious than one really is. It is often wrongly used to label people who are merely narrow-minded or genuinely pious. Do not confuse this word with "hypercritical," which describes people who are picky.

hysterical/hilarious

People say of a bit of humor or a comical situation that it was "hysterical"—shorthand for "hysterically funny"—meaning "hilarious." But when you speak of a man being "hysterical" it means he is having a fit of hysteria, and that may not be funny at all.

I/me/myself
See "me/I/myself."

i.e./e.g.
See "e.g./i.e."

-ic

In the Cold War era, anti-socialists often accused their enemies of being "socialistic," by which they meant that although they were not actually socialists, some of their beliefs were like those of socialists. But the "-ic" suffix is recklessly used in all kinds of settings, often without understanding its implications. Karl Marx was not "socialistic"; he was actually socialist.

ice tea/iced tea

Iced tea is not literally made of ice, it simply is "iced": has ice put in it.

idea/ideal

Any thought can be an idea, but only the best ideas worth pursuing are ideals.

ie/ei

See "ei/ie."

if/whether

"If" is used frequently in casual speech and writing where some others would prefer "whether": "I wonder if you would be willing to dress up as a giant turnip for the parade?" Revise to "I wonder whether. . . ." "If" can't really be called an error, but when you are discussing two alternative possibilities, "whether" sounds more polished. (The two possibilities in this example are: 1) you would be willing or 2) you wouldn't. In sentences using "whether," "or not" is often understood.) Don't substitute the very different word "whither," which means "where."

if I was/if I were

The subjunctive mood, always weak in English, has been dwindling away for centuries until it has almost vanished. According to traditional thought, statements about the conditional future such as "If I were a carpenter . . ." require the subjunctive "were"; but "was" is certainly much more common. Still, if you want to impress those in the know with your usage, use "were." The same goes for other pronouns: "you," "she," "he," and "it." In the case of the plural pronouns "we" and "they" the form "was" is definitely nonstandard, of course, because it is a singular form.

ignorant/stupid

A person can be ignorant (not knowing some fact or idea) without being stupid (incapable of learning because of a basic mental deficiency). And those who say, "That's an ignorant idea," when they mean "stupid idea" are expressing their own ignorance.

illicit/elicit

See "elicit/illicit."

Illinois

The "S" at the end of "Illinois" is silent.

illiterate/alliterate

See "alliterate/illiterate."

illusion/allusion

See "allusion/illusion."

imbedded/embedded

The proper spelling is "embedded."

immaculate conception/virgin birth

The doctrine of "immaculate conception" (the belief that Mary was conceived without inheriting original sin) is often confused with the doctrine of the "virgin birth" (the belief that Mary gave birth to Jesus while remaining a virgin).

immanent/imminent/eminent

See "eminent/imminent/immanent."

immigrate/emigrate

See "emigrate/immigrate."

immoral/amoral

See "amoral/immoral."

impact

One (very large) group of people thinks that using "impact" as a verb is just nifty: "The announcement of yet another bug in the software will strongly impact the price of the company's stock." Another (very passionate) group of people thinks that "impact" should be used only as a noun and considers the first group to be barbarians. Although the first group may well be winning the usage struggle, you risk offending more people by using "impact" as a verb than you will by substituting more traditional words like "affect" or "influence."

impertinent/irrelevant

"Impertinent" looks as if it ought to mean the opposite of "pertinent," and indeed it once did; but for centuries now its meaning in ordinary speech has been narrowed to "impudent," specifically in regard to actions or speech toward someone regarded as socially superior. Only snobs and very old-fashioned people use "impertinent" correctly; most people would be well advised to forget it and use "irrelevant" instead to mean the opposite of "pertinent."

imply/infer

These two words, which originally had quite distinct meanings, have become so blended together that most people no longer distinguish between them. If you want to avoid irritating the rest of us, use "imply" when something is being suggested without being explicitly stated and "infer" when someone is trying to arrive at a conclusion based on evidence. "Imply" is more assertive, active: I *imply* that you need to revise your paper; and based on my hints, you *infer* that I didn't think highly of your first draft.

important/large

See "large/important."

importantly/important

When speakers are trying to impress audiences with their rhetoric, they often seem to feel that the extra syllable in "importantly" lends weight to their remarks: "And more importantly, I have an abiding love for the American people." However, these pompous speakers are wrong. It is rarely correct to use this form of the phrase because it is

109

seldom adverbial in intention. Say "more important" instead. The same applies to "most importantly"; it should be "most important."

in accordance with/as per
See "as per/in accordance with."

in another words/in other words
"In other words" is the correct expression.

in depth/indepth
See "indepth/in depth."

in fact/infact
See "infact/in fact."

in lieu of/in light of
"In lieu of" (with "lieu" often misspelled) means "instead of" and should not be used in place of "in light of" in sentences like the following: "In light of the fact that Fred has just knocked the doughnuts on the floor, the meeting is adjourned."

in proximity to/close proximity/close
See "close proximity/close/in proximity to."

in sink/in synch
"In synch" is short for "in synchronization" and has nothing to do with sinking.

in the fact that/in that
Many people mistakenly write "in the fact that" when they mean simply "in that" in sentences like "It seemed wiser not to go to work in the fact that the boss had discovered the company picnic money was missing." Omit "the fact." While we're at it, "infact" is not a word; "in fact" is always a two-word phrase.

in to/into
See "into/in to."

incent/incentivize

Business folks sometimes use "incent" to mean "create an incentive," but it's not standard English. "Incentivize" is even more widely used, but strikes many people as an ugly substitute for "encourage."

incidence/incidents/instances

These three overlap in meaning just enough to confuse a lot of people. Few of us have a need for "incidence," which most often refers to the degree or extent of the occurrence of something ("the incidence of measles in Whitman County has dropped markedly since the vaccine has been provided free"). "Incidents," which is pronounced identically, is merely the plural of "incident," meaning "occurrences" ("police reported damage to three different outhouses in separate incidents last Halloween"). Instances are examples ("semicolons are not required in the first three instances given in your query"). Incidents can be used as instances only if someone is using them as examples.

incredible

The other day I heard a film reviewer praise a director because he created "incredible characters," which would literally mean unbelievable characters. What the reviewer meant to say, of course, was precisely the opposite: characters so lifelike as to seem like real people. Intensifiers and superlatives tend to get worn down quickly through overuse and become almost meaningless, but it is wise to be aware of their root meanings so that you don't unintentionally utter absurdities. "Fantastic" means "as in a fantasy," just as "fabulous" means "as in a fable." A "wonderful" sight should make you pause in wonder (awe). Some of these words are worn down beyond redemption, however. For instance, who now expects a "terrific" sight to terrify?

See also "intensifiers."

indepth/in depth

You can make an "in-depth" study of a subject by studying it "in depth," but never "indepth." Like "a lot," this is two words often mistaken for one. The first, adjectival, use of the phrase given above is commonly hyphenated, which may lead some people to splice the words even more closely together. "Indepth" is usually used as an adverb by people of limited vocabulary who would be better off saying "profoundly" or "thoroughly." Some of them go so far as to say that they have studied a subject "indepthly." Avoid this one if you don't want to be snickered at.

Indian/Native American

Although academics have long promoted "Native American" as a more accurate label than "Indian," most of the people so labeled continue to refer to themselves as "Indians" and prefer that term. In Canada, there is a move to refer to descendants of the original inhabitants as "First Peoples," but so far that has not spread to the U.S.

Indiana University/University of Indiana

See "University of Indiana/Indiana University."

indifferent/ambivalent

See "ambivalent/indifferent."

individual/person

Law-enforcement officers often use "individual" as a simple synonym for "person" when they don't particularly mean to stress individuality: "I pursued the individual who had fired the weapon at me for three blocks." This sort of use of "individual" lends an oddly formal air to your writing. When "person" works as well, use it.

infact/in fact

"In fact" is always two words.

infamous

"Infamous" means "famous in a bad way." It is related to the word "infamy." Humorists have for a couple of centuries jokingly used the word in a positive sense, but the effectiveness of the joke depends on the listener knowing that this is a misuse of the term. Because this is a very old joke indeed you should stick to using "infamous" only for people like Hitler and Billy the Kid.

    See also "notorious."

infer/imply
See "imply/infer."

infinite
When Shakespeare's Enobarbus said of Cleopatra that "age cannot wither her, nor custom stale her infinite variety," he was obviously exaggerating. So few are the literal uses of "infinite" that almost every use of it is metaphorical. There are not an infinite number of possible positions on a chessboard, nor number of stars in the universe. Things can be innumerable (in one sense of the word) without being infinite; in other words, things which are beyond the human capacity to count them can still be limited in number. "Infinite" has its uses as a loose synonym for "a very great many," but it is all too often lazily used when one doesn't want to do the work to discover the order of magnitude involved. When you are making quasi-scientific statements you do a disservice to your reader by implying infinity when mere billions are involved.

inflammable/flammable
The prefix "in-" does not indicate negation here; it comes from the word "inflame." "Flammable" and "inflammable" both mean "easy to catch on fire," but so many people misunderstand the latter term that it's better to stick with "flammable" in safety warnings.

-ing/-ed
See "-ed/-ing."

input
Some people object to "input" as computer jargon that's proliferated unjustifiably in the business world. Be aware that it's not welcome in all settings; but whatever you do, don't misspell it "imput."

inquire/enquire
See "enquire/inquire."

install/instill
People conjure up visions of themselves as upgradable robots when they write things like "My Aunt Tillie tried to install the spirit of

giving in my heart." The word they are searching for is "instill." You install equipment; you instill feelings or attitudes.

instances/incidence/incidents
See "incidence/incidents/instances."

instances/instants
Brief moments are "instants," and examples of anything are "instances."

insure/ensure/assure
See "assure/ensure/insure."

integral
Often mispronounced "in-tra-gul" as if it were related to "intricate" instead of the more proper "in-tuh-grul," related to "integrate."

intense/intensive
If you are putting forth an intense effort, your work is "intense": "My intense study of Plato convinced me that I would make a good leader." But when the intensity stems not so much from your effort as it does from outside forces, the usual word is "intensive": "The village endured intensive bombing."

intensifiers
People are always looking for ways to emphasize how really, really special the subject under discussion is. (The use of "really" is one of the weakest and least effective of these.) A host of words have been worn down in this service to near-meaninglessness. It is good to remember the etymological roots of such words to avoid such absurdities as "fantastically realistic," "absolutely relative," and "incredibly convincing." When you are tempted to use one of these vague intensifiers consider rewriting your prose to explain more precisely and vividly what you mean: "Fred's cooking was incredibly bad" could be changed to "When I tasted Fred's cooking I almost thought I was back in the middle-school cafeteria." *See also* "incredible."

intensive purposes/intents and purposes

This is another example of the oral transformation of language by people who don't read much. "For all intents and purposes" is an old cliché that won't thrill anyone, but using the mistaken alternative is likely to elicit guffaws.

interesting

The second syllable is normally silent in "interesting." It's nonstandard to go out of your way to pronounce the "ter," and definitely substandard to say "innaresting."

interface/interact

The use of the computer term "interface" as a verb, substituting for "interact," is widely objected to.

interment/internment

Interment is burial; internment is merely imprisonment.

Internet/intranet

"Internet" is the proper name of the network most people connect to, and the word needs to be capitalized. However "intranet," a network confined to a smaller group, is a generic term that does not deserve capitalization. In advertising, we often read things like "unlimited Internet, $19." It would be more accurate to refer in this sort of context to "Internet *access*."

interpretate/interpret

"Interpretate" is mistakenly formed from "interpretation," but the verb form is simply "interpret."

    See also "orientate/orient."

into/in to

"Into" is a preposition that often answers the question, "where?" For example, "Tom and Becky had gone far into the cave before they realized they were lost." Sometimes the "where" is metaphorical, as in "He went into the army" or "She went into business." It can also refer by analogy to time: "The snow lingered on the ground well into

April." In old-fashioned math talk, it could be used to refer to division: "Two into six is three." In other instances where the words "in" and "to" just happen to find themselves neighbors, they must remain separate words. For instance, "Rachel dived back in to rescue the struggling boy." Here "to" belongs with "rescue" and means "in order to," not "where." (If the phrase had been "dived back into the water," "into" would be required.)

Try speaking the sentence concerned aloud, pausing distinctly between "in" and "to." If the result sounds wrong, you probably need "into."

Then there is the '60s colloquialism that lingers on in which "into" means "deeply interested or involved in": "Kevin is into baseball cards." This is derived from usages like, "The committee is looking into the fund-raising scandal." The abbreviated form is not acceptable formal English, but is quite common in informal communications.

intranet/Internet
See "Internet/intranet."

intrigue
Something fascinating or alluring can be called "intriguing," but "intrigue" as a noun means something rather different: scheming and plotting. Don't say people or situations are full of intrigue when you mean they are intriguing. The name of the Oldsmobile car model called the Intrigue is probably based on this common confusion.

ironic/sarcastic
See "sarcastic/ironic."

ironically/coincidentally
An event that is strikingly different from or the opposite of what one would have expected, usually producing a sense of incongruity, is ironic: "The sheriff proclaimed a zero-tolerance policy on drugs, but ironically flunked his own test." Other striking comings-together of events lacking these qualities are merely coincidental: "The lovers leapt off the tower just as a hay wagon coincidentally happened to be passing below."

irregardless/regardless

Regardless of what you have heard, "irregardless" is a redundancy. The suffix "-less" on the end of the word already makes the word negative. It doesn't need the negative prefix "ir-" added to make it even more negative.

irrelevant/impertinent

See "impertinent/irrelevant."

is, is

In speech, people often lose track in the middle of a sentence and repeat "is" instead of saying "that": "The problem with the conflict in the Balkans is, is the ethnic tensions seem exacerbated by everything we do." This is just a nervous tic, worth being alert against when you're speaking publicly. Of course, I suppose it all depends on what you think the meaning of "is" is.

Islams/Muslims

Followers of Islam are called "Muslims," not "Islams." (Although the Associated Press still does not accept it, 'Muslim" is now widely preferred over the older and less phonetically accurate "Moslem.")

isn't/aren't/ain't/am not

See "ain't/am not/isn't/aren't."

Isreal/Israel

To remember how to spell "Israel" properly, try pronouncing it the way Israelis do when they're speaking English: "ISS-rah-el."

Issac/Isaac

Words with a double "A" are rare in English, causing many to misspell the Biblical name "Isaac."

issues/problems

In many circles people speak of "having issues" when they mean they have problems with some issue or objections of some kind. Traditionalists are annoyed by this.

itch/scratch

Strictly speaking, you scratch an itch. If you're trying to get rid of a tingly feeling on your back, scratch it, don't itch it.

its/it's

The exception to the general rule that one should use an apostrophe to indicate possession is in possessive pronouns. Some of them are not a problem. "Mine" has no misleading "S" at the end to invite an apostrophe. And few people are tempted to write "hi's," though the equally erroneous "her's" is fairly common, as are "our's" and "their's"—all wrong, wrong, wrong. The problem with avoiding "it's" as a possessive is that this spelling is perfectly correct as a contraction meaning "it is." Just remember two points and you'll never make this mistake again. 1) "It's" always means "it is" or "it has" and nothing else. 2) Try changing the "its" in your sentence to "his" and if it doesn't make sense, then go with "it's."

See also "apostrophes."

Jacuzzi
See "brand names."

jealous/envious
See "envious/jealous."

jerry-built/jury-rigged

Although their etymologies are obscure and their meanings overlap, these are two distinct expressions. Something poorly built is "jerry-built." Something rigged up temporarily in a makeshift manner with materials at hand, often in an ingenious manner, is "jury-rigged." "Jerry-built" always has a negative connotation, whereas one can be impressed by the cleverness of a jury-rigged solution. Many people cross-pollinate these two expressions and mistakenly say "jerry-rigged" or "jury-built."

Jew/Jewish

"Jew" as an adjective ("Jew lawyer") is an ethnic insult; the word is "Jewish." But people who object to "Jew" as a noun are being oversensitive. Most Jews are proud to be called Jews. The expression "to Jew someone down"—an expression meaning "to bargain for a lower price"—reflects a grossly insulting stereotype and should be avoided in all contexts.

jewelry

Often mispronounced "joolereee." To remember the standard pronunciation, just say "jewel" and add "-ree" on the end. The British spelling is much fancier: "jewellery."

And we pronounce this jewelry . . . marvelous!

jibe/jive/gibe
See "gibe/jibe/jive."

jig/gig
See "gig/jig."

John Henry/John Hancock
John Hancock signed the Declaration of Independence so flamboyantly that his name became a synonym for "signature." Don't mix him up with John Henry, who was a steel-drivin' man.

journey/sojourn
See "sojourn/journey."

judgement/judgment
In Great Britain and many of its former colonies, "judgement" is still the correct spelling; but ever since Noah Webster decreed the first *E* superfluous, Americans have omitted it. Many of Webster's crotchets have faded away (each year fewer people use the spelling "theater," for instance); but even the producers of *Terminator 2: Judgment Day,* chose the traditional American spelling. If you write "judgement" you should also write "colour" and "tyre."

jump-start/kick-start
See "kick-start/jump-start."

jury-rigged/jerry-built
See "jerry-built/jury-rigged."

karat/carat/caret/carrot
See "carat/caret/carrot/karat."

kick-start/jump-start

You revive a dead battery by jolting it to life with a jumper cable: an extraordinary measure used in an emergency. So if you hope to stimulate a foundering economy, you want to jump-start it. Kick-starting is just the normal way of getting a motorcycle going.

kind/kind of

See "that kind/that kind of."

knelt/kneeled

See "-ed/-t."

koala bear/koala

A koala is not a bear. People who know their marsupials refer to them simply as "koalas." The same goes for pandas, which are not bears either.

⚜

lackaidasical/laxidaisical

See "laxidaisical/lackaidasical."

laissez-faire

The mispronunciation "lazy-fare" is almost irresistible in English, but this is a French expression meaning "let it be" or, more precisely, "the economic doctrine of avoiding state regulation of the economy," and it has retained its French pronunciation (though with an English *R*): "lessay fare." It is most properly used as an adjective, as in "laissez-faire capitalism," but is also commonly used as if it were a noun phrase: "the Republican party advocates laissez-faire."

lamblast/lambaste

"Lambaste" has its roots in words having to do with beating, not blasting.

lapse/elapse
See "elapse/lapse."

large/important
In colloquial speech it's perfectly normal to refer to something as a "big problem," but when people create analogous expressions in writing, the result is awkward. Don't write "This is a large issue for our firm" when what you mean is "This is an important issue for our firm." Size and intensity are not synonymous.

larnyx/larynx
"Larynx" is often mispronounced and sometimes misspelled "larnyx."

last name/family name
Now that few people know what a "surname" is, we usually use the term "last name" to designate a family name; but in a host of languages the family name comes first. "Julius" was the family name of Julius Caesar, and "Kawabata" was the family name of author Kawabata Yasunari. For Asians, this situation is complicated because publishers and immigrants often switch names to conform to Western practice, so you'll find most of Kawabata's books in an American bookstore by looking under "Yasunari Kawabata." It's safer with international names to write "given name" and "family name" rather than "first name" and "last name."

late/former
If you want to refer to your former husband, don't call him your "late husband" unless he's dead.

later/latter
Except in the expression "latter-day" (modern), the word "latter" usually refers back to the last-mentioned of a set of alternatives. "We gave the kids a choice of a vacation in Paris, Rome, or Disney World. Of course the latter was their choice." In other contexts not referring back to such a list, the word you want is "later."

Latino/Chicano/Hispanic
See "Chicano/Latino/Hispanic."

laxidaisical/lackaidasical

"Laxidaisical" is a dialectical pronunciation of the more traditional "lackadaisical."

lay/lie

You lay down the book you've been reading, but you lie down when you go to bed. In the present tense, if the subject is acting on some other object, it's "lay." If the subject is lying down, then it's "lie." This distinction is often not made in informal speech, partly because in the past tense the words sound much more alike: "He lay down for a nap," but "He laid down the law." If the subject is already at rest, you might "let it lie." If a helping verb is involved, you need the past participle forms. "Lie" becomes "lain" and "lay" becomes "laid": "He had just lain down for a nap," and "His daughter had laid the gerbil on his nose."

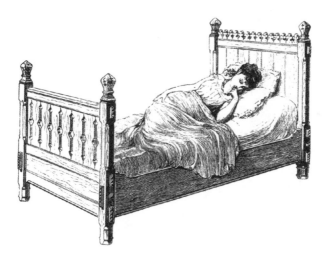

You may lay your thoughts to rest before you lie down.

leach/leech

Water leaches chemicals out of soil or color out of cloth; your brother-in-law leeches off the family by constantly borrowing money to pay his gambling debts (he behaves like a bloodsucking leech).

lead/led

When you're hit over the head, the instrument could be a *lead* pipe. But when it's a verb, "lead" is the present and "led" is the past tense. The problem is that the past tense is pronounced exactly like the above-mentioned plumbing material, so people confuse the two. ("Plumb," by the way, comes from a word meaning "lead.") In a sentence like "She led us to the scene of the crime," always use the three-letter spelling.

leant/leaned

See "-ed/-t."

leapt/leaped

See "-ed/-t."

leave/let

The colloquial use of "leave" to mean "let" in phrases like "leave me be" is not standard. "Leave me alone" is fine, though.

lectern/podium

See "podium/lectern."

led/lead

See "lead/led."

leech/leach

See "leach/leech."

leery/wary/weary

See "wary/weary/leery."

legend/myth

Myths are generally considered to be traditional stories whose importance lies in their significance, like the myth of the Fall in Eden; whereas legends can be merely famous deeds, like the legend of Davy Crockett. In common usage "myth" usually implies fantasy. Enrico Caruso was a legendary tenor, but Hogwarts is a mythical school. Legends may or may not be true. But be cautious about using "myth" to mean "untrue story" in a mythology, theology, or literature class, where teachers can be quite touchy about insisting that the true significance of a myth lies not in its factuality but in its meaning for the culture that produces or adopts it.

lend/loan

"Loan me your hat" was just as correct everywhere as "lend me your ears" until the British made "lend" the preferred verb, relegating "loan" to the thing being lent. However, as in so many cases, Americans kept the older pattern, which in its turn has influenced modern British usage so that those insisting that "loan" can only be a noun are in the minority.

See also "borrow/loan."

lense/lens

Although the variant spelling "lense" is listed in some dictionaries, the standard spelling for those little disks that focus light is "lens."

less/fewer

See "amount/number."

let/leave

See "leave/let."

liable/libel

If you are likely to do something you are *liable* to do it; and if a debt can legitimately be charged to you, you are *liable* for it. A person who defames you with a false accusation *libels* you. There is no such word as "lible."

library

The first "R" in "library" is often slurred or omitted in speech. It sometimes drops out in writing as well, and "librarian" is often turned into "libarian."

lie/lay

See "lay/lie."

light-year

"Light-year" is always a measure of distance rather than of time; in fact it is the distance that light travels in a year. "Parsec" is also a measure of distance, equaling 3.26 light-years, though the term was used incorrectly as a measure of time by Han Solo in *Star Wars*, as director George Lucas has since admitted.

lighted/lit

Don't fret over the difference between these two words; they're interchangeable.

lightening/lightning

Those bright flashes in the storm clouds used indeed to be referred to as "lightening," later as "light'ning," but now they are simply "lightning."

like

Since the 1950s, when it was especially associated with hipsters, "like" as a sort of meaningless verbal hiccup has been common in speech. The earliest uses had a sort of sense to them in which "like" introduced feelings or perceptions which were then specified: "When I learned my poem had been rejected I was, like, devastated." However, "like" quickly migrated elsewhere in sentences: "I was, like, just going down the road, when, like, I saw this cop, like, hiding behind the billboard." This habit has spread throughout American society, affecting people of all ages. Those who have the irritating "like" habit are usually unaware of it, even if they use it once or twice in every sentence. But if your job involves much speaking with others, it's a habit worth breaking.

Recently young people have extended its uses by using "like" to introduce thoughts and speeches: "When he tells me his car broke down on the way to my party I'm like, 'I know you were with Cheryl because she told me so.'" To be reacted to as a grown-up, avoid this pattern.

See also "goes."

like/as if

"As if" is generally preferred in formal writing over "like" in sentences such as "The conductor looks as if he's ready to begin the symphony." But in colloquial speech, "like" prevails, and when recording expressions such as "He spends money like it's going out of style," it would be artificial to substitute "as if." In expressions where the verb is implied rather than expressed, "like" is standard rather than "as": "She took to gymnastics like a duck to water."

like for/like

I would like you to remember that saying, "I'd like for you to take out the garbage," is not formal English. The "for" is unnecessary.

liquor

Although it may be pronounced "LIK-ker," you shouldn't spell it that way, and it's important to remember to include the "U" when writing the word.

LISTSERV

"LISTSERV" is the brand name of one kind of electronic mail-handling software for distributing messages to a list of subscribers. Other common brand names are "Majordomo" and "Listproc." You can subscribe to the poodle-fluffing list, but not the LISTSERV. People at my university, where only Listproc is used, often (and erroneously) refer to themselves as managers of "listservs." English teachers are frequently tripped up when typing "listserv" as part of a computer command; they naturally want to append an "E" on the end of the word. According to L-Soft, the manufacturer of LISTSERV, the name of its software should always be set in all capital letters. See the LISTSERV Web site for the details.

lit/lighted

See "lighted/lit."

"lite" spelling

Attempts to "reform" English spelling to render it more phonetic have mostly been doomed to failure—luckily for us. These proposed changes, if widely adopted, would make old books difficult to read and obscure etymological roots, which are often a useful guide to meaning. A few—like "lite" for "light," "nite" for "night," and "thru" for "through"—have attained a degree of popular acceptance, but none of these should be used in formal writing. "Catalog" has become an accepted substitute for "catalogue," but I don't like it and refuse to use it. "Analog" has triumphed in technical contexts, but humanists are still more likely to write "analogue."

literally

Like "incredible," "literally" has been so overused as a sort of vague intensifier that it is in danger of losing its literal meaning. It should be used to distinguish between a figurative and a literal meaning of a phrase. It should not be used as a synonym for "actually" or "really." Don't say of someone that he "literally blew up" unless he swallowed a stick of dynamite.

little/few

See "amount/number."

lived

In expressions like "long-lived," pronouncing the last part to rhyme with "dived" is more traditional, but rhyming it with "sieved" is so common that it's now widely acceptable.

loan/borrow

See "borrow/loan."

loan/lend

See "lend/loan."

long-lived
See "lived."

loosen/unloosen
See "unloosen/loosen."

lose/loose
This confusion can easily be avoided if you pronounce the word intended aloud. If it has a voiced "Z" sound, then it's "lose." If it has a hissy "S" sound, then it's "loose." Here are examples of correct usage: "He tends to lose his keys." "She lets her dog run loose." Note that when "lose" turns into "losing" it loses its "E."

a lot/alot
See "alot/a lot."

low and behold/lo and behold
The "lo" is a sort of poetic synonym for "behold." Don't substitute the nonsensical "low."

lustful/lusty
"Lusty" means "brimming with vigor and good health" or "enthusiastic." Don't confuse it with "lustful," which means "filled with sexual desire."

mantle/mantel
Though they stem from the same word, a "mantle" today is usually a cloak, while the shelf over a fireplace is most often spelled "mantel."

many/much
See "amount/number."

marital/martial

"Marital" refers to marriage, "martial" to war, whose ancient god was Mars. These two are often swapped, with comical results.

Whether theirs was marital or martial bliss no one ever knew.

marshall/marshal

You may write "The Field Marshal marshalled his troops," but you cannot spell his title with a double "L." A marshal is always a marshal, never a marshall.

marshmellow/marshmallow

Your s'mores may taste mellow, but that gooey confection you use in them is not "marshmellow," but "marshmallow." It was originally made from the root of a mallow plant which grew in marshes.

mass/massive

When the dumb Coneheads on *Saturday Night Live* talked about consuming "mass quantities" of beer they didn't know any better, but native Earth humans should stick with "massive" unless they are trying to allude to *SNL*. "Mass" is often used by young people in expressions where "many" or even the informal "a lot of" would be more appropriate.

masseuse/masseur

"Masseuse" is a strictly female term; Monsieur Philippe, who gives back rubs down at the men's gym, is a *masseur*. Because of the unsavory associations that have gathered around the term "masseuse," serious practitioners generally prefer to be called "massage therapists."

mathmatics/mathematics

Don't subtract its second syllable from "mathematics." The British logically abbreviate this word to "maths," but Americans use plain "math."

mauve

"Mauve" (a kind of purple) is pronounced to rhyme with "grove," not "mawv."

may/might

Most of the time "might" and "may" are almost interchangeable, with "might" suggesting a somewhat lower probability. You're more likely to get wet if the forecaster says it may rain than if she says it might rain; but substituting one for the other is unlikely to get you into trouble—so long as you stay in the present tense.

But "might" is also the past tense of the auxiliary verb "may" and is required in sentences like "Chuck might have avoided arrest for the robbery if he hadn't given the teller his business card before asking for the money." When speculating that events might have been other than they were, don't substitute "may" for "might."

As an aside: if you are an old-fashioned child, you will ask, "May I go out to play?" rather than "Can I go out to play?" Despite the prevalence of the latter pattern, some adults still feel strongly that "may" has to do with permission whereas "can" implies only physical ability. But then if you have a parent like this you've had this pattern drilled into your head long before you encountered this book.

me/I/myself

In the old days when people studied traditional grammar, we could simply say, "The first person singular pronoun is 'I' when it's a subject and 'me' when it's an object," but now few people know what that means. Let's see if we can apply some common sense here. The misuse of "I" and "myself" for "me" is caused by nervousness about "me." Educated people know that "Jim and me is goin' down to slop the hogs" is not elegant speech, not "correct." It should be "Jim and I" because if I were slopping the hogs alone I would never say "Me is going. . . ." So far so good. But the notion that there is something wrong with "me" leads people to overcorrect and avoid it where it is perfectly appropriate. People will say, "The document had to be signed by both Susan and I" when the correct statement would be, "The document had to be signed by both Susan and me."

Trying even harder to avoid the lowly "me," many people will substitute "myself," as in "The suspect uttered epithets at Officer O'Leary and myself." "Myself" is no better than "I" as an object. "Myself" is not a sort of all-purpose intensive form of "me" or "I." Use "myself" only when you have used "I" earlier in the same sentence: "I am not particularly fond of goat cheese myself." "I kept half the loot for myself." All this confusion can easily be avoided if you just remove the second party from the sentences where you feel tempted to use "myself" as an object or feel nervous about "me." You wouldn't say, "The IRS sent the refund check to I," so you shouldn't say, "The IRS sent the refund check to my wife and I," either. And you shouldn't say, "to my wife and myself." The only correct way to say this is, "The IRS sent the refund check to my wife and me." Still sounds too casual? Get over it.

On a related point, those who continue to announce "It is I" have traditional grammatical correctness on their side, but they are vastly outnumbered by those who proudly boast "It's me!" There's not much that can be done about this now. Similarly, if a caller asks for Susan and Susan answers, "This is she," her somewhat antiquated correctness is likely to startle the questioner into confusion.

See also "first person."

mean time/meantime
"In the mean time" should not have its two final words compressed into one.

medal/metal/meddle/mettle

A person who proves his or her mettle displays courage or stamina. The word "mettle" is seldom used outside of this expression, so people constantly confuse it with other similar-sounding words.

media/medium

There are several words with Latin or Greek roots whose plural forms ending in "A" are constantly mistaken for singular ones. Radio is a broadcast medium. Television is another broadcast medium. Newspapers are a print medium. Together they are media. Following the tendency of Americans to abbreviate phrases, with "transistor radio" becoming "transistor" (now fortunately obsolete) and "videotape" becoming "video," "news media" and "communications media" have been abbreviated to "media." Remember that watercolor on paper and oil on black velvet are also media, though they have nothing to do with the news. When you want to get a message from your late Uncle Fred, you may consult a medium. The word means a vehicle between some source of information and the recipient of it. The "media" are the transmitters of the news; they are not the news itself.

See also "criteria/criterion" and "data/datum."

medieval ages/Middle Ages

The "eval" of "medieval" means "age," so by saying "medieval ages" you are saying "middle ages ages." Medievalists also greatly resent the common misspelling "midevil."

mediocre

Although some dictionaries accept the meaning of this word as "medium" or "average," in fact its connotations are almost always more negative. When something is distinctly not as good as it could be, it is mediocre. If you want to say that you are an average student, don't proclaim yourself mediocre, or you'll convey a worse impression of yourself than you intend.

medium/media
See "media/medium."

medium/median
That strip of grass separating the lanes going opposite directions in the middle of a freeway is a *median*.

memento/momento
See "momento/memento."

memorium/memoriam
The correct spelling of the Latin phrase is "in memoriam."

metal/medal/meddle/mettle
See "medal/metal/meddle/mettle."

metaphor
See "parallel/symbol."

mic/mike
Until very recently the casual term for a microphone was "mike," not "mic." Young people now mostly imitate the technicians who prefer the shorter "mic" label on their soundboards, but it looks distinctly odd to those used to the traditional term. There are no other words in English in which "-ic" is pronounced to rhyme with "bike"—that's the reason for the traditional "mike" spelling in the first place.

Middle Ages
See "medieval ages/Middle Ages."

might/may
See "may/might."

militate against/mitigate against
See "mitigate against/militate against."

minature/miniature

Few people pronounce the second syllable in "miniature" distinctly, so it often gets dropped in spelling.

minister/administer

See "administer/minister."

mischievious/mischievous

The correct pronunciation of this word is "MISS-chuh-vuss," not "miss-CHEE-vee-uss." Don't let that mischievous extra "I" sneak into the word.

misnomer

A misnomer a is mistake in naming a thing; calling a debit card a "credit card" is a misnomer. Do not use the term more generally to designate other sorts of confusion, misunderstood concepts, or fallacies, and above all do not render this word as "misnamer."

mitigate against/militate against

"Mitigate" means "soften, make less harsh," and has nothing to do with the expression "militate against," which means "to conflict with." "Mitigate" should never be used with "against."

momentarily

"The plane will be landing momentarily," says the flight attendant, and the grumpy grammarian in seat 36B thinks to himself, "So we're going to touch down for just a moment?" Everyone else thinks, "Just a moment now before we land." Back in the 1920s when this use of "momentarily" was first spreading on both sides of the Atlantic, one might have been accused of misusing the word; but by now it's listed without comment as one of the standard definitions in most dictionaries.

momento/memento

A memento is something associated with a memory and has nothing to do with "moment."

Moon/moon
See "Earth/earth/Moon/moon."

moot point
See "mute point/moot point."

moral/morale
If you are trying to make people behave properly, you are policing their morals; if you are just trying to keep their spirits up, you are trying to maintain their morale. "Moral" is accented on the first syllable, "morale" on the second.

more than/over
See "over/more than."

moreso/more so
"More so" should always be spelled as two distinct words.

most always/almost always
"Most always" is a casual, slangy way of saying "almost always." The latter expression is better in writing.

motion/move
When you make a motion in a meeting, say simply "I move," as in "I move to adjourn"; and if you're taking the minutes, write "Barbara moved," not "Barbara motioned" (unless Barbara was making wild arm-waving gestures to summon the servers to bring in the lunch). Instead of "I want to make a motion . . ." it's simpler and more direct to say "I want to move. . . ."

Mount Fujiyama/Fujiyama
Yama means "mountain" in Japanese, so when you say "Mount Fujiyama" you are saying "Mount Fuji Mountain." The Japanese usually say *Fuji-san*, but "Fujiyama" or "Mount Fuji" is standard in English—just be aware that both sound "foreign" to Japanese native speakers.

Ms.
See "gender."

much/many
See "amount/number."

much differently/very differently
Say, "We consistently vote very differently," not "much differently."
But you can say, "My opinion doesn't much differ from yours."

muchly/much
Drop the nonstandard "-ly" ending from "much," or substitute the word "very" when appropriate.

murmer/murmur
Think of "murmur" as a gentle repetition of sounds like "blahblah."

music/singing
After my wife—an accomplished soprano—reported indignantly that a friend of hers had stated that her church had "no music, only singing," I began to notice the same tendency among my students to equate music strictly with instrumental music. I was told by one that "the singing interfered with the music" (i.e., the accompaniment). In the classical realm most listeners seem to prefer instrumental to vocal performances, which is odd given the distinct unpopularity of strictly instrumental popular music. People rejoice at the sound of choral works at Christmas but seldom seek them out at other times of the year. Serious music lovers rightly object to the linguistic sloppiness that denies the label "music" to works by such composers as Palestrina, Schubert, and Verdi. From the Middle Ages to the late 18th century, vocal music reigned supreme, and instrumentalists strove to achieve the prized compliment of "sounding like the human voice." The dominance of orchestral works is a comparatively recent phenomenon.

In contrast, my students often call instrumental works "songs," being unfamiliar with the terms "composition" and "piece." All singing is music, but not all music is singing.

After establishing that their singing was, indeed, music, they began in earnest.

Muslims/Islams
See "Islams/Muslims."

mute point/moot point
"Moot" is a very old word related to "meeting," specifically a meeting where serious matters are discussed. Oddly enough, a moot point can be a point worth discussing at a meeting (or in court)—an unresolved question—or it can be the opposite: a point already settled and not worth discussing further. At any rate, "mute point" is simply wrong.

myriad of/myriad

Some traditionalists object to the word "of" after "myriad" or an "a" before, though both are fairly common in formal writing. The word is originally Greek, meaning "10,000," but now usually means "a great many." Its main function is as a noun, and the adjective derived from it shows its origins by being reluctant to behave like other nouns expressing amount, like "ton" as in "I've got a ton of work to do." In contrast: "I have myriad tasks to complete at work."

myself
See "me/I/myself."

myth/legend
See "legend/myth."

❦

naive/nieve
See "nieve/naive.

Native American/Indian
See "Indian/Native American."

nauseous/nauseated

Many people say, when sick to their stomachs, that they feel "nauseous" (pronounced "NOSH-uss" or "NOZH-uss"), but traditionalists insist that this word should be used to describe something that makes you want to throw up: something nauseating. They hear you as saying that you make people want to vomit, and it tempers their sympathy for your plight. Better to say you are "nauseated," or simply that you feel like throwing up. Note that the English use "sick" exclusively for vomiting; when Americans say they feel sick, the English say they feel ill. Americans visiting Great Britain who tell their hosts they feel sick may cause them to worry needlessly about the carpeting.

near miss

It is futile to protest that "near miss" should be "near collision." This expression is a condensed version of something like "a miss that came very near to being a collision" and is similar to "narrow escape." Everyone knows what is meant by it and almost everyone uses it. It should be noted that the expression can also be used in the sense of almost succeeding in striking a desired target: "His Cointreau soufflé was a near miss."

neice/niece

Despite the fact that the rule "I before E except after C" holds true most of the time, many people have trouble believing that words with the "ee" sound in them should be spelled with an "IE." The problem is that in English (and only in English), the letter "I" sounds like "aye" rather than "ee," as it does in the several European languages from which we have borrowed a host of words. If you had studied French in high school you would have learned that this word is pronounced "knee-YES" in that language, and it would be easier to remember. Americans in particular misspell a host of German-Jewish names because they have trouble remembering that in German "IE" is pronounced "ee" and "EI" is pronounced "aye." The possessors of such names are inconsistent about this matter in English. "Wein" changes from "vine" to "ween," but "Klein" remains "kline."

 See also "ie/ei."

Nevada

"Nuh-VAH-duh" is a little closer to the original Spanish pronunciation than the way Nevadans pronounce the name of their home state, but the correct middle syllable is the same "A" sound as in "sad." When East Coast broadcasters use the first pronunciation, they mark themselves as outsiders.

new beginning
See "redundancies."

next store/next door
You can adore the boy next door, but not "next store."

next to last/penultimate

See "penultimate/next to last."

niece/neice

See "neice/niece."

nieve/naive

People who spell this French-derived word "nieve" make themselves look naive. In French there is also a masculine form: *naif*, and both words can be nouns meaning "naive person" as well as adjectives. *Nieve* is actually the Spanish word for "snow." "Naiveté" is the French spelling of the related noun in English. If you prefer more nativized spelling, "naivety" is also acceptable.

19th century/1800s

See "1800s/19th century."

nip it in the butt/nip it in the bud

To nip something in the bud is to stop it from flowering fully. The alternate expression is hilarious, but doesn't convey the same idea at all.

nite

See "'lite' spelling."

no sooner when/no sooner than

The phrase "No sooner had Paula stopped petting the cat when it began to yowl" should be instead "No sooner had Paula stopped petting the cat than it began to yowl."

none

Some people insist that since "none" is derived from "no one" it should always be singular: "none of us is having dessert." However, in standard usage, the word is most often treated as a plural. "None of us are having dessert" will do just fine.

nonplussed

"Nonplussed" means to be stuck, often in a puzzling or embarrassing way, unable to go further ("non"="no" + "plus"="further"). It does not mean, as many people seem to think, "calm, in control."

noone/no one

Shall we meet at Ye Olde Sandwyche Shoppe at Noone? "No one" is always two separate words, unlike "anyone" and "someone."

not all that/not very

The slangy phrase "not all that," as in "The dessert was not all that tasty," doesn't belong in formal writing. "Not very" would work, but something more specific would be even better: "The pudding tasted like library paste."

not hardly/not at all

"Not hardly" is slang, fine when you want to be casual—but in a formal document? Not hardly!

notorious

"Notorious" means famous in a bad way, as in "Nero was notorious for giving long recitals of his tedious poetry." Occasionally writers deliberately use it in a positive sense to suggest irony or wit, but this is a very feeble and tired device. Nothing admirable should be called "notorious."

See also "infamous."

nuclear

This isn't a writing problem, but a pronunciation error. President Eisenhower used to consistently insert a "U" sound between the first and second syllables, leading many journalists to imitate him and say "nuk-yuh-lar" instead of the correct "nuk-lee-ar." The confusion extends also to "nucleus." Many people can't even hear the mistake when they make it, and only scientists and a few others will catch the mispronunciation; but you lose credibility if you are an anti-nuclear protester who doesn't know how to pronounce "nuclear." Here's one way to remember: we need a new, clear understanding of the issues; let's stop saying "Nuke you!"

number/amount

See "amount/number."

number of verb

In long, complicated sentences, people often lose track of whether the subject is singular or plural and use the wrong sort of verb. "The ultimate effect of all of these phone calls to the detectives were to make them suspicious of the callers" is an error because "effect," which is singular, is the subject. If you are uncertain about whether to go with singular or plural, condense the sentence down to its skeleton: "The effect . . . was to make them suspicious."

Another situation that creates confusion is the use of interjections like "along with," "as well as," and "together with," where they are often treated improperly as if they meant simply "and." "Aunt Hilda, as well as her pet dachshund, is coming to the party" (not "are coming").

numbers

If your writing contains numbers, the general rule is to spell out in letters all the numbers from zero to nine and use numerals for larger numbers, but there are exceptions. If what you're writing is full of numbers and you're doing math with them, stick with numerals. Approximations like "about thirty days ago" and catch-phrases like "his first thousand days" are spelled out. Large round numbers are often rendered thus: "50 billion sold." With measurements, use numerals: "4 inches long." Never start a sentence with a numeral. Either spell out the number involved or rearrange the sentence to move the number to a later position.

See also "'50s."

nuptual/nuptial

"Nuptial" is usually a pretentious substitute for "wedding," but if you're going to use it, be sure to spell it properly.

of

"Of" is often shoved in where it doesn't belong in phrases like "not that big of a deal" and "not that great of a writer." Just leave it out.

of/'s

Phrases combining "of" with a noun followed by "'s" may seem redundant, since both indicate possession; nevertheless, "a friend of Karen's" is standard English, just as "a friend of Karen" and "Karen's friend" are.

off of

For most Americans, the natural thing to say is, "Climb down off of [pronounced 'offa'] that horse, Tex, with your hands in the air," but many U.K. authorities urge that the "of" should be omitted as redundant. Where British English reigns you may want to omit the "of" as superfluous, but common usage in the U.S. has rendered "off of" so standard as to generally pass unnoticed, though some American authorities also discourage it in formal writing. However, "off of" meaning "from" in phrases like "borrow five dollars off of Clarice" is definitely nonstandard.

offense/offence

In the U.S. "offense" is standard; in the U.K. use "offence." The sports pronunciation accenting the first syllable should not be used when discussing military, legal, or other sorts of offense.

often

People striving for sophistication often pronounce the "T" in this word, but true sophisticates know that the masses are correct in saying "offen."

OK/okay

This may be the most universal word in existence; it seems to have spread to most of the world's languages. Etymologists now generally agree that it began as a humorous misspelling of "all correct": "oll korrect." "OK" without periods is the most common form in written American English now, though "okay" is not incorrect.

old fashion/old-fashioned
Although "old fashion" appears in advertising a good deal, the traditional spelling is "old-fashioned."

old-timer's disease/Alzheimer's disease
I've always thought that "old-timer's disease" was a clever if tasteless pun on "Alzheimer's disease," but many people have assured me that this is a common and quite unintentional error.

on accident/by accident
Although you can do things *on* purpose, you do them *by* accident.

on sale/for sale
See "for sale/on sale."

on to/onto
See "onto/on to."

once and a while/once in a while
"Once and a while" is based on a mishearing of the traditional expression "once in a while."

one-dimensional/two-dimensional
Once upon a time most folks knew that "three-dimensional" characters or ideas were rounded, fleshed out, and complex and "two-dimensional" ones were flat and uninteresting. It seems that the knowledge of basic geometry has declined in recent years, because today we hear uninteresting characters and ideas described as "one-dimensional." According to Euclid, no object can be one-dimensional (of course, according to modern physics, even two-dimensionality is only an abstract concept). If you are still bothered by the notion that two dimensions are one too many, just use "flat."

one in the same/one and the same
The old expression "they are one and the same" is now often mangled into the roughly phonetic equivalent "one in the same." The use of

145

"one" here to mean "identical with each other" is familiar from phrases like "Jane and John act as one." They are one, they are the same.

one of the (singular)

In phrases like "pistachio is one of the few flavors that appeals to me," use the singular form for the verb "appeals" because its subject is "one," not "flavors."

one of the only/one of the few

"Only" has its root in "one," as should be obvious from looking at it. But we lose sight of this because of phrases like "only a few" and "only some," which lead in turn to the mistaken "one of the only." "The only" always refers to just one item, so the correct expression is "one of the few." Compare this with the similarly mistaken "very unique."

only

Writers often inadvertently create confusion by placing "only" incorrectly in a sentence. It should go immediately before the word or phrase it modifies. "I lost my only shirt" means that I had but one to begin with. "I lost only my shirt" means I didn't lose anything else. "Only I lost my shirt" means that I was the only person in my group to lose a shirt. Strictly speaking, "I only lost my shirt" should mean I didn't destroy it or have it stolen—I just lost it, but in common speech this is usually understood as being identical with "I lost only my shirt." Scrutinize your uses of "only" to make sure you are not creating unwanted ambiguities.

onto/on to

"Onto" and "on to" are often interchangeable, but not always. Consider the effect created by wrongly using "onto" in the following sentence when "on to" is meant: "We're having hors d'oeuvres in the garden, and for dinner moving onto the house." If the "on" is part of an expression like "moving on," it can't be shoved together with a "to" that just happens to follow it.

146

oppress/repress

Dictators commonly oppress their citizens and repress dissent, but these words don't mean exactly the same thing. "Repress" just means "keep under control." Sometimes repression is a good thing: "During the job interview, repress the temptation to tell Mr. Brown that he has toilet paper stuck to his shoe." Oppression is always bad, and implies serious persecution.

oral/aural

See "aural/oral."

orders of magnitude

Many pretentious writers have begun to use the expression "orders of magnitude" without understanding what it means. The concept derives from the scientific notation of very large numbers in which each order of magnitude is 10 times the previous one. When the bacteria in a flask have multiplied from some hundreds to some thousands, it is very handy to say that their numbers have increased by an order of magnitude, and when they have increased to some millions, that their numbers have increased by four orders of magnitude.

Number language generally confuses people. Many seem to suppose that a 100 percent increase must be pretty much the same as an increase by an order of magnitude, but in fact such an increase represents merely a doubling. A "hundredfold increase" is even bigger: one 100 times as much. If you don't have a firm grasp on such concepts, it's best to avoid the expression altogether. After all, "Our audience is 10 times as big now as when the show opened" makes the same point more clearly than "Our audience has increased by an order of magnitude."

Compare with "quantum leap."

ordinance/ordnance

A law is an ordinance, but a gun is a piece of ordnance.

Oregon

Oregon natives and other Westerners pronounce the state name's last syllable to sound like "gun," not "gone."

organic

The word "organic" is used in all sorts of contexts, often in a highly metaphorical manner; the subject here is its use in the phrase "organic foods" in claims of superior healthfulness. Various jurisdictions have various standards for "organic" food, but generally the label is applied to foods that have been grown without artificial chemicals or pesticides. Literally, of course, the term is a redundancy: all food is composed of organic chemicals (complex chemicals containing carbon). There is no such thing as an inorganic food (unless you count water as a food). Natural fertilizers and pesticides may or may not be superior to artificial ones, but the proper distinction is not between organic and inorganic. Many nitrogen-fixing plants like peas do a great job of fertilizing the soil with plain old inorganic atmospheric nitrogen.

When it comes to nutrition, people tend to generalize rashly from a narrow scientific basis. After a few preservatives were revealed to have harmful effects in some consumers, many products were proudly labeled "No Preservatives!" I don't want harmful preservatives in my food, but that label suggests to me a warning: "Deteriorates quickly! May contain mold and other kinds of rot!" Salt is a preservative.

Oriental/Asiatic/Asian

"Oriental" is generally considered old-fashioned now, and many find it offensive. "Asian" is preferred, but not "Asiatic." It's better to write the nationality involved, for example "Chinese" or "Indian," if you know it. "Asian" is often taken to mean exclusively "East Asian," which irritates South Asian and Central Asian people.

orientate/orient

Although some dictionaries have now begun to accept it, "orientate" was mistakenly formed from "orientation." The proper verb form is simply "orient." Similarly, "disorientated" is an error for "disoriented."

See also "interpretate/interpret."

ostensively/ostensibly
This word, meaning "apparently," is spelled "ostensibly."

ought/had ought
See "had ought/ought."

outlet/plug-in
See "plug-in/outlet."

over/more than
Some people insist that "over" cannot be used to signify "more than," as in "Over a thousand baton-twirlers marched in the parade." "Over," they insist, always refers to something physically higher: say, the blimp hovering over the parade route. This absurd distinction ignores the role metaphor plays in language. If I write "1" on the blackboard and "10" beside it, "10" is still the "higher" number. "Over" has been used in the sense of "more than" for over a thousand years.

over-exaggerated/exaggerated
"Over-exaggerated" is a redundancy. If something is exaggerated, it's already overstressed.

overdo/overdue
If you *overdo* the cocktails after work you may be *overdue* for your daughter's soccer game at 6:00.

overhang indents
See "hanging indents."

oversee/overlook
When you *oversee* the preparation of dinner, you take control and manage the operation closely. But if you *overlook* the preparation of dinner you forget to prepare the meal entirely—better order pizza.

Pacific

See "specific/Pacific."

pair (number)

"This is a left-handed pair of scissors." "There is a pair of glasses on the mantelpiece." "Pair" is singular in this sort of expression. Note that we say, "That is a nice pair of pants," even though we also say, "Those are nice pants."

palate/palette/pallet

Your "palate" is the roof of your mouth, and by extension, your sense of taste. A "palette" is the flat board an artist mixes paint on (or by extension, a range of colors). A "pallet" is either a bed (now rare) or a flat platform onto which goods are loaded.

palm off/pawn off

See "pawn off/palm off."

parallel/symbol

Beginning literature students often write sentences like "He uses the rose as a parallel for her beauty" when they mean "a symbol for her beauty." If you are taking a literature class, it's good to master the distinctions between several related terms relating to symbolism. An eagle clutching a bundle of arrows and an olive branch is a symbol of the U.S. government in war and peace.

Students often misuse the word "analogy" in the same way. An analogy has to be specifically spelled out by the writer, not simply referred to: "My mother's attempts to find her keys in the morning were like early expeditions to the South Pole: prolonged and mostly futile."

A *metaphor* is a kind of symbolism common in literature. When Shakespeare writes "That time of year thou mayst in me behold/ When yellow leaves, or none, or few, do hang/Upon those boughs which shake against the cold," he is comparing his aging self to a tree in late autumn, perhaps even specifically suggesting that he is going bald by referring to the tree shedding its leaves. This autumnal tree is a metaphor for the human aging process.

A *simile* resembles a metaphor except that "like" or "as" or something similar is used to make the comparison explicitly. Byron admires a dark-haired woman by saying of her "She walks in beauty, like the night/Of cloudless climes and starry skies." Her darkness is said to be *like* that of the night.

An *allegory* is a symbolic narrative in which characters may stand for abstract ideas and the story conveys a philosophy. Allegories are no longer popular, but the most commonly read one in school is Dante's *Divine Comedy* in which the poet Virgil is a symbol for human wisdom, Dante's beloved Beatrice is a symbol of divine grace, and the whole poem tries to teach the reader how to avoid damnation. Aslan in C. S. Lewis' *Narnia* tales is an allegorical figure meant to symbolize Christ: dying to save others and rising again. (*Aslan* is Turkish for "lion").

parallelism in a series
Phrases in a series separated by commas or conjunctions must all have the same grammatical form. "They loved mountain-climbing, to gather wild mushrooms, and first-aid practice" should be corrected to something like this: "They loved to climb mountains, gather wild mushrooms, and practice first aid" (all three verbs are dependent on that initial "to"). Fear of being repetitious often leads writers into awkward inconsistencies when creating such series.

parallelled/paralleled
In British English two pairs of parallel "L's" are a handy spelling reminder, but in American English the spelling of the past tense of "parallel" is "paralleled." The same pattern holds for British "parallelling" and American "paralleling."

paralyzation/paralysis
Some people derive the noun "paralyzation" from the verb "paralyze," but the proper term is "paralysis."

parameters/perimeters
When parameters were spoken of only by mathematicians and scientists, the term caused few problems; but now that it has become

widely adopted by other speakers, it is constantly confused with "perimeters." A parameter is a quantity or constant that varies depending on the instance being examined. The parameters of distance between the axles of a car and its turning radius are related. The perimeter of something is its boundary. The two words shade into each other because we often speak of factors of an issue or problem being parameters, simultaneously thinking of them as limits; but this is to confuse two distinct, if related, ideas. A safe rule is to avoid using "parameters" altogether unless you are confident you know what it means.

parentheses

The most common error in using parenthesis marks (besides using them too much) is to forget to enclose the parenthetical material with a final, closing parenthesis mark. The second most common is to place concluding punctuation incorrectly. The simplest sort of example is one in which the entire sentence is enclosed in parentheses. (Most people understand that the final punctuation must remain inside the closing parenthesis mark, like this.) More troublesome are sentences in which only a clause or phrase is enclosed in parentheses. Normally a sentence's final punctuation mark—whether period, exclamation point, or question mark—goes outside such a parenthesis (like this). However, if the material inside the parenthesis requires a concluding punctuation mark like an exclamation point or question mark (but not a period!), that mark is placed inside the closing mark even though another mark is outside it. This latter sort of thing is awkward, however, and best avoided if you can help it.

For some reason, many writers have begun to omit the space before a parenthetic page citation, like this:(p. 17). Always preserve the space, like this: (p. 17).

parliment/parliament

Americans unfamiliar with parliamentary systems often mistakenly leave the second "A" out of "parliament" and "parliamentary."

a part/apart

See "apart/part."

pass/progress

See "progress/pass."

passed/past

If you are referring to time or distance, use "past": "The team performed well in the past" and "The police car drove past the suspect's house." If you are referring to the action of passing, however, you need to use "passed": "When John passed the gravy, he spilled it on his lap" and "The teacher was astonished that none of the students had passed the test."

passive voice

There are legitimate uses for the passive voice: "This absurd regulation was of course written by a committee." But it's true that you can make your prose more lively and readable by using the active voice much more often. "The victim was attacked by three men in ski masks" isn't nearly as striking as "Three men in ski masks attacked the victim." The passive voice is often used to avoid taking responsibility for an action: "My term paper was accidentally deleted" avoids stating the truth: "I accidentally deleted my term paper." Over-use of passive constructions is irritating, though not necessarily erroneous. But it does lead to real clumsiness when passive constructions get piled on top of each other: "No exception in the no-pets rule was sought to be created so that angora rabbits could be raised in the apartment" can be made clearer by shifting to the active voice: "The landlord refused to make an exception to the no-pets rule to allow Eliza to raise angora rabbits in the apartment."

past/passed

See "passed/past."

past history

See "redundancies."

past time/pastime

An agreeable activity like knitting with which you pass the time is your pastime. Spell it as one word, with one "S" and one "T."

pawn off/palm off

Somebody defrauds you by using sleight of hand (literal or figurative) to "palm" the object you wanted and give you something inferior instead. The expression is not "to pawn off," but "to palm off."

peace/piece

It's hard to believe many people really confuse the meaning of these words, but the spellings are frequently swapped, probably out of sheer carelessness. "Piece" has the word "pie" buried in it, which should remind you of the familiar phrase "a piece of pie." You can meditate to find peace of mind, or you can get angry and give someone a piece of your mind. Classical scholars will note that *pax* is the Latin word for "peace," suggesting the need for an "A" in the latter word.

See also "hold your peace/say your piece."

peak/peek/pique

It is tempting to think that your attention might be aroused to a high point by "peaking" your curiosity, but in fact, *pique* is a French word meaning "prick," in the sense of "stimulate." The expression has nothing to do with "peek," either. Therefore the expression is "my curiosity was piqued."

peasant/pheasant

See "pheasant/peasant."

penultimate/next to last

To confuse your readers, use the term "penultimate," which means "next to last," but which most people assume means "the very last." And if you really want to baffle them, use "antepenultimate" to mean "third from the end." Many people also mistakenly use "penultimate" when they mean "quintessential" or "archetypical."

peoples

In the Middle Ages "peoples" was not an uncommon word, but later writers grew wary of it because "people" has a collective, plural meaning that seemed to make "peoples" superfluous. It lived on in the sense of "nations" ("the peoples of the world") and from this social scientists (anthropologists in particular) derived the extended meaning "ethnic groups" ("the peoples of the upper Amazon Basin"). However, in ordinary usage "people" is usually understood to be plural, so much so that in the bad old days when dialect humor was popular having a speaker refer to "you peoples" indicated illiteracy. If you are not referring to national or ethnic groups, it is better to avoid "peoples" and use "people."

See also "behaviors/behavior."

per/according to
Using "per" to mean "according to," as in "ship the widgets as per the instructions of the customer," is rather old-fashioned business jargon and is not welcome in other contexts. "Per" is fine when used in phrases involving figures like "miles per gallon."

per se/perse
See "perse/per se."

percent decrease
When something has been reduced by one hundred percent, it's all gone (or if the reduction was in its price, it's free). You can't properly speak of reducing anything by more than a hundred percent (unless it's a deficit or debt, in which case you wind up with a surplus).

See also "orders of magnitude."

peremptory/preemptory
See "preemptory/peremptory."

perimeters/parameters
See "parameters/perimeters."

permiscuous/promiscuous
The influence of "permissiveness" may influence this misspelling of "promiscuous."

pernickety/persnickety
The original Scottish dialect form was "pernickety," but Americans changed it to "persnickety" a century ago. "Pernickety" is generally unknown in the U.S. though it's still in wide use across the Atlantic.

perogative/prerogative

"Prerogative" is frequently both mispronounced and misspelled as "perogative." It may help to remember that the word is associated with *pr*ivileges of *pr*ecedence.

perpetuate/perpetrate

"Perpetrate" is something criminals do (criminals are sometimes called "perps" in slang). When you seek to continue something you are trying to "perpetuate" it.

perscription/prescription

"Prescription" is often mispronounced "perscription."

perse/per se

This legal term meaning "in, of, or by itself" is a bit pretentious, but you gain little respect if you misspell *per se* as a single word. Worse is the mistaken "per say."

persecute/prosecute

When you persecute someone, you're treating them badly, whether they deserve it or not; but only legal officers can prosecute someone for a crime.

persnickety/pernickety

See "pernickety/persnickety."

person/individual

See "individual/person."

personal/personnel

Employees are personnel, but private individuals considered separately from their jobs have personal lives.

personality

In show business personalities are people famous for being famous (mostly popular actors and singers); people with more substantial accomplishments like distinguished heads of state and Nobel Prize winners should not be referred to as "personalities" even when they appear on *The Tonight Show*.

perspective/prospective

"Perspective" has to do with sight, as in painting, and is usually a noun. "Prospective" generally has to do with the future (compare with "What are your prospects, young man?") and is usually an adjective. But beware: there is also a rather old-fashioned but fairly common meaning of the word "prospect" that has to do with sight: "As he climbed the mountain, a vast prospect opened up before him."

persuade/convince

See "convince/persuade."

peruse

This word, which means "examine thoroughly," is often misused to mean "glance over hastily." Although some dictionaries accept the latter meaning, it is not traditional.

phase/faze

See "faze/phase."

pheasant/peasant

When I visited the former Soviet Union I was astonished to learn that farmworkers were still called "peasants" there. In English-speaking countries we tend to think of the term as belonging strictly to the feudal era. However you use it, don't confuse it with "pheasant," a favorite game bird. Use the sound of the beginning consonants to remind you of the difference: pheasants are food, peasants are people.

phenomena/phenomenon

"Phenomena" is the plural form. It's "this phenomenon," but "these phenomena."

Philippines/Filipinos

The people of the Philippines are called "Filipinos." Don't switch the initial letters of these two words.

physical/fiscal
See "fiscal/physical."

picaresque/picturesque
"Picaresque" is a technical literary term you are unlikely to have a use for. It labels a sort of literature involving a *picaro* (Spanish), a lovable rogue who roams the land having colorful adventures. A landscape that looks as lovely as a picture is "picturesque."

picture
The pronunciation of "picture" as if it were "pitcher" is common in some dialects, but not standard. The first syllable should sound like "pick."

piece/peace
See "peace/piece."

PIN number/PIN
Those who object to "PIN number" on the grounds that the "N" in "PIN" stands for "number" in the phrase "personal identification number" are quite right, but it may be difficult to get people to say anything else. "PIN" was invented to meet the objection that a "password" consisting of nothing but numbers is not a word. Pronouncing each letter of the acronym as "P-I-N" blunts its efficiency. Saying just "PIN" reminds us of another common English word, though few people are likely to think when they are told to "enter PIN" that they should shove a steel pin into the terminal they are operating. In writing, anyway, "PIN" is unambiguous and should be used without the redundant "number."

The same goes for "VIN number"; "VIN" stands for "vehicle identification number." "UPC code" is redundant because "UPC" stands for "universal product code."

pique/peak/peek
See "peak/peek/pique."

playwrite/playwright

It might seem as if a person who writes plays should be called a "playwrite" but in fact a playwright is a person who has wrought words into a dramatic form, just as a wheelwright has wrought wheels out of wood and iron. All the other words ending in "-wright" are archaic, or we'd be constantly reminded of the correct pattern.

plead innocent

Lawyers frown on the phrase "plead innocent" (it's "plead guilty" or "plead not guilty"), but outside of legal contexts the phrase is standard English.

please RSVP/please reply

R.S.V.P. stands for the French phrase *répondez s'il vous plaît* ("reply, please"), so it doesn't need an added "please." However, since few people seem to know its literal meaning, and fewer still take it seriously, it's best to use plain English: "Please reply." And for those of you receiving such an invitation, yes, you have to let the host know whether you're coming or not, and no, you can't bring along the kids or other uninvited guests.

plug-in/outlet

That thing on the end of an electrical cord is a plug, which goes into the socket of the wall outlet.

PM/AM

See "AM/PM."

podium/lectern

Strictly speaking, a podium is a raised platform on which you stand to give a speech; the piece of furniture on which you place your notes and behind which you stand is a lectern.

point being is that

"The point being is that" is redundant; say just "the point is that" or "the point being that."

point in time/point, time
This redundancy became popular because it was used by astronauts seeking to distinguish precisely between a point in time and a point in space. Since most people use the expression in contexts where there is no ambiguity, it makes more sense to say simply "at this point" or "at this time."

pole/poll
A "pole" is a long stick. You could take a "poll" (survey or ballot) to determine whether voters want lower taxes or better education.

pompom/pompon
To most people that fuzzy ball on the top of a knit hat and the implement wielded by a cheerleader are both "pompoms," but to traditionalists they are "pompons," spelled the way the French—who gave us the word—spell it. A pompom, say these purists, is only a sort of large gun. Though you're unlikely to bother many people by falling into the common confusion, you can show off your education by observing the distinction.

populace/populous
The population of a country may be referred to as its "populace," but a crowded country is "populous."

pore/pour
When used as a verb, "pore" has the unusual sense of "scrutinize," as in "She pored over her receipts." If it's coffee or rain, the stuff pours.

portentious/portentous
People being pretentious get confused about "portentous," which is related to "portents"—omens.

portray/protray
See otray/portray."

posses/possess
Posses chase after bank robbers. If you own something, you *possess* it.

possessed of/possessed by/possessed with
If you own a yacht, you're possessed *of* it. If a demon takes over your body, you're possessed *by* it. If that which possesses you is more metaphorical, as in the case of an executive determined to get ahead, he or she can be possessed *by* or *with* the desire to win.

pour/pore
See "pore/pour."

practice/practise
In the United Kingdom, "practice" is the noun, "practise" the verb; but in the U.S. the spelling "practice" is commonly used for both, though the distinction is sometimes observed. "Practise" as a noun is, however, always wrong in both places: a doctor always has a "practice," never a "practise."

practicle/practical
Some words end in "-icle" and others in "-ical" without the result being any difference in pronunciation. But when you want somebody really practical, call on good old Al.

pray/prey
If you want a miracle, pray to God. If you're a criminal, you prey on your victims.
Incidentally, it's "praying mantis," not "preying mantis." The insect holds its forefeet in a position suggesting prayer.

precede/proceed
"Precede" means "to go before." "Proceed" means "to go on." Let your companion precede you through the door, then proceed to follow her. Interestingly, the second "E" is missing in "procedure."

precedence/precedents
Although these words sound the same, they work differently. The pop star is given precedence over the factory worker at the entrance to the dance club. "Precedents" is just the plural of "precedent": "If we let

the kids adopt that rattlesnake as a pet and agree to let them take it for a walk in Death Valley, we'll be setting some bad precedents."

precipitate/precipitous

Both of these adjectives are based on the image of plunging over the brink of a precipice, but "precipitate" emphasizes the suddenness of the plunge, "precipitous," the steepness of it. If you make a "precipitate" decision, you are making a hasty and probably unwise one. If the stock market declines "precipitously," it goes down sharply.

predicts/calls for

See "calls for/predicts."

predominate/predominant

"Predominate" is a verb: "In the royal throne room, the color red predominates." "Predominant" is an adjective: "The predominant view among the touts is that Fancy Dancer is the best bet in the third race."

predominately/predominantly

"Predominantly" is formed on the adjective "predominant," not the verb "predominate."

preemptory/peremptory

"Peremptory" (meaning "imperative") is often misspelled and mispronounced "preemptory" through confusion caused by the influence of the verb "preempt," whose adjectival form is actually "preemptive." "Preemptory" exists only as an obscure legal term you're not likely to have use for.

preferably

Although some U.S. dictionaries now recognize the pronunciation of "preferably" with the first two syllables pronounced just like "prefer"—first "E" long and the stress on the second syllable—the standard pronunciation is "PREFFerublee," with the first syllable stressed, just like in "preference." The alternative pronunciation sounds awkward to some people.

prejudice/prejudiced

People not only misspell "prejudice" in a number of ways, they sometimes say "he's prejudice" when they mean "he's prejudiced."

See also "bias/biased."

premier/premiere

These words are, respectively, the masculine and feminine forms of the word for "first" in French; but they have become differentiated in English. Only the masculine form is used as an adjective, as in "Tidy-Pool is the premier pool-cleaning firm in Orange County." The confusion arises when these words are used as nouns. The prime minister of a parliamentary government is known as a "premier." The opening night of a film or play is its "premiere."

"Premiere" as a verb is common in the arts and in show business ("The show premiered on PBS"), but it is less acceptable in other contexts ("The state government premiered its new welfare system"). Use "introduced" or, if real innovation is involved, "pioneered."

premise/premises

Some people suppose that since "premises" has a plural form, a single house or other piece of property must be a "premise," but that word is reserved for use as a term in logic meaning something assumed or taken as given in making an argument. Your lowly one-room shack is still your "premises."

preplan

See "redundancies."

prepone

South Asian speakers have evolved the logical word "prepone" to mean the opposite of "postpone": to move forward in time. It's a handy word, but users of it should be aware that those unfamiliar with their dialect will be baffled by it.

preposition, ending a sentence with a

See "ending a sentence with a preposition."

prepositions (repeated)

In the sentence "Alex liked Nancy, with whom he shared his Snickers bar with," only one "with" is needed—eliminate either one. Look out for similarly duplicated prepositions.

Incidentally, an often-cited example of this pattern is from Paul McCartney's "Live and Let Die": "In this ever-changing world in which we live in." But if you listen closely, you'll hear instead a quite correct "In this ever-changing world in which we're livin'." Americans have a hard time hearing the soft British "R" in "we're."

prepositions (wrong)

One of the clearest indications that a person reads little and doesn't hear much formal English is a failure to use the right preposition in a common expression. You aren't ignorant *to* a fact; you're ignorant *of* it. Things don't happen *on* accident, but *by* accident (though they do happen "on purpose"). There are no simple rules governing preposition usage; you just have to immerse yourself in good English in order to write it naturally.

See also "different than/different from/different to."

prerogative/perogative

See "perogative/prerogative."

prescribe/proscribe

You recommend something when you prescribe it, but you forbid it when you proscribe it. The usually positive function of "pro-" confuses many people.

prescription/perscription

See "perscription/prescription."

presently/currently

Some argue that "presently" doesn't mean "in the present." It means "soon." If you want to talk about something that's happening right now, they urge you to say it's going on "currently."

For a moment he was confused—
was he being attacked by a bear presently or currently?

preservatives
See "organic."

presumably/assumably
See "assumably/presumably."

pretty/somewhat
It's pretty common to use "pretty" to mean "somewhat" in ordinary speech; but it should be avoided in formal writing, where sometimes "very" is more appropriate. The temptation to use "pretty" usually indicates the writer is being vague, so changing to something more specific may be an even better solution: "a pretty bad mess" might be "chocolate syrup spilled all over the pizza which had been dumped upside down on the carpet."

preventive/preventative
It is sometimes argued that "preventive" is the adjective, "preventative" the noun. I must say I like the sound of this distinction, but in fact the two are interchangeable as both nouns and adjectives, though many prefer "preventive" as being shorter and simpler. "Preventative" used as an adjective dates back to the 17th century, as does "preventive" as a noun.

prey/pray
See "pray/prey."

primer
When this word is used in the U.S. to mean "elementary textbook" it is pronounced with a short "I": "primmer" (rhymes with "dimmer"). All other meanings are pronounced with a long "I": "prymer" (rhymes with "timer").

principal/principle
Generations of teachers have tried to drill this one into students' heads by reminding them, "The principal is your pal." Many don't seem convinced. "Principal" is a noun and adjective referring to someone or something which is highest in rank or importance. (In a loan, the principal is the more substantial part of the money, the interest is—or should be—the lesser.) "Principle" is only a noun and has to do with law or doctrine: "The workers fought hard for the principle of collective bargaining."

prioritize
Many people disdain "prioritize" as bureaucratic jargon for "rank" or "make a high priority."

priority
It is common to proclaim, "In our business, customer service is a priority," but it would be better to say "a high priority," since priorities can also be low.

proactive
See "reactionary/reactive."

probably

The two "B's" in this word are particularly difficult to pronounce in sequence, so the word often comes out as "probly" and is even occasionally misspelled that way. When even the last "B" disappears, the pronunciation "prolly" suggests drunken slurring or, at best, an attempt at humor.

problems/issues

See "issues/problems."

proceed/precede

See "precede/proceed."

progress/pass

Events may progress in time, but time itself does not progress—it just passes.

promiscuous/permiscuous

See permiscuous/promiscuous."

prone/supine

"Prone" (face down) is often confused with "supine" (face up). "Prostrate" technically also means "face down," but is most often used to mean simply "devastate."

　　See also "prostate/prostrate."

pronounciation/pronunciation

"Pronounce" is the verb, but the "O" is omitted for the noun: "pronunciation." This mistake ranks right up there in incongruity with "writting."

proof is in the pudding/proof of the pudding is in the eating

This common truncated version of an old saying conjures up visions of poking around in your dessert looking for prizes, but "the proof of the pudding is in the eating" means that you don't really know that your dessert has come out right until you taste it.

prophecy/prophesy

"Prophecy," the noun (pronounced "PROF-a-see"), is a prediction. The verb "to prophesy" (pronounced "PROF-a-sigh") means to predict something. When a prophet prophesies he or she utters prophecies.

proscribe/prescribe

See "prescribe/proscribe."

prosecute/persecute

See "persecute/prosecute."

prospective/perspective

See "perspective/prospective."

prostate/prostrate

The gland men have is called the "prostate." "Prostrate" is an adjective meaning "lying face downward."

protagonist/hero

See "hero/protagonist."

protray/portray

There are a lot of words in English that begin in "pro-." This is not one of them. When you make a portrait, you portray someone.

proved/proven

For most purposes either form is a fine past participle of "prove," though in a phrase like "a proven talent" where the word is an adjective preceding a noun, "proven" is standard.

publically/publicly

There's no particular logic to the spelling of "publicly." Maybe it would help to remember not to include wastefully unnecessary letters at the public expense.

purposely/purposefully
If you do something on purpose (not by accident), you do it purposely. But if you have a specific purpose in mind, you are acting *purposefully*.

❦

q/g
See "g/q."

quantum leap
The thing about quantum leaps is that they mark an abrupt change from one state to a distinctly different one, with no in-between transitional states being possible; but they are not large. In fact, in physics a quantum leap is one of the smallest sorts of changes worth talking about. Leave "quantum leap" to the subatomic physicists unless you know what you're talking about.

queue
If you're standing in a queue you'll have plenty of time to ponder the unusual spelling of this word. Remember, it contains two "U's."

quiet/quite
This is probably caused by a slip of the fingers more often than by a slip of the mental gears, but one often sees "quite" (very) substituted for "quiet" (shhh!). This is one of those common errors your spelling checker will not catch, so look out for it.

quotation marks
The examples below are set off in order to avoid confusion over the use of single and double quotation marks.

There are many ways to go wrong with quotation marks. They are often used ironically:

> She ran around with a bunch of "intellectuals."

The quotation marks around "intellectuals" indicate that the writer believes that these are in fact so-called intellectuals, not real intellectuals at all. The ironic use of quotation marks is very much overdone and is usually a sign of laziness indicating that the writer has not bothered to find the precise word or expression necessary.

Advertisers unfortunately tend to use quotation marks merely for emphasis:

"FRESH" TOMATOES 59 CENTS A POUND

The influence of the more common ironic usage tends to make the reader question whether these tomatoes are really fresh. Underlining, bold lettering, capitalizing—there are several less ambiguous ways to emphasize words than placing them between quotation marks.

In American usage, single quotation marks are used normally only for quoted words and phrases within quotations:

> Angela had the nerve to tell me, "When I saw 'BYOB' on your invitation, I assumed it meant 'Bring Your Old Boyfriend.'"

British usage tends to reverse this relationship, with single quotation marks being standard and double ones being used only for quotations within quotations. (The English also call quotation marks "inverted commas," though only the opening quotation mark is actually inverted—and flipped as well.)

Single quotation marks are also used in linguistic, phonetic, and philosophical studies to surround words and phrases under discussion; but the common practice of using single quotation marks for short phrases and words and double ones for complete sentences is otherwise an error.

> Block quotations like this should not be surrounded by any quotation marks at all. A very short passage should not be rendered as a block quotation; you need at least three lines of verse or five lines of prose to justify a block quotation. Normally you should leave extra space above and below a block quotation.

When quoting a long passage involving more than one paragraph, quotation marks go at the beginning of each paragraph, but at the end of only the final one. Dialogue in which the speaker changes with each paragraph has each speech enclosed in its own quotation marks.

Titles of books and other long works that might be printed as books are usually italicized (except, for some reason, in newspapers); but the titles of short poems, stories, essays, and other works that would be more commonly printed within larger works (anthologies, collections, periodicals, etc.) are enclosed in quotation marks.

There are different patterns for regulating how quotation marks relate to other punctuation. Find out which one your teacher or editor prefers and use it, or choose one of your own liking, but stick to it consistently. One widely accepted authority in America is *The Chicago Manual of Style*, whose guidelines are outlined below. Writers in England, Canada, Australia, and other British-influenced countries should be aware that their national patterns will be quite different and variable.

In standard American practice, commas are placed inside quotation marks:

> I spent the morning reading Faulkner's "Barn Burning,"
> which seemed to be about a pyromaniac.

Periods are also normally placed inside quotation marks. Colons and semicolons, however, are placed outside quotation marks.

If a question mark or exclamation point ends the quoted matter, it is placed inside the quotation marks:

> John asked, "When's dinner?"

But if it is the enclosing sentence which asks the question, then the question mark comes after the quotation marks:

> What did she mean, John wondered, by saying
> "as soon as you make it"?

Similarly:

> Fred shouted, "Look out for the bull!"

but

> When I was subsequently gored, all Timmy
> said was "this is kinda boring"!

See also "single quotes."

quote

A passage doesn't become a quote (or—better—"quotation") until you've quoted it. The only time to refer to a "quote" is when you are referring to someone quoting something. When referring to the original words, simply call it a "passage."

racism

The "C" in "racism" and "racist" is pronounced as a simple "S" sound. Don't confuse it with the "SH" sound in "racial."

rack/wrack

If you are racked with pain or you feel nerve-racked, you are feeling as if you were being stretched on that medieval instrument of torture, the rack. You rack your brains when you stretch them vigorously to search out the truth like a torturer. "Wrack" has to do with ruinous accidents, so if the stock market is wracked by rumors of imminent recession, it's wrecked.

raise/rear

Old-fashioned writers insist that you raise crops and rear children, but in modern American English children are usually "raised."

ran/run

Computer programmers have been heard to say "the program's been ran," when what they mean is "the program's been run."

rapport

Many more people hear this word, meaning "affinity," than read it, judging by the popularity of various popular misspellings such as "rapore" and "rapoire." If you get along really well with someone, the two of you have rapport.

rather/sooner

See "sooner/rather."

ratio

A ratio is a way of expressing the relationship between one number and another. If there is one teacher to fifty students, the teacher/student ratio is one to fifty, and the student/teacher ratio is fifty to one. If a very dense but wealthy prince were being tutored by fifty teachers, the teacher/student ratio would be fifty to one, and the student/teacher ratio would be one to fifty. As you can see, the order in which the numbers are compared is important.

The ratios discussed so far have been "high"—the difference between the numbers is large. The lowest possible ratio is one to one: one teacher to one student. If you are campaigning for more individual attention in the classroom, you want a higher number of teachers, but a *lower* student/teacher ratio.

rationale/rationalization

When you're explaining the reasoning behind your position, you're presenting your *rationale.* But if you're just making up some lame excuse to make your position appear better—whether to yourself or others—you're engaging in *rationalization.*

ravaging/ravishing/ravenous

To ravage is to pillage, sack, or devastate. The only time "ravaging" is properly used is in phrases like "When the pirates had finished ravaging the town, they turned to ravishing the women." Which brings us to "ravish": meaning to rape or rob violently. A trailer court can be ravaged by a storm (nothing is stolen, but a lot of damage is done), but not ravished. The crown jewels of Ruritania can be ravished (stolen using violence) without being ravaged (damaged).

To confuse matters, people began back in the 14th century to speak metaphorically of their souls being "ravished" by intense spiritual or aesthetic experiences. Thus we speak of a "ravishing woman" (the term is rarely applied to men) today not because she literally rapes men who look at her but because her devastating beauty penetrates their hearts in an almost violent fashion. Despite contemporary society's heightened sensitivity about rape, we still remain (perhaps fortunately) unconscious of many of the transformations of the root meaning in words with positive connotations such as "rapturous."

Originally, "raven" as a verb was synonymous with "ravish" in the sense of "to steal by force." One of its specialized meanings became "devour," as in "The lion ravened her prey." By analogy, hungry people became "ravenous" (as hungry as beasts), and that remains the only common use of the word today.

If a woman smashes your apartment up, she ravages it. If she looks stunningly beautiful, she is ravishing. If she eats the whole platter of hors d'oeuvres you've set out for the party before the other guests come, she's ravenous.

reactionary/reactive

Many people incorrectly use "reactionary" to mean "acting in response to some outside stimulus." That's "reactive." "Reactionary" actually has a very narrow meaning; it is a noun or adjective describing a form of looking backward that goes beyond conservatism (wanting to prevent change and maintain present conditions) to reaction—wanting to recreate a lost past. The advocates of restoring Czarist rule in Russia are reactionaries. While we're on the subject, the term "proactive" formed by analogy with "reactive" seems superfluous to many of us. Use "active," "assertive," or "positive" whenever you can instead.

real/really

The correct adverbial form is "really" rather than "real," but even that form is generally confined to casual speech, as in, "When you complimented me on my speech I felt really great!" To say "real great" instead moves the speaker several steps downscale socially. However "really" is a feeble qualifier. "Wonderful" is an acceptable substitute for "really great" and you can give a definite up-scale slant to your speech by adopting the British "really quite wonderful." Usually, however, it is better to replace the expression altogether with something more precise: "almost seven feet tall" is better than "really tall." To strive for intensity by repeating "really" as in "That dessert you made was really, really good" demonstrates an impoverished vocabulary.

realtor

For some reason, this word is often mispronounced as "real-a-ter" instead of the proper "ree-ul-ter." Incidentally, realtors insist that this is a term originally trademarked by the National Association of Real Estate Boards (now renamed the National Association of Realtors), that it must be capitalized, and that all non-members of that association are mere "real estate associates." Common usage, however, calls both "real estate agents," despite their protests.

rear/raise

See "raise/rear."

reason because

We often hear people say things like, "The reason there's a hole in the screen door is because I tripped over the cat on my way out." The phrase "is because" should be "is that." If you want to use "because," the sentence should be phrased, "There's a hole in the screen door because I tripped over the cat." Using both is a redundancy, as is the common expression "the reason why." "The reason being is" should be simply "the reason being."

rebelling/revolting

Even though the verbs "rebel" and "revolt" mean more or less the same thing, people who are revolting are disgusting, not taking up arms against the government.

rebut/refute

See "refute/rebut."

recent/resent

There are actually three words to distinguish here. "Recent," always pronounced with an unvoiced hissy "S" and with the accent on the first syllable, means "not long ago," as in "I appreciated your recent encouragement." "Resent" has two different meanings with two different pronunciations, both with the accent on the second syllable. In the most common case, where "resent" means "feel bad about," the word is pronounced with a voiced "Z" sound: "I resent your implica-

175

tion that I gave you the chocolates only because I was hoping you'd share them with me." In the less common case, the word means "to send again" and is pronounced with an unvoiced hissy "S" sound: "The e-mail message bounced, so I resent it." So say the intended word aloud. If the accent is on the second syllable, "resent" is the spelling you need.

recognize

In sloppy speech, this often comes out "reck-uh-nize." Sound the "G."

recreate/reinvent

The expression "no need to reinvent the wheel" loses much of its wit when "recreate" is substituted for the original verb. While we're at it, "recreate" does not mean "to engage in recreation." If you play basketball, you may be exercising, but you're not recreating.

recuperate/recoup

If you are getting over an illness, you are recuperating; but if you insist on remaining at the roulette table when your luck has been running against you, you are seeking to recoup your losses.

recurring/reoccurring

See "reoccurring/recurring."

redundancies

There are many examples of redundancies in these pages: phrases which say twice what needs to be said only once, like "past history." Advertisers are particularly liable to redundancy in hyping their offers: "as an added bonus" (as a bonus), "preplan" (plan), and "free gift" (but look out for the shipping charges!). Two other common redundancies that are clearly errors are "and plus" (plus) and "end result" (result). But some other redundancies are contained in phrases sanctioned by tradition: "safe haven," "hot water heater," "new beginning," and "tuna fish."

reeking havoc/wreaking havoc

"Reeking" means "smelling strongly," so that can't be right. The phrase simply means "working great destruction." "Havoc" has always referred to general destruction in English, but one very old phrase incorporating the word was "cry havoc," which meant to give an army the signal for pillage. To "play havoc with" means the same thing as to "wreak havoc." Avoid as well the mistaken "wreck havoc."

refer/allude

See "allude/refer."

reference

Nouns are often turned into verbs in English, and "reference" in the sense "to provide references or citations" has become so widespread that it's generally acceptable, though some teachers and editors still object.

See also "vague reference."

refute/rebut

When you rebut someone's argument you argue against it. To refute someone's argument is to prove it incorrect. Unless you are certain you have achieved success, use "rebut."

regard/regards

Business English is deadly enough without scrambling it. "As regards your downsizing plan . . ." is acceptable, if stiff. "In regard to" and "with regard to" are also correct. But "in regards to" is nonstandard. You can also convey the same idea with "in respect to" or "with respect to."

regardless/irregardless

See "irregardless/regardless."

regime/regimen

Some people insist that "regime" should be used only in reference to governments and that people who say they are following a dietary regime should instead use "regimen"; but "regime" has been a synonym of "regimen" for over a century and is widely accepted in that sense.

regretfully/regrettably
Either word can be used as an adverb to introduce an expression of regret, though conservatives prefer "regrettably" in sentences like "Regrettably, it rained on the 4th of July." Within the body of a sentence, however, "regretfully" may be used only to describe the manner in which someone does something: "John had to regretfully decline his beloved's invitation to go hang-gliding because he was terrified of heights." If no specified person in the sentence is doing the regretting, but the speaker is simply asserting "it is to be regretted," the word is "regrettably": "Their boss is regrettably stubborn."

reign/rein
A king or queen reigns, but you rein in a horse. The expression "to give rein" means to give in to an impulse as a spirited horse gives in to its impulse to gallop when you slacken the reins. Similarly, the correct expression is "free rein," not "free reign."

reinvent/recreate
See "recreate/reinvent."

relevant/revelant
See elant/relevant."

religion
Protestants often refer incorrectly to "the Catholic religion." Catholicism is a faith or a church. (Only Protestants belong to "denominations.") Both Catholics and Protestants follow the Christian religion.

religion believes/religion teaches
People often write things like "Buddhism believes" when they mean to say "Buddhism teaches" or "Buddhists believe." Religions do not believe, they are the objects of belief.

remotely close

"Not even remotely close" is a fine example of an oxymoron. An idea can be "not even remotely correct," but closeness and remoteness are opposites; it doesn't make sense to have one modify the other.

remuneration/renumeration

Although "remuneration" looks as if it might mean "repayment," it usually means simply "payment." In speech it is often confused with "renumeration," re-counting (counting again).

reoccurring/recurring

It might seem logical to form this word from "occurring" by simply adding a "re-" prefix—logical, but wrong. The word is "recurring." The root form is "recur," not "reoccur." For some reason "recurrent" is seldom transformed into "reoccurrent."

repel/repulse

In most of their meanings these are synonyms, but if you are disgusted by someone, you are repelled, not repulsed. The confusion is compounded by the fact that "repellent" and "repulsive" mean the same thing. Go figure.

repress/oppress

See "oppress/repress."

resent/recent

See "recent/resent."

resister/resistor

A *resistor* is part of an electrical circuit; a person who resists something is a *resister*.

respect/aspect

See "aspect/respect."

retch/wretch

If you vomit, you *retch;* if you behave in a wretched manner or fall into wretched circumstances, you are a *wretch*.

reticent/hesitant

"Reticent" most often means "reluctant to speak." It can also mean "reserved" or "restrained," though conservatives prefer to use it to apply only to speech. If you're feeling nervous about *doing* something, you're hesitant: "I'm hesitant about trying to ride a unicycle in public." "Hesitant" is by far the more common word; so if you hesitate to choose between the two, go with "hesitant."

return back/return

"Return back" is a redundancy. Use just "return," unless you mean to say instead "turn back."

revelant/relevant

"Relevant" matters are *related* to the subject at hand. "Revelant" is both spoken and written frequently when "relevant" is intended.

revolting/rebelling

See "rebelling/revolting."

revolve around/center around/center on

See "center around/center on/revolve around."

revue/review

You can attend a musical *revue* in a theatre, but when you write up your reactions for a newspaper, you're writing a *review*.

right of passage/rite of passage

The more common phrase is "rite of passage"—a ritual one goes through to move on to the next stage of life. Learning how to work the combination on a locker is a rite of passage for many entering middle school students. A "right of passage" would be the right to travel through a certain territory, but you are unlikely to have any use for the phrase.

Rio Grande River/Rio Grande

Rio is Spanish for "river," so "Rio Grande River" is a redundancy. Just write "Rio Grande." Non-Hispanic Americans have traditionally failed to pronounce the final "E" in "Grande," but they've learned to do it to designate the large size of latte, so perhaps it's time to start saying it the proper Spanish way: "REE-oh GRAHN-day." Or to be really international we could switch to the Mexican name: "Rio Bravo."

risky/risqué
People unfamiliar with the French-derived word "risqué" ("slightly indecent") often write "risky" by mistake. Bungee-jumping is risky, but nude bungee-jumping is *risqué*.

rite of passage
See "right of passage/rite of passage."

road to hoe/row to hoe
Out in the cotton patch you have a tough row to hoe. This saying has nothing to do with road construction.

rob/steal
When you rob a bank, you steal its money. You can't rob the money itself. The stuff taken in a robbery is always "stolen, " not "robbed."

role/roll
An actor plays a role. Bill Gates is the entrepreneur's role model. But you eat a sausage on a roll and roll out the barrel.

roomate/roommate
You have to crowd *two* "M's" into "roommate."

root/rout/route
You can *root* for your team (cheer them on) and hope that they utterly smash their opponents (create a *rout*), then come back in triumph on *Route* 27 (a road).

rot iron/wrought iron
Wrought iron is metal which has been worked (wrought) into decorative shapes.

row to hoe/road to hoe
See "road to hoe/row to hoe."

run/ran
See "ran/run."

✦✦✦

sacred/scared
This is one of those silly typos which your spelling checker won't catch: gods are sacred, the damned in Hell are scared.

sacreligious/sacrilegious
Doing something sacrilegious involves committing sacrilege. Don't let the related word "religious" trick you into misspelling the word as "sacreligious."

safe haven
See "redundancies."

safety deposit box/safe-deposit box
"Safety" is rarely pronounced very differently from "safe-D" so it is natural that many people suppose they are hearing the word at the beginning of this phrase, but the correct expression is in fact "safe-deposit box."

sail/sale/sell
These simple and familiar words are surprisingly often confused in writing. You sail a boat which has a sail of canvas. You sell your old fondue pot at a yard sale.

sale
See "for sale/on sale" and "sail/sale/sell."

salsa sauce/salsa
Salsa is Spanish for "sauce," so "salsa sauce" is redundant. Here in the U.S., where people now spend more on salsa than on ketchup (or

182

catsup, if you prefer), few people are unaware that it's a sauce. Anyone so sheltered as not to be aware of that fact will need a fuller explanation: "chopped tomatoes, onions, chilies, and cilantro."

same difference

This is a jokey, deliberately illogical slang expression that doesn't belong in formal writing.

sameo, sameo/same old, same old

See "deja vu."

sarcastic/ironic

Not all ironic comments are sarcastic. Sarcasm is meant to mock or wound. Irony can be amusing without being maliciously aimed at hurting anyone.

satellite

Originally a satellite was a follower. Astronomers applied the term to smaller bodies orbiting about planets, like our moon. Then we began launching artificial satellites. Since few people were familiar with the term in its technical meaning, the adjective "artificial" was quickly dropped in popular usage. So far so bad. Then television began to be broadcast via satellite. Much if not all television now wends its way through a satellite at some point, but in the popular imagination only broadcasts received at the viewing site via a dish antenna aimed at a satellite qualify to be called "satellite television." Thus we see motel signs boasting:

AIR CONDITIONING,* SATELLITE

People say things like, "The fight's going to be shown on satellite." The word has become a pathetic fragment of its former self. The technologically literate speaker will avoid these slovenly abbreviations.

---

* At least motels have not yet adopted the automobile industry's truncation of "air conditioning" to "air."

saw/seen

In standard English, it's "I've seen" not "I've saw." The helping verb "have" (abbreviated here to "'ve") requires "seen." Any time you use a helping verb to introduce it, the word you need is "seen": "Mine eyes have seen the glory of the coming of the Lord."

In the simple past (no helping verb), the expression is "I saw," not "I seen." "I've seen a lot of ugly cars, but when I saw that old beat-up Rambler I couldn't believe my eyes." Or "I saw the game on TV."

say/tell

You *say*, "Hello, Mr. Chips," to the teacher and then *tell* him about what you did last summer. You can't "tell that" except in expressions like "go tell that to your old girlfriend."

say your piece/hold your peace

See "hold your peace/say your piece."

says that/expresses that

See "expresses that/says that."

scan/skim

Those who insist that "scan" can never be a synonym of "skim" have lost the battle. It is true that the word originally meant "to scrutinize," but it has now evolved into one of those unfortunate words with two opposite meanings: "to examine closely" (now rare) and "to glance at quickly" (much more common). It would be difficult to say which of these two meanings is more prominent in the computer-related usage to "scan a document."

scared/sacred

See "sacred/scared."

schizophrenic

In popular usage, "schizophrenic" (and the more slangy and now dated "schizoid") indicates "split between two attitudes." This drives people with training in psychiatry crazy. "Schizo-" does indeed mean "split," but it is used here to mean "split off from reality." Someone with a Jekyll-and-Hyde personality is suffering from "multiple personality disorder" (or, more recently, "dissociative identity disorder"), not "schizophrenia."

sci-fi/science fiction/SF

"Sci-fi," the widely used abbreviation for "science fiction," is objectionable to most professional science fiction writers and scholars, and to many fans. Some of them scornfully designate alien monster movies and other trivial entertainments "sci-fi" (which they pronounce "skiffy") to distinguish them from true science fiction. The preferred abbreviation in these circles is "SF." The problem with this abbreviation is that to the general public "SF" means "San Francisco." "The Sci-Fi Channel" has exacerbated the conflict over this term. If you are a reporter approaching a science fiction writer or expert you immediately mark yourself as an outsider by using the term "sci-fi."

scratch/itch

See "itch/scratch."

sea change

In Shakespeare's *The Tempest*, Ariel deceitfully sings to Ferdinand:

> Full fathom five thy father lies;
> Of his bones are coral made;
> Those are pearls that were his eyes:
> Nothing of him that doth fade
> But doth suffer a sea-change
> Into something rich and strange.

This rich language has so captivated the ears of generations of writers that they feel compelled to describe as "sea changes" not only alterations that are "rich and strange," but, less appropriately, those that are simply large or sudden. Always popular, this cliché has recently become so pervasive as to make "sea" an almost inextricable companion to "change" whatever its meaning. In its original context, it meant nothing more complex than "a change caused by the sea." Since the phrase is almost always improperly used and is greatly overused, it has suffered a swamp change into something dull and tiresome. Avoid the phrase; otherwise you will irritate those who know it and puzzle those who do not.

seam/seem

"Seem" is the verb, "seam" the noun. Use "seam" only for things like the line produced when two pieces of cloth are sewn together or a thread of coal in a geological formation.

She sewed a seam, or so it seemed.

second of all/second

"First of all" makes sense when you want to emphasize the primacy of the first item in a series, but it should not be followed by "second of all," where the expression serves no such function. And "secondly" is an adverbial form that makes no sense at all in enumeration (neither does "firstly"). As you go through your list, say simply "second," "third," "fourth," etc.

seem/seam

See "seam/seem."

seen/saw

See "saw/seen."

select/selected

"Select" means "special, chosen because of its outstanding qualities." If you are writing an ad for a furniture store offering low prices on some of its recliners, call them "selected recliners," not "select recliners," unless they are truly outstanding and not just leftovers you're trying to move out of the store.

self-worth/self-esteem

To say that a person has a low sense of self-worth makes sense, though it's inelegant. But people commonly truncate the phrase, saying instead, "He has low self-worth." This would literally mean that he isn't worth much rather than that he has a low opinion of himself. "Self-esteem" sounds much more literate.

sell

See "sail/sale/sell."

semicolons

See "colons/semicolons."

semiweekly/biweekly

See "biweekly/semiweekly."

sense/since

"Sense" is a verb meaning "feel" ("I sense you near me") or a noun meaning "intelligence" ("have some common sense!"). Don't use it when you need the adverb "since" ("since you went away," "since you're up anyway, would you please let the cat out?").

sensual/sensuous

"Sensual" usually relates to physical desires and experiences and often means "sexy." But "sensuous" is more often used for aesthetic pleasures, like "sensuous music." The two words do overlap a good deal. The leather seats in your new car may be sensuous; but if they turn you on, they might be sensual. "Sensual" often has a slightly racy or even judgmental tone lacking in "sensuous."

sentence fragments

There are actually many fine uses for sentence fragments. Here's a brief scene from an imaginary Greek tragedy composed entirely of fragments:

> *Menelaus:* Aha! Helen!
> *Helen (startled)*: Beloved husband!
> *Menelaus:* Slut!
> *Paris (entering, seeing Menelaus)*: Oops. 'Bye.
> *Menelaus:* Not so fast! *(stabs Paris)*.
> *Paris:* Arrggh!

But some people get into trouble by breaking a perfectly good sentence in two: "We did some research in newspapers. Like the *National Inquirer*." The second phrase belongs in the same sentence with the first, not dangling off on its own.

A more common kind of troublesome fragment is a would-be sentence introduced by a word or phrase that suggests it's part of some other sentence: "By picking up the garbage the fraternity had strewn around the street the weekend before got the group a favorable story in the paper." Just lop off "by" to convert this into a proper complete sentence.

seperate/separate

"Separate" has two "A's" separated by an "R."

service/serve

A mechanic services your car and a stallion services a mare, but most of the time when you want to talk about the goods or services you supply, the word you want is "serve": "Our firm serves the hotel industry."

set/sit

In some dialects people say, "Come on in and set a spell," but in standard English the word is "sit." You *set* down an object or a child you happen to be carrying; those seating themselves *sit*.

setup/set up

Technical writers sometimes confuse "setup" as a noun ("check the setup") with the phrase "set up" ("set up the experiment").

several/various

See "various/several."

SF/sci-fi/science fiction

See "sci-fi/science fiction/SF."

shall/will

"Will" has almost entirely replaced "shall" in American English except in legal documents and in questions like "Shall we have red wine with the duck?"

Shepard/shepherd

"Shepard" can be a family name, but the person who herds the sheep is a "shepherd."

sherbert/sherbet

The name for these icy desserts is derive   Turkish/Persian *sorbet*, but the "R" in the first syllable seems to seduce many speakers into adding one in the second, where it doesn't belong. A California chain called "Herbert's Sherbets" had me confused on this point for years when I was growing up.

shock/electrocute

See "electrocute/shock."

should of

See "could of, should of, would of/could have, should have, would have."

Sierra Nevada Mountains/Sierra Nevadas

Sierra is Spanish for "mountain range," so knowledgeable Westerners usually avoid a redundancy by simply referring to "the Sierra Nevadas" or simply "the Sierras." Transplanted weather forecasters often get this wrong.

Some object to the familiar abbreviation "Sierras," but this form, like "Rockies" and "Smokies" is too well established to be considered erroneous.

See also "Nevada."

sight/site/cite
See "cite/site/sight."

silicon/silicone
Silicon is a chemical element, the basic stuff of which microchips are made. Silicones are plastics and other materials containing silicon, the most commonly discussed example being silicone breast implants. Less used by the general public is "silica": the oxide of silicon.

simile
See "parallel/symbol."

simplistic
"Simplistic" means "overly simple" and is always used negatively. Don't substitute it when you just mean to say "simple" or even "very simple."

since/because
Some assert that "since" must always refer only to time, but since the 14th century, when it was often spelled "syn," it has also meant "seeing that" or "because."

since/sense
See "sense/since."

singing/music
See "music/singing."

single quotes
In standard American writing, the only use for single quotation marks is to designate a quotation within a quotation. Students are exposed by Penguin Books and other publishers to the British practice of using single quotes for normal quotations and become confused. Some

strange folkloric process has convinced many people that while entire sentences and long phrases are surrounded by conventional double quotation marks, single words and short phrases take single quotation marks. "Wrong," I insist.

See also "quotation marks."

sit/set
See "set/sit."

site/cite/sight
See "cite/site/sight."

skim/scan
See "scan/skim."

slash/backslash
See "backslash/slash."

slaughter
See "decimate/annihilate, slaughter, etc."

slight of hand/sleight of hand
"Sleight" is an old word meaning "cleverness, skill," and the proper expression is "sleight of hand." It's easy to understand why it's confused with "slight" since the two words are pronounced in exactly the same way.

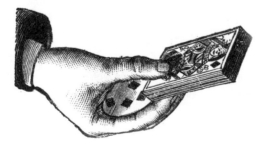

His sleight-of-hand skills were not slight.

sluff off/slough off
You use a loofah to *slough* off dead skin.

snuck/sneaked
When Huckleberry Finn "snuck" out of a house, he was acting according to his character—and dialect. This is one of many cases in which people's humorously self-conscious use of dialect has influenced others to adopt it as standard and it is now often seen even in sophisticated writing in the U.S. But it is safer to use the traditional form: "sneaked."

so/very
Originally people said things like, "I was so delighted with the wrapping that I couldn't bring myself to open the package." But then they began to lazily say, "You made me so happy," no longer explaining just how happy that was. This pattern of using "so" as a simple intensifier meaning "very" is now standard in casual speech, but is out of place in formal writing, where "very" or another intensifier works better. Without vocal emphasis, the "so" conveys little in print.

so fun/so much fun
Strictly a young person's usage: "That party was so fun!" If you don't want to be perceived as a gum-chewing airhead, say "so much fun."

societal/social
"Societal" as an adjective has been in existence for a couple of centuries, but has become widely used only in the recent past. People who imagine that "social" has too many frivolous connotations of mere partying often resort to it to make their language more serious and impressive. It is best used by social scientists and others in referring to the influence of societies: "societal patterns among the Ibo of western Nigeria." When used in place of "social" in ordinary speech and writing, it sounds pretentious.

sojourn/journey
Although the spelling of this word confuses many people into thinking it means "journey," a sojourn is actually a temporary stay in

one place. If you're constantly on the move, you're not engaged in a sojourn.

sometime/some time
"Let's get together sometime." When you use the one-word form, it suggests some indefinite time in the future. "Some time" is not wrong in this sort of context, but it is required when being more specific: "Choose some time that fits in your schedule." "Some" is an adjective here modifying "time." The same pattern applies to "someday" (vague) and "some day" (specific).

somewhat/pretty
See "pretty/somewhat."

somewhat of a/somewhat, something of a
This error is the result of confusing two perfectly good usages: "She is somewhat awkward" and "He is something of a klutz." Use one or the other instead.

song
See "music/singing."

sooner/rather
"I'd sooner starve than eat what they serve in the cafeteria" is less formal than "I'd rather starve."

sort of
"Sort of" is not only slangy, it is often vague. "Dinner was sort of expensive" does not convey nearly as much as "The bill for dinner came to more than he earned in a week." The same applies to the similarly vague "kind of."

soup du jour of the day/soup of the day
Soupe du jour (note the "E" on the end of *soupe*) means "soup of the day." If you're going to use French to be pretentious on a menu, it's important to learn the meaning of the words you're using. Often what is offered is *potage*, anyway. Keep it simple, keep it in English, and you can't go wrong.

193

sour grapes

In a famous fable by Aesop, a fox declared that he didn't care that he could not reach an attractive bunch of grapes because he imagined they were probably sour anyway. You express sour grapes when you put down something you can't get: "Winning the lottery is just a big headache anyway." The phrase is misused in all sorts of ways by people who don't know the original story and imagine it means something more general like "bitterness" or "resentment."

spaded/spayed

If you have sterilized your dog, you've spayed it; save the spading until it dies.

specific/Pacific

An astonishing number of people mispronounce "Pacific" as "specific."

spelt/spelled

See "-ed/-t."

spit and image/spitting image

According to the *Oxford English Dictionary,* the earlier form was "spitten image," which may have evolved from "spit and image." It's a crude figure of speech: someone else is enough like you to have been spat out by you, made of the very stuff of your body. In the early 20th century the spelling and pronunciation gradually shifted to the less logical "spitting image," which is now standard. It's too late to go back. There is no historical basis for the claim sometimes made that the original expression was "spirit and image."

split infinitives

For the hyper-critical, "to boldly go where no man has gone before" should be "to go boldly. . . ." It is good to be aware that the insertion of one or more words between "to" and a verb is not strictly speaking an error, and is often more expressive and graceful than moving the intervening words elsewhere. But so many people are offended by split infinitives that it is better to avoid them except when the alternatives sound strained and awkward.

stain glass/stained glass
The proper spelling is "stained."

stalactites/stalagmites
There's an old joke that will help you keep these straight. Remember "ants in the pants"; the *mites* go up and the *tights* come down.

stamp/stomp
See "stomp/stamp."

states/countries
Citizens of the United States, where states are smaller subdivisions of the country, are sometimes surprised to see "states" referring instead to foreign countries. Note that the U.S. Department of State deals with foreign affairs, not those of U.S. states. Clearly distinguish these two uses of "state" in your writing.

stationary/stationery
When something is standing still, it's "stationary." That piece of paper you write a letter on is "stationery."

steal/rob
See "rob/steal."

stereo
"Stereo" refers properly to a means of reproducing sound in two or more discrete channels to create a solid, apparently three-dimensional sound. Because in the early days only fanciers of high fidelity (or hi-fi) equipment could afford stereophonic sound, "stereo" came to be used as a substitute for "high fidelity" and even "record player." Stereo equipment (for instance a cheap, portable cassette player) is not necessarily high fidelity equipment. Visual technology creating a sense

of depth by using two different lenses can also use the root "stereo," as in "stereoscope."

stomp/stamp

"Stomp" is colloquial, casual. A professional wrestler stomps his opponent. In more formal contexts "stamp" is preferred. But you will probably not be able to stamp out the spread of "stomp."

straightjacket/straitjacket

The old word "strait" ("narrow, tight") has survived only as a noun in geography referring to a narrow body of water ("the Bering Strait") and in a few adjectival uses such as "straitjacket" (a narrowly confining garment) and "strait-laced" (literally laced up tightly, but usually meaning narrow-minded). Its unfamiliarity causes many people to mistakenly substitute the more common "straight."

stupid/ignorant

See "ignorant/stupid."

subjunctive

See "if I was/if I were."

substance-free

An administrator at our university announced recently that his goal was a "substance-free" campus, which I suppose fits in with the growing fad of "virtual education." What he really meant was, of course, a campus free of illegal drugs and alcohol, designated "controlled substances" in the law. This is a very silly expression, but if he'd just said "sober and straight" he would have sounded too censorious. How about "drug- and alcohol-free"?

substitute with/substitute for

You can substitute pecans for the walnuts in a brownie recipe, but many people mistakenly say "substitute with" instead, perhaps influenced by the related expression "replace with." It's always "substitute for."

subtle/suttle
See "suttle/subtle."

suffer with/suffer from
Although technical medical usage sometimes differs, in normal speech we say that a person suffers from a disease rather than suffering with it.

suit/suite
Your bedroom suite consists of the bed, the nightstand, and whatever other furniture goes with it. Your pajamas would be your bedroom suit.

summary/summery
When the weather is warm and summery and you don't feel like spending a lot of time reading that long report from the restructuring committee, just read the summary.

supercede/supersede
"Supersede," meaning "to replace," originally meant "to sit higher" than, from Latin *sedere*, "to sit." In the 18th century, rich people were often carried about as they sat in sedan chairs. Don't be misled by the fact that this word rhymes with words having quite different roots, such as "intercede."

supine/prone
See "prone/supine."

supposably/supposingly/supposedly
"Supposedly" is the standard form. "Supposably" can be used only when the meaning is "capable of being supposed," and then only in the U.S. You won't get into trouble if you stick with "supposedly."

suppose to/supposed to
Because the "D" and the "T" are blended into a single consonant when this phrase is pronounced, many writers are unaware that the

"D" is even present and omit it in writing. You're supposed to get this one right if you want to earn the respect of your readers.

See also "use to/used to."

supremist/supremacist

"Supremacist" is the correct spelling.

surfing the Internet

"Channel-surfing" developed as an ironic term to denote the very unathletic activity of randomly changing channels on a television set with a remote control. Its only similarity to surfboarding on real surf has to do with the aesthetic of "going with the flow." The Internet could be a fearsomely difficult place to navigate until the World Wide Web was invented; casual clicking on Web links was naturally quickly compared to channel-surfing, so the expression "surfing the Web" was a natural extension of the earlier expression. But the Web is only one aspect of the Internet, and you label yourself as terminally uncool if you say "surfing the Internet." (Cool people say "Net" anyway.) It makes no sense to refer to targeted, purposeful searches for information as "surfing"; for that reason I call my classes on Internet research techniques "scuba-diving the Internet."

suttle/subtle

It's a not-so-subtle hint to the reader that your spelling is weak if you misspell "subtle" as "suttle."

symbol

See "parallel/symbol."

sympathy/empathy

See "empathy/sympathy."

-t/-ed

See "-ed/-t."

tact/tack

The expression "take a different tack" has nothing to do with tactfulness and everything to do with sailing, in which it is a direction taken. One tacks—abruptly turns—a boat. To "take a different tack" is to try another approach.

take/bring

See "bring/take."

taken back/taken aback

When you're startled by something, you're taken aback by it. When you're reminded of something from your past, you're taken back to that time.

taught/taut

Students are taught, ropes are pulled taut.

taunt/taut/tout

I am told that medical personnel often mistakenly refer to a patient's abdomen as "taunt" rather than the correct "taut." "Taunt" ("tease" or "mock") can be a verb or noun, but never an adjective. "Taut" means "tight, distended," and is always an adjective. Don't confuse "taunt" with "tout," which means "promote," as in "Senator Bilgewater has been touted as a Presidential candidate." You tout somebody you admire and taunt someone that you don't.

teenage/teenaged

Some people object that the word should be "teenaged"; but unlike the still nonstandard "ice tea" and "stain glass," "teenage" is almost universally accepted now.

tell/say

See "say/tell."

tenant/tenet

These two words come from the same Latin root, *tenere*, meaning "to hold," but they have very different meanings. "Tenet" is the rarer of the two, meaning a belief that a person holds: "Avoiding pork is a tenet of the Muslim faith." In contrast, the person leasing an apartment from you is your tenant. (She holds the lease.)

tender hooks/tenterhooks

A "tenter" is a canvas-stretcher, and to be "on tenterhooks" means to be as tense with anticipation as a canvas stretched on one.

tense

See "verb tense."

tentative

This is often all-too-tentatively pronounced "tennative." Sound all three "T's."

than/then

When comparing one thing with another you may find that one is more appealing "than" another. "Than" is the word you want when doing comparisons. But if you are talking about time, choose "then": "First you separate the eggs; then you beat the whites." Alexis is smarter than I, not "then I."

thankyou/thank you

When you thank someone, write "thank you" as two words. A phrase like "thank-you note" requires a hyphen between the two words.

that/what

See "what/that."

that/which

I must confess that I do not myself observe the distinction between "that" and "which." Furthermore, there is little evidence that this distinction is or has ever been regularly made in past centuries by careful writers of English. However, a small but impassioned group of authorities has urged the distinction; so here is the information you will need to pacify them.

If you are defining something by distinguishing it from a larger class of which it is a member, use "that": "I chose the lettuce that had the fewest wilted leaves." When the general class is not being limited or defined in some way, then "which" is appropriate: "He made an iceberg Caesar salad, which didn't taste quite right." Note the comma preceding "which" in the previous sentence.

that/who
See "who/that."

that kind/that kind of
Although expressions like "that kind thing" are common in some dialects, standard English requires "of" in this kind of phrase.

thaw/unthaw
See "unthaw/thaw."

the/ye
See "ye/the."

their/there/they're
See "they're/their/there."

their/they (singular)
See "they/their (singular)."

theirselves/themselves
There is no such word as "theirselves" (and you certainly can't spell it "theirselfs" or "thierselves"); it's "themselves." And there is no correct singular form of this non-word; instead of "theirself" use "himself" or "herself."

them/those
One use of "them" for "those" has become a standard catch phrase: "How do you like them apples?" This is deliberate dialectical humor. But "I like them little canapés with the shrimp on top" is gauche; say instead "I like those little canapés."

then/than
See "than/then."

there/their/they're
See "they're/their/there."

therefor/therefore
The form without a final "E" is an archaic bit of legal terminology meaning "for." The word most people want is "therefore."

there's
People often forget that "there's" is a contraction of "there is" and mistakenly say, "There's three burrs caught in your hair," when they mean "there're" ("there are"). Use "there's" only when referring to one item. "There's" can also be a contraction of "there has," as in "There's been some mistake in this bill, clerk!"

these are them/these are they
Although only the pickiest listeners will cringe when you say "these are them," the traditionally correct phrase is "these are they," because "they" is the predicate nominative of "these." However, if people around you seem more comfortable with "it's me" than "it's I," you might as well stick with "these are them."

these kind/this kind
In a sentence like "I love this kind of chocolates," "this" modifies "kind" (singular) and not "chocolates" (plural), so it would be incorrect to change it to "I love these kind of chocolates." Only if "kind" itself is pluralized into "kinds" should "this" shift to "these": "You keep making these kinds of mistakes!"

these ones/these
By itself, there's nothing wrong with the word "ones" as a plural: "surrounded by her loved ones." However, "this one" should not be pluralized to "these ones." Just say "these." The same pattern applies to "those."

they/their (singular)
Using the plural pronoun to refer to a single person of unspecified gender is an old and honorable pattern in English, not a newfangled

bit of degeneracy or a politically correct plot to avoid sexism (though it often serves the latter purpose). People who insist that "Everyone has brought his own lunch" is the only correct form ignore the usage of centuries of fine writers. A good general rule is that only when the singular noun does not specify an individual can it be replaced plausibly with a plural pronoun: "Everybody" is a good example. We know that "everybody" is singular because we say "everybody is here," not "everybody are here," yet we tend to think of "everybody" as a group of individuals, so we usually say "everybody brought their own grievances to the bargaining table." "Anybody" is treated similarly.

However, in many written sentences the use of singular "their" and "they" creates an irritating clash even when it would pass unnoticed in speech. It is wise to shun this popular pattern in formal writing. Often expressions can be pluralized to make the "they" or "their" indisputably proper: "All of them have brought their own lunches." "People" can often be substituted for "each." Americans seldom avail themselves of the otherwise very handy British "one" to avoid specifying gender because it sounds to our ears rather preten-tious: "One's hound should retrieve only one's own grouse." If you decide to try "one," don't switch to "they" in mid-sentence: "One has to be careful about how they speak" sounds absurd because the word "one" so emphatically calls attention to its singleness. The British also quite sensibly treat collective bodies like governmental units and corporations as plural ("Parliament have approved their agenda"), whereas Americans insist on treating them as singular.

they're/their/there

Many people are so spooked by apostrophes that a word like "they're" seems to them as if it might mean almost anything. In fact, it's always a contraction of "they are." If you've written "they're," ask yourself whether you can substitute "they are." If not, you've made a mistake. "Their" is a possessive pronoun like "her" or "our": "They eat their hot dogs with sauerkraut." Everything else is "there." "There goes the ball, out of the park! See it? Right there! There aren't very many home runs like that." "Thier" is a common misspelling, but you can avoid it by remembering that "they" and "their" begin with the same three letters. Another hint: "there" has "here" buried inside it to remind you it refers to place, while "their" has "heir" buried in it to remind you that it has to do with possession.

think on/think about
An archaic form that persists in some dialects is seen in statements like "I'll think on it" when most people would say "I'll think about it."

this kind/these kind
See "these kind/this kind."

those/them
See "them/those."

though/thought/through
Although most of us know the differences between these words, people often type one of them when they mean another. Spelling checkers won't catch this sort of slip, so look out for it.

throne/thrown
A throne is that chair a king sits on, at least until he gets thrown out of office.

thru
See "'lite' spelling."

thusly/thus
"Thusly" has been around for a long time, but it is widely viewed as nonstandard. It's safer to go with plain old "thus."

tie me over/tide me over
That little something that enables you to get through the dry spell between tides (or any other periods of plenty), *tides* you over.

tilde
See "accent marks."

till/until

Since it looks like an abbreviation for "until," some people argue that this word should always be spelled "'til" (though not all insist on the apostrophe). However, "till" has regularly occurred as a spelling of this word for over 800 years; it's actually older than "until." It is perfectly good English.

time period

The only kinds of periods meant by people who use this phrase are periods of time, so it's a redundancy. Say simply "time" or "period."

times smaller

Mathematically literate folks object to expressions like "My paycheck is three times smaller than it used to be" because "times" indicates multiplication and should logically apply only to increases in size. Say "one third as large" instead.

titled/entitled

See "entitled/titled."

to/too/two

People seldom mix "two" up with the other two; it obviously belongs with words that also begin with "TW," like "twice" and "twenty," that involve the number 2. But the other two are confused all the time. Just remember that the only meanings of "too" are "also" ("I want some ice cream too") and "in excess" ("Your walkman is playing too loudly"). Note that extra "O." It should remind you that this word has to do with adding more on to something. "To" is the proper spelling for all the other uses.

to home/at home

In some dialects people say, "I stayed to home to wait for the mail," but in standard English the expression is "stayed *at* home."

today's modern society/today
People seeking to be up to the minute often indulge in such redundancies as "in today's modern society" or "in the modern society of today." This is empty arm-waving which says nothing more than "now" or "today." A reasonable substitute is "contemporary society." Such phrases are usually indulged in by people with a weak grasp of history to substitute for such more precise expressions as "for the past five years" or "this month."

See also "from the beginning of time."

tolled/told
Some people imagine that the expression should be "all tolled" as if items were being ticked off to the tolling of a bell or it involved the paying of a toll, but in fact this goes back to an old meaning of "tell": "to count." You could "tell over" your beads if you were counting them in a rosary. "All told" means "all counted."

tongue and cheek/tongue in cheek
When people want to show they are kidding or have just knowingly uttered a falsehood, they stick their tongues in their cheeks, so it's "tongue in cheek," not "tongue and cheek."

tout/taunt/taut
See "taunt/taut/tout."

tow the line/toe the line
"Toe the line" has to do with lining your toes up on a precise mark, not with pulling on a rope.

toward/towards
These two words are interchangeable, but "toward" is more common in the U.S. and "towards" in the U.K.

track home/tract home
Commuters from a tract home may well feel that they are engaged in a rat race, but that does not justify them in describing their housing

development as a "track." "Tract" here means an area of land on which inexpensive, uniform houses have been built.

tradegy/tragedy
Not only do people often misspell "tragedy" as "tradegy," they mispronounce it that way too. Just remember that the adjective is "tragic" to recall that it's the "G" that comes after the "A." Also common is the misspelling "tradgedy."

troop/troupe
A group of performers is a troupe. Any other group of people, military or otherwise, is a troop.

truely/truly
"True" has to give up its final "E" when it changes into "truly."

try and/try to
Although "try and" is common in colloquial speech and will usually pass unremarked there, in writing try to remember to use "try to" instead of "try and."

tuna fish
See "redundancies."

two/to/too
See "to/too/two."

two-dimensional/one-dimensional
See "one-dimensional/two-dimensional."

UFO
"UFO" stands for "unidentified flying object," so if you're sure that a silvery disk is an alien spacecraft, there's no point in calling it a

"UFO." I love the sign in a Seattle bookstore labeling the alien-invasion section: "Incorrectly Identified Flying Objects."

And now for a few correctly identified flying objects . . .

ulterior/alterior
See "alterior/ulterior."

umlaut
See "accent marks."

unconscience/unconscious
Do people confuse the unconscious with conscience because the stuff fermenting in one's unconscious is often stuff that bothers one's conscience? Whatever the cause, there is no such word as "unconscience." And while we're on the subject, Freudian psychology does not use the term "subconscious," which implies something that is merely not consciously thought of, rather than something that is suppressed, though the term is used by Jungians.

uninterested/disinterested
See "disinterested/uninterested."

unique

See "very unique/unique."

University of Indiana/Indiana University

There is no such place as "the University of Indiana"; it's "Indiana University." I should know; I went there.

unloosen/loosen

Think about it. "Unloosen" would mean "tighten." The word is "loosen."

unquote/endquote

See "endquote/unquote."

unrest

Journalists often use this mild term to describe all manner of civil disorders, but it's silly to call mayhem or chaos merely "unrest" when there are bullets flying about and bodies lying in the streets.

unthaw/thaw

"Unthaw" is another illogical negative. Use "thaw."

until/till

See "till/until."

upmost/utmost

The word is "utmost" and is related to words like "utter," as in "The birthday party was utter chaos." "Upmost" may seem logical, but it's a sure sign of a person who knows spoken English better than written English.

use to/used to

Because the "D" and the "T" are blended into a single consonant when this phrase is pronounced, many writers are unaware that the "D" is even present and omit it in writing.

    See also "suppose to/supposed to."

vague reference

Vague reference is a common problem in sentences where "this," "it," "which," or other such words don't refer back to any one specific word or phrase, but a whole situation. "I hitchhiked back to town, got picked up by an alien spacecraft, and was subjected to humiliating medical experiments, which is why I didn't get my paper done on time." In conversation this sort of thing goes unnoticed, but more care needs to be taken in writing. There are lots of ways to reorganize this sentence to avoid the vague reference. You could replace "which is why" with "so," for instance.

Sometimes the referent is only understood and not directly expressed at all: "Changing your oil regularly is important, which is one reason your engine burned up." The "which" refers to an implied *failure* to change the oil regularly, but doesn't actually refer back to any of the specific words used earlier in the sentence.

Sometimes there is no logical referent: "In the book it says that Shakespeare was in love with some 'dark lady.'" This is a casual way of using "it" that is not acceptable in formal written English. Write instead "Arthur O. Williams says in *The Sonnets* that Shakespeare. . . ."

A reference may be ambiguous because it's not clear which of two referents is meant: "Most women are attracted to guys with a good sense of humor unless they are into practical jokes." Does "they" refer to "women" or "guys"? It would be clearer if the sentence said, "Most women are attracted to guys with a good sense of humor, though not usually to practical jokers."

vale of tears/veil of tears
See "veil of tears/vale of tears."

valuble/valuable
Few of us pronounce the second "A" in "valuable" distinctly; just be sure to include it when writing the word.

various/several
Many people say, "She heard from various of the committee members that they wanted to cancel the next meeting." "Several of the committee members" would be better.

vary/differ

See "differ/vary."

vary/very

"Vary" means "to change." Don't substitute it for "very" in phrases like "very nice" or "very happy."

veil of tears/vale of tears

The expression "vale of tears" goes back to pious sentiments that consider life on earth to be a series of sorrows to be left behind when we go on to a better world in heaven. It conjures up an image of a suffering traveler laboring through a valley ("vale") of troubles and sorrow. "Veil of tears" is poetic sounding, but it's a mistake.

verb tense

If the situation being described is an ongoing or current one, the present tense is needed, even in a past-tense context: "Last week she admitted that she is really a brunette" (not "was").

Pairs of verbs that go together logically have to be kept in the same tense. "Patricia described her trip to China and writes that the Great Wall really impressed her." Since "described" is in the past tense, and the writing contains her descriptions, "writes" should be "wrote."

Lots of people get into trouble with sentences that describe a hypothetical situation in the past: "If he would have packed his own suitcase, he would have noticed that the cat was in it." That first "would have" should be a simple "had": "If he had packed his own suitcase he would have noticed that the cat was in it." Also, "The game would have been more fun if we had [not "would have"] won." This sort of construction consists of two parts: a hypothetical cause in the past and its logical effect. The hypothetical cause needs to be put into the past tense: "had." Only the *effect* is made conditional: "would have." Note that in the second example above the effect is referred to before the cause.

Students summarizing the plot of a play, movie, or novel are often unfamiliar with the tradition of doing so in the present tense: "Hester embroiders an 'A' on her dress." Think of the events in a piece of fiction as happening whenever you read them—they exist in an eternal present even if they are narrated in the past tense. Even those who are familiar with this pattern get tripped up when they begin to discuss the historical or biographical context of a work, properly using the past tense, and forget to shift back to the present when they return to plot summary. Here's how it's done correctly: "Mark Twain's days on the Mississippi were long past when he wrote *Huckleberry Finn;* but Huck's love for life on the river clearly reflects his youthful experience as a steamboat pilot." The verb "reflects" is in the present tense. Often the author's activity in writing is also rendered in the present tense as well: "Twain depicts Pap as a disgusting drunk." What about when you are comparing events that occur at two different times in the same narrative? You still have to stick to the present: "Tom puts Jim through a lot of unnecessary misery before telling him that he is free." Just remember when you go from English to your history class that you have to shift back to the past tense for narrating historical events: "Napoleon lost the battle of Waterloo."

verbage/verbiage

"Verbiage" is an insulting term usually meant to disparage needlessly wordy prose. Don't use it to mean simply "wording." There is no such word as "verbage."

verses/versus

The "vs." in a law case like "Brown vs. The Board of Education" stands for Latin *versus* (meaning "against"). Don't confuse it with the word for lines of poetry—"verses"—when describing other conflicts, like the upcoming football game featuring Oakesdale versus Pinewood.

very/so

See "so/very."

very/vary

See "vary/very."

very differently/much differently

See "much differently/very differently."

very unique/unique

"Unique" singles out one of a kind. That "un" at the beginning is a form of "one." A thing is unique (the only one of its kind) or it is not. Something may be almost unique (there are very few like it), but nothing is "very unique."

vice versa/visa versa

See "visa versa/vice versa."

vicious/viscous circle/cycle

The term "vicious circle" was invented by logicians to describe a form of fallacious circular argument in which each term of the argument draws on the other: "Democracy is the best form of government because democratic elections produce the best governments." The phrase has been extended in popular usage to all kinds of self-exacerbating processes such as this: "Poor people often find themselves borrowing money to pay off their debts, but in the process create even more onerous debts which in their turn will need to be financed by further borrowing." Sensing vaguely that such destructive spirals are not closed loops, people have transmuted "vicious circle" into "vicious cycle." The problem with this perfectly logical change is that a lot of people know what the original "correct" phrase was and are likely to scorn users of the new one. They go beyond scorn to contempt, however, toward those poor souls who render the phrase as "viscous cycle." Don't use this expression unless you are discussing a Harley-Davidson in dire need of an oil change.

video/film

Many of us can remember when portable transistorized radios were ignorantly called "transistors." We have a tendency to abbreviate the names of various sorts of electronic technology (see "stereo" and "satellite"), often in the process confusing the medium with the content. Video is the electronic reproduction of images and applies to broadcast and cable television, prerecorded videocassette recordings (made on a videocassette recorder, or VCR), and related technologies. MTV appropriated this broad term for a very narrow meaning: "videotaped productions of visual material meant to accompany popular music recordings." This is now what most people mean when they speak of "a video," unless they are "renting a video," in which case they mean a videocassette or DVD recording of a film. One also hears people referring to theatrical films that they happened to have viewed in videotaped reproduction as "videos." This is simply wrong. A film is a film (or movie), whether it is projected on a screen from 35 or 70 mm film or broadcast via the NTSC, SECAM or PAL standard. Orson Welles' *Citizen Kane* is not now and never will be a "video."

villian/villain
Villainous misspellings of "villain" have lain in wait to trip up unwary writers for many years.

vinegarette/vinaigrette
Naïve diners and restaurant workers alike commonly mispronounce the classic French dressing called "vinaigrette" as if it were "vinegarette." To be more sophisticated, say "vin-uh-GRETT" (the first syllable rhymes with "seen").

viola/voila
A viola is a flower or a musical instrument. The expression that means "behold!" is "voila." It comes from a French expression literally meaning "look there!" In French it is spelled with a grave accent over the "A," as *voilà*, but when it was adopted into English, it lost its accent. Such barbarous misspellings as "vwala" are even worse, caused by the reluctance of English speakers to believe that "OI" can represent the sound "wah," as it usually does in French.

virgin birth/immaculate conception
See "immaculate conception/virgin birth."

visa versa/vice versa
This expression, meaning "just the opposite," begins with "vice" (Latin for "turn"). The expression has nothing to do with charges on your Visa card.

Voila! A viola.

visable/visible

To make things clearly visible, you need both your eyes, and both its "I's."

vitae/vita

Unless you are going to claim credit for accomplishments you had in previous incarnations, you should refer to your "vita," not your "vitae." All kidding aside, the "AE" in *vitae* supposedly indicates the genitive rather than the plural, but the derivation of *vita* from *curriculum vitae* is purely speculative (see the *Oxford English Dictionary*), and *vitae* on its own makes no sense grammatically.

Résumé, by the way, is a French word with both "E's" accented. It literally means "summary." In English one often sees it without the accents or with only the second accent, neither of which is a serious error. But if you're trying to show how multilingual you are, remember the first accent.

vocal chords/vocal cords
The musical meaning of "chords" influences some folks to misspell "vocal cords." The "cords" in question are long, thin muscles that look like pieces of fat string.

vocation/avocation
See "avocation/vocation."

voila/viola
See viola/voila."

volumptuous/voluptuous
Given the current mania for slim, taut bodies, it is understandable—if amusing—that some folks should confuse voluptuousness with lumpiness. In fact, "voluptuous" is derived from Latin *voluptas*, which refers to sensual pleasure and not to shape at all. A voluptuous body is a luxurious body.

vunerable/vulnerable
"Vulnerable" is often mispronounced, and sometimes misspelled, without its first "L."

❧

warrantee/warranty
Confused by the spelling of "guarantee," people often misspell the related word "warrantee" rather than the correct "warranty." "Warrantee" is a rare legal term that means "the person to whom a warrant is made." Although "guarantee" can be a verb ("we guarantee your satisfaction"), "warranty" can not. The rarely used verb form is "to warrant."

wary/weary/leery

People sometimes write "weary" (tired) when they mean "wary" (cautious), which is a close synonym with "leery." "Leery" in the psychedelic era was often misspelled "leary," but since Timothy Leary faded from public consciousness, the correct spelling has prevailed.

wash

In my mother's Oklahoma dialect, "wash" was pronounced "warsh," and I was embarrassed to discover in school that the inclusion of the superfluous "R" sound was considered ignorant. This has made me all the more sensitive now that I live in Washington to the mispronunciation "Warshington." Some people tell you that after you "warsh" you should "wrench" ("rinse").

way more/far more/much more

Young people frequently use phrases like "way better" to mean "far better" or "very much better." In formal writing, it would be gauche to say that Impressionism is "way more popular" than Cubism instead of "much more popular."

ways/way

In some dialects it's common to say, "You've got a ways to go before you've saved enough to buy a Miata," but in standard English it's "a *way* to go."

weary/leery/wary

See "wary/weary/leery."

weather/wether/whether

The climate is made up of "weather"; whether it is nice out depends on whether it is raining or not. A wether is just a castrated sheep.

Web

See "World Wide Web."

well/good

See "good/well."

Wensday/Wednesday
Wednesday was named after the Nordic god "Woden" (or "Wotan").
Almost no one pronounces this word's middle syllable, but it's
important to remember the correct spelling in writing.

went/gone
See "gone/went."

were/where
Sloppy typists frequently leave the "H" out of "where." Spelling
checkers do not catch this sort of error, of course, so look for it as you
proofread.

wet your appetite/whet your appetite
It is natural to think that something mouth-watering "wets your
appetite," but actually the expression is "whet your appetite"—
sharpen your appetite, as a whetstone sharpens a knife.

wether/whether/weather
See "weather/wether/whether."

what/that
In some dialects it is common to substitute "what" for "that," as in "You
should dance with him what brung you." This is not standard usage.

wheat/whole wheat
Waiters routinely ask, "Wheat or white?" when bread is ordered, but
the white bread is also made of wheat. The correct term is "whole
wheat," in which the whole grain, including the bran and germ, has
been used to make the flour. "Whole wheat" does not necessarily
imply that no white flour has been used in the bread; most whole
wheat breads incorporate some white flour.

where/were
See "were/where."

where it's at

This slang expression gained widespread currency in the 1960s as a hip way of stating that the speaker understood the essential truth of a situation: "I know where it's at." Or more commonly, "You don't know where it's at." It is still heard from time to time with that meaning, but the user risks being labeled as a quaint old baby boomer. However, standard usage never accepted the literal sense of the phrase. Don't say, "I put my purse down and now I don't know where it's at," unless you want to be regarded as uneducated. "Where it is" will do fine; the "at" is redundant.

whereabouts are/whereabouts is

Despite the deceptive "S" on the end of the word, "whereabouts" is normally singular, not plural. "The whereabouts of the stolen diamond is unknown." Only if you were simultaneously referring to two or more persons having separate whereabouts would the word be plural, and you are quite unlikely to want to do so.

whether/if

See "if/whether."

whether/weather/wether

See "weather/wether/whether."

whether/whether or not

"Whether" works fine on its own in most contexts: "I wonder whether I forgot to turn off the stove?" But when you mean "regardless of whether," it has to be followed by "or not" somewhere in the sentence: "We need to leave for the airport in five minutes whether you've found your teddy bear or not."

See also "if/whether."

which/that

See "that/which."

while away/wile away

See "wile away/while away."

whilst/while
Although "whilst" is a perfectly good traditional synonym of "while," in American usage it is considered pretentious and old-fashioned.

whimp/wimp
The original and still by far the most common spelling of this common bit of slang meaning "weakling, coward" is "wimp." If you use the much less common "whimp" instead, people may regard you as a little wimpy.

whim and a prayer/wing and a prayer
A 1943 hit song depicted a fighter pilot just barely managing to bring his shot-up plane back to base, "comin' in on a wing and a prayer" (lyrics by Harold Adamson, music by Jimmy McHugh). Some people who don't get the allusion mangle this expression as "a whim and a prayer." Whimsicality and fervent prayerfulness don't go together.

whisky/whiskey
Scots prefer the spelling "whisky"; Americans follow instead the Irish spelling, so Kentucky bourbon is "whiskey."

who/that
Some argue that "who" should be used only of people, "that" of animals and inanimate objects and processes.

In fact there are many instances in which the most conservative usage is to refer to a person using "that": "All the politicians that were at the party later denied even knowing the host" is actually somewhat more traditional than the more popular "politicians who." An aversion to "that" referring to human beings as somehow diminishing their humanity may be praiseworthily sensitive, but it cannot claim the authority of tradition. In some sentences, "that" is clearly preferable to "who": "She is the only person I know of that prefers whipped cream on her granola." In the following example, to exchange "that" for "who" would be absurd: "Who was it that said, 'A woman without a man is like a fish without a bicycle'?"*

---

* This is commonly attributed to Gloria Steinem, but at least one source says she was quoting Irina Dunn.

"Whose" can also be used properly of things: "*The Matrix* was a film whose plot made absolutely no sense."

who/whom

"Whom" has been dying an agonizing death for decades—you'll notice there are no Whoms in Dr. Seuss's Whoville. Many people never use the word in speech at all. However, in formal writing, critical readers still expect it to be used when appropriate. The distinction between "who" and "whom" is basically simple: "who" is the subject form of this pronoun and "whom" is the object form. "Who was wearing that awful dress at the Academy Awards banquet?" is correct because "who" is the subject of the sentence. "The M.C. was so startled by the neckline that he forgot to whom he was supposed to give the Oscar" is correct because "whom" is the object of the preposition "to." So far so good.

Now consider this sort of question: "Who are you staring at?" Although strictly speaking the pronoun should be "whom," nobody who wants to be taken seriously would use it in this case, though it is the object of the preposition "at." "Whom" is very rarely used even by careful speakers as the first word in a question, and many authorities have now conceded the point.

There is another sort of question in which "whom" appears later in the sentence: "I wonder whom he bribed to get the contract?" This may seem at first similar to the previous example, but here "whom" is not the subject of any verb in the sentence; rather it is part of the noun clause which itself is the object of the verb "wonder." Here an old gender-biased but effective test for "whom" can be used. Try rewriting the sentence using "he" or "him." Clearly "He bribed he" is incorrect; you would say "he bribed him." Where "him" is the proper word in the paraphrased sentence, use "whom."

Instances in which the direct object appears at the beginning of a sentence are tricky because we are used to having subjects in that position and are strongly tempted to use "who": "Whomever Susan admired most was likely to get the job." (Test: "She admired *him*." Right?)

Where things get really messy is in statements in which the object or subject status of the pronoun is not immediately obvious.

For example, "The police gave tickets to whoever had parked in front of the fire hydrant." The object of the preposition "to" is the entire noun clause, "whoever had parked in front of the fire hydrant," but "whoever" is the subject of that clause, the subject of the verb "had parked." Here's a case where the temptation to use "whomever" should be resisted.

Confused? Just try the "he or him" test, and if it's still not clear, go with "who." You'll bother fewer people and have a fair chance of being right.

a whole 'nother/a completely different
It is one thing to use the expression "a whole 'nother" as a consciously slangy phrase suggesting rustic charm and a completely different matter to use it mistakenly. The "A" at the beginning of the phrase is the common article "a" but is here treated as if it were simultaneously the first letter of "another," interrupted by "whole."

whole wheat/wheat
See "wheat/whole wheat."

wholely/wholly
"Whole" loses its concluding "E" when it changes to "wholly."

wholistic/holistic
This trendy word is correctly spelled "holistic."

who's/whose
This is one of those cases where it is important to remember that possessive pronouns never take apostrophes, even though possessive nouns do. "Who's" always and forever means only "who is," as in "Who's that guy with the droopy mustache?" or "who has," as in "Who's been eating my porridge?" "Whose" is the possessive form of "who" and is used as follows: "Whose dirty socks are these on the breakfast table?"
See also "its/it's."

why/how come
See "how come/why."

wile away/while away

The traditional phrase is "while away the time." Some dictionaries accept the illogical "wile away," but it is distinctly less standard.

will/shall

See "shall/will."

wimp/whimp

See "whimp/wimp."

wing and a prayer/whim and a prayer

See "wing and a prayer/whim and a prayer."

-wise

In political and business jargon it is common to append "-wise" to nouns to create novel adverbs: "Revenue-wise, last quarter was a disaster." Critics of language are united in objecting to this pattern, and it is often used in fiction to satirize less than eloquent speakers.

without further adieu/without further ado

This familiar cliché introducing speakers and performing acts has nothing to do with saying *adieu* (goodbye) to them. It means "without further blather, fuss, or to-do." The last word is "ado."

women/woman

The singular "woman" probably gets mixed up with the plural "women" because although both are spelled with an "O" in the first syllable, only the pronunciation of the "O" really differentiates them. Just remember that this word is treated no differently than "man" (one person) and "men" (more than one person). A woman is a woman—never a women.

wonderful

See "incredible."

wont/won't

People often leave the apostrophe out of "won't," meaning "will not." "Wont" is a completely different and rarely used word meaning "habitual custom." Perhaps people are reluctant to believe this is a contraction because it doesn't make obvious sense like "can not" being contracted to "can't." The *Oxford English Dictionary* suggests that "won't" is a contraction of a nonstandard form: "woll not."

world-renown/world-renowned
Your hamburgers may have world renown, but they are world-renowned hamburgers.

World Wide Web
"World Wide Web" is a name that needs to be capitalized, like "Internet." It is made up of Web pages and Web sites (or, less formally, Websites).

worse comes to worse/worst comes to worst
The traditional idiom is "if worst comes to worst." The modern variation "worse comes to worst" is a little more logical. "Worse comes to worse" is just a mistake.

would have liked to have/would have liked
"She would liked to have had another glass of champagne" should be "She would have liked to have another glass. . . ."

would of
See "could of, should of, would of/could have, should have, would have."

wrack/rack
See "rack/wrack."

wreaking havoc/reeking havoc
See "reeking havoc/wreaking havoc."

wreckless/reckless
This word has nothing to do with creating the potential for a wreck. Rather it involves not reckoning carefully all the hazards involved in an action. The correct spelling is therefore "reckless."

wretch/retch

See "retch/wretch."

writting/writing

One of the comments English teachers dread to see on their evaluations is "The professor really helped me improve my writting." When "-ing" is added to a word that ends in a short vowel followed only by a single consonant, that consonant is normally doubled, but "write" has a silent "E" on the end to ensure the long "I" sound in the word. Doubling the "T" in this case would make the word rhyme with "flitting."

wrongly/wrong

"Wrongly" always precedes the verb it modifies: "He was wrongly suspected of having used garlic powder in the lasagna." "Wrong" is the word you want after the verb: "She answered wrong."

wrought iron/rot iron

See "rot iron/wrought iron."

Xmas/Christmas

"Xmas" is not originally an attempt to exclude Christ from Christmas, but uses an abbreviation of the Greek spelling of the word "Christ" with the "X" representing the Greek letter *chi*. However, so few people know this that it is probably better not to use this popular abbreviation in religious contexts.

ya'll/y'all

"How y'all doin'?" If you are rendering this common Southernism in print, be careful where you place the apostrophe, which stands for the second and third letters in "you." "Ya'll" is properly used only when addressing two or more people.

ye/the

Those who study the history of English know that the word often misread as "ye" in Middle English is good old "the" spelled with an unfamiliar character called a *thorn* which looks vaguely like a "Y" but which is pronounced "TH." So all those quaint shop names beginning with "Ye Olde" are based on a confusion: people never *said* "ye" to mean "the." However, if you'd rather be cute than historically accurate, go ahead. Very few people will know any better.

yea/yeah/yay

"Yea" is a very old-fashioned, formal way of saying "yes," used mainly in voting. It's the opposite of—and rhymes with—"nay." When you want to write the common casual version of "yes," the correct spelling is "yeah" (sounds like "yeh"). When the third grade teacher announced a class trip to the zoo, we all yelled "yay!" (the opposite of "boo!"). That was back when I was only *yay* big.

yet/as of yet

See "as of yet/yet."

yoke/yolk

The yellow center of an egg is its *yolk*. The link that holds two oxen together is a *yoke*; they are *yoked*.

you have mail/you've got mail

See "you've got mail/you have mail."

your/you

"I appreciate your cleaning the toilet" is more formal than "I appreciate you cleaning the toilet."

your/you're

"You're" is always a contraction of "you are." If you've written "you're," try substituting "you are." If it doesn't work, the word you want is "your." Your writing will improve if you're careful about this.

you've got another thing coming/
you've got another think coming
Here's a case in which eagerness to avoid error leads to error. The original expression is the last part of a deliberately ungrammatical joke: "If that's what you think, you've got another think coming."

you've got mail/you have mail
Some object groundlessly to this perfectly correct common e-mail alert as a redundancy. The "have" contracted in phrases like this is merely an auxiliary verb indicating the present perfect tense, not an expression of possession. Compare: "You've sent the mail."

Category
Listings

Commonly Confused Expressions

These entries explain words and expressions that are, in most cases,
correct in some contexts. The trouble is that they are sometimes
switched for one another.

accede/exceed

accept/except

adapt/adopt

administer/minister

advance/advanced

adverse/averse

advice/advise

affluence/effluence

alliterate/illiterate

allude/elude

allude/refer

allusion/illusion

altogether/all together

ambiguous/ambivalent

ambivalent/indifferent

among/between

amoral/immoral

anecdote/antidote

anxious/eager

apart/a part

appraise/apprise

apropos/appropriate

aspect/respect

assure/ensure/insure

augur/auger

aural/oral

avocation/vocation

backslash/slash

bazaar/bizarre

bemuse/amuse

beside/besides

biweekly/semiweekly

borrow/loan

both/each

breach/breech

breath/breathe

bring/take

callous/callused

calls for/predicts

Calvary/cavalry

cannot/can not

caramel/Carmel

celibate/chaste

cement/concrete

chunk/chuck

cite/site/sight

compare to/compare with

comprised of/composed of

continual/continuous

convince/persuade

core/corps/corpse

council/counsel/consul

credible/credulous

crescendo/climax

criteria/criterion

critique/criticize

cut and paste/copy and paste

damped/dampened

data/datum

defuse/diffuse

depreciate/deprecate

desert/dessert

device/devise

differ/vary

dilemma/difficulty

disburse/disperse

disc/disk

discreet/discrete

disinterested/uninterested

dolly/handcart

dominate/dominant

done/finished

doubt that/doubt whether/doubt if

downfall/drawback

downgrade/degrade/denigrate

dribble/drivel

drive/disk

e.g./i.e.

ecology/environment

economical/economic

1800s/19th century

elapse/lapse

elicit/illicit

emergent/emergency

emigrate/immigrate

eminent/imminent/immanent

empathy/sympathy

enormity/enormousness

entitled/titled

envelop/envelope

epigram/epigraph/
    epitaph/epithet

exact same/exactly the same

exasperated/exacerbated

farther/further

fatal/fateful

fearful/fearsome

flammable/inflammable

flaunt/flout

flesh out/flush out

floppy disk/hard disk

flounder/founder

forbidding/foreboding/formidable

forceful/forcible/forced

formally/formerly

fortuitous/fortunate

forward/forwards/foreword

g/q

gamut/gauntlet

gibe/jibe/jive

gig/jig

gratis/gratuitous

grisly/grizzly

group (plural vs. singular)

hanged/hung

healthy/healthful

historic/historical

hold your peace/say your piece

homophobic

hysterical/hilarious

idea/ideal

if/whether

ignorant/stupid

immaculate conception/virgin birth

impertinent/irrelevant

imply/infer

importantly/important

in lieu of/in light of

incidence/incidents/instances

install/instill

instances/instants

intense/intensive

interment/internment

Internet/intranet

into/in to

ironically/coincidentally

itch/scratch

jerry-built/jury-rigged

kick-start/jump-start

last name/family name

later/latter

lay/lie

lead/led

leave/let

legend/myth

lend/loan

lighted/lit

like/as if

lose/loose

lustful/lusty

mass/massive

masseuse/masseur

medal/metal/meddle/mettle

media/medium

medium/median

mitigate against/militate against

moral/morale

motion/move

nauseous/nauseated

oppress/repress

Oriental/Asian

overdo/overdue

oversee/overlook

palate/palette/pallet

parallel/symbol

parameters/perimeters

passed/past

peace/piece

peak/peek/pique

perpetuate/perpetrate

persecute/prosecute

personal/personnel

perspective/prospective

pheasant/peasant

phenomena/phenomenon

picaresque/picturesque

podium/lectern

pole/poll

populace/populous

pore/pour

posses/possess

pray/prey

precede/proceed

precedence/precedents

precipitate/precipitous

predominate/predominant

premier/premiere

prescribe/proscribe

presently/currently

pretty/somewhat

preventive/preventative

principal/principle

progress/pass

prone/supine

prophecy/prophesy

prostate/prostrate

purposely/purposefully

quiet/quite

rack/wrack

raise/rear

ran/run

rationale/rationalization

ravaging/ravishing/ravenous

reactionary/reactive

real/really

rebelling/revolting

recent/resent

recreate/reinvent

recuperate/recoup

refute/rebut

regard/regards

regime/regimen

regretfully/regrettably

reign/rein

remuneration/renumeration

repel/repulse

resister/resistor

retch/wretch

reticent/hesitant

revue/review

risky/risqué

rob/steal

role/roll

root/rout/route

sail/sale/sell

sarcastic/ironic

say/tell

scan/skim

seam/seem

seen/saw

self-worth/self-esteem

sense/since

sensual/sensuous

service/serve

set/sit

setup/set up

shall/will

silicon/silicone

since/because

societal/social

sojourn /journey

somewhat of a/
   somewhat, something of a

sooner/rather

spaded/spayed

stalactites/stalagmites

states/countries

stomp/stamp

suit/suite

summary/summery

tact/tack

taken back/taken aback

taught/taut

taunt/taut

tenant/tenet

than/then

that/which

them/those

these kind/this kind

they're/their/there

throne/thrown

to/too/two

tolled/told

toward/towards

troop/troupe

University of Indiana/
    Indiana University

unloosen/loosen

unthaw/thaw

various/several

vary/very

verses/versus

video/film

viola/voila

wary/weary/leery

way more/far more/much more

ways/way

weather/wether/whether

were/where

who's/whose

without further adieu/
    without further ado

women/woman

wont/won't

world-renown/
    world-renowned

wrongly/wrong

ye/the

yea/yeah/yay

yoke/yolk

your/you

your/you're

Of Foreign Origin

These entries explain words and phrases that are misspelled, mispronounced, or misused, often due to their foreign-language roots.

accent marks

amature/amateur

apropos/appropriate

bazaar/bizarre

beaurocracy/bureaucracy

bonafied/bona fide

bourgeois

cache/cachet

chai tea/chai

chaise longue

chick/chic

cliché/clichéd

click/clique

connaisseur/connoisseur

coupe de gras/coup de grace

criteria/criterion

data/datum

deja vu

ect./etc.

French dip with au jus/French dip

gaff/gaffe

genre

hoi polloi

hors d'oeuvres

laissez-faire

Mount Fujiyama/Fujiyama

nieve/naive

peak/peek/pique

pernickety/persnickety

picaresque/picturesque

please RSVP/please reply

pompom/pompon

premier/premiere

Rio Grande River/
   Rio Grande

risky/risqué

salsa sauce/salsa

Sierra Nevada Mountains/
   Sierra Nevadas

soup du jour of the day/
   soup of the day

verses/versus

vinegarette/vinaigrette

vitae/vita

viola/voila

whisky/whiskey

Xmas/Christmas

ye/the

Grammar, Spelling & Style

These entries cover grammar, spelling, and style topics.

accent marks

accidently/accidentally

acronyms & apostrophes

all

all ready/already

almost

alright/all right

AM/PM

among/between

amount/number

any

anymore/any more

anyways/anyway

apostrophes

as far as/as far as . . . is concerned

awhile/a while

backward/backwards

bad/badly

better

between

between you and I/
   between you and me

borrow/loan

both/each

boughten/bought

bouyant/buoyant

brang/brung/brought

by/'bye/buy

capitalization

cents

Church/church

cleanup/clean up

cliché /clichéd

colons/semicolons

commas

conjunction, beginning
   a sentence with a

conversate/converse

definate/definite

device/devise

dialogue/discuss

done/did

don't/doesn't

double negatives

dove/dived

drank/drunk

drug/dragged

each

-ed/-ing

ei/ie

either

either are/either is

ellipses

ending a sentence with a preposition

every (plural vs. singular)

everyday

fastly/fast

'50s

first annual

first person

from . . . to

from the beginning of time

-ful/-fuls

gender

God/god

gone/went

good/well

got/gotten

group (plural vs. singular)

had ought/ought

hanging indents

heighth/height

him, her/he, she

an historic/a historic

homophobic

hopefully

hyphenation

hyphens & dashes

-ic

if I was/if I were

impact

Indian/Native American

individual/person

input

intensifiers

interface/interact

is, is

Islams/Muslims

its/it's

lay/lie

"lite" spelling

may/might

me/I/myself

momentarily

near miss

not all that/not very

not hardly/not at all

number of verb

numbers

of

of/'s

off of

OK/okay

one of the (singular)

only

onto/on to

orientate/orient

over/more than

pair (number)

parallelism in a series

paralyzation/paralysis

parentheses

passive voice

peoples

phenomena/phenomenon

prepone

proved/proven

quotation marks

reference

remotely close

saw/seen

second of all/second

seen/saw

sentence fragments

single quotes

snuck/sneaked

so fun/so much fun

split infinitives

that/which

that kind/that kind of

theirselves/themselves

there's

these are them/these are they

these kind/this kind

these ones/these

they/their (singular)

thusly/thus

vague reference

verb tense

very unique/unique

what/that

whereabouts are/
 whereabouts is

whether/whether or not

whilst/while

who/that

who/whom

who's/whose

-wise

World Wide Web

would have liked to have/
 would have liked

Xmas/Christmas

your/you

you've got mail/you have mail

Homonyms

These entries cover words that sound alike but are not spelled alike.

adviser/advisor

all ready/already

altar/alter

altogether/all together

anymore/any more

axel/axle

bare/bear

by/'bye/buy

canon/cannon

capital/capitol

carat/caret/carrot/karat

cite/site/sight

cleanup/clean up

close/clothes

coarse/course

Colombia/Columbia

complement/compliment

complementary/
 complimentary

core/corps/corpse

council/counsel/consul

currant/current

discreet/discrete

drier/dryer

dual/duel

dyeing/dying

eminent/imminent/immanent

fair/fare

faze/phase

flair/flare

flak/flack

for/fore/four

forego/forgo

forward/forwards/foreword

foul/fowl

gaff/gaffe

gibe/jibe/jive

gild/guild

hairbrained/harebrained

hangar/hanger

hardy/hearty

hear/here

heroin/heroine

hippy/hippie

hoard/horde

incidence/incidents/instances

into/in to

its/it's

leach/leech

lead/led

liable/libel

mantle/mantel

medal/metal/meddle/mettle

onto/on to

palate/palette/pallet

passed/past

peace/piece

peak/peek/pique

pole/poll

populace/populous

pore/pour

pray/prey

precedence/precedents

premier/premiere

principal/principle

rack/wrack

reign/rein

resister/resistor

retch/wretch

revue/review

role/roll

root/rout/route

sail/sale/sell

seam/seem

slight of hand/sleight of hand

sluff off/slough off

stationary/stationery

stomp/stamp

suit/suite

summary/summery

taught/taut

they're/their/there

throne/thrown

to/too/two

tolled/told

troop/troupe

vary/very

verses/versus

weather/wether/whether

who's/whose

wile away/while away

without further adieu/
   without further ado

yea/yeah/yay

yoke/yolk

your/you're

Commonly Misspelled

These entries cover words that are commonly misspelled. See the end of this list for an added list of entries covering words to be especially careful with when running a spelling checker on your computer.

absorbtion/absorption

accidently/accidentally

acrosst/accrossed/across

add/ad

adultry/adultery

adviser/advisor

all ready/already

alot/a lot

alright/all right

amature/amateur

angel/angle

anticlimatic/anticlimactic

artical/article

ashfault/asphalt

asterick/asterisk

athiest/atheist

augur/auger

basicly/basically

bazaar/bizarre

bonafied/bona fide

bouyant/buoyant

breach/breech

breath/breathe

by/'bye/buy

callous/callused

caramel/Carmel

Ceasar/Caesar

chick/chic

click/clique

close/clothes

concensus/consensus

Confusionism/Confucianism

congradulations/congratulations

connaisseur/connoisseur

copywrite/copyright

cortage/cortege

council/counsel/consul

coupe de gras/coup de grace

crucifiction/crucifixion

defence/defense

definate/definite

deja vu

desert/dessert

device/devise

dialate/dilate

dieties/deities

dire straights/dire straits

disburse/disperse

disc/disk

diswraught/distraught

do to/due to

doctorial/doctoral

doggy dog world/dog-eat-dog world

drownding/drowning

duck tape/duct tape

due to the fact that/because

Earth/earth/Moon/moon

ect./etc.

-ed/-t

electorial college/electoral college

elicit/illicit

email/e-mail

embaress/embarrass

enviroment/environment

epitomy/epitome

excape/escape

exceptional/exceptionable

exhileration/exhilaration

expecially/especially

expresso/espresso

Febuary/February

firey/fiery

fiscal/physical

flustrated/frustrated

forsee/foresee

gaurd/guard

genre

Ghandi/Gandhi

government

grammer/grammar

greatful/grateful

grievious/grievous

harbringer/harbinger

hone in/home in

hors d'oeuvres

ice tea/iced tea

imbedded/embedded

in sink/in synch

indepth/in depth

infact/in fact

input

interment/internment

interpretate/interpret

into/in to

Isreal/Israel

Issac/Isaac

judgement/judgment

lamblast/lambaste

larnyx/larynx

laxidaisical/lackadaisical

lense/lens

library

lightening/lightning

liquor

LISTSERV

marshmellow

mathmatics/mathematics

mean time/meantime

medal/metal/meddle/mettle

medieval ages/Middle Ages

memorium/memoriam

mic/mike

minature/miniature

mischievious/mischievous

momento/memento

moreso/more so

murmer/murmur

mute point/moot point

neice/niece

nieve/naive

noone/no one

nuptual/nuptial

old fashion/old-fashioned

ostensively/ostensibly

parallelled/paralleled

parliment/parliament

past time/pastime

peace/piece

peoples

permiscuous/promiscuous

pernickety/persnickety

perogative/prerogative

perscription/prescription

perse/per se

phenomena/phenomenon

Philippines/Filipinos

playwrite/playwright

pompom/pompon

posses/possess

practice/practise

practicle/practical

precede/proceed

predominately/predominantly

preemptory/peremptory

prejudice/prejudiced

premise/premises

principal/principle

pronounciation/pronunciation

protray/portray

publically/publicly

queue

quiet/quite

rapport

reeking havoc/wreaking havoc

regard/regards

reign/rein

relevant/revelant

remuneration/renumeration

reoccurring/recurring

resister/resistor

right of passage/rite of passage

risky/risqué

roomate/roommate

rot iron/wrought iron

sacred/scared

sacreligious/sacrilegious

safety deposit box/
   safe-deposit box

seperate/separate

shepard/shepherd

sherbert/sherbet

sluff off/slough off

sometime/some time

spaded/spayed

stain glass/stained glass

stationary/stationery

straightjacket/straitjacket

summary/summery

supercede/supersede

supposably/supposingly/
   supposedly

suppose to/supposed to

supremist/supremacist

suttle/subtle

teenage/teenaged

tender hooks/tenterhooks

thankyou/thank you

theirselves/themselves

there's

therefor/therefore

they're/their/there

though/thought/through

till/until

to/too/two

toward/towards

track home/tract home

tradegy/tragedy

troop/troupe

truely/truly

unconscience/unconscious

upmost/utmost

use to/used to

valuble/valuable

veil of tears/vale of tears

verbage/verbiage

verses/versus

villian/villain

vinegarette/vinaigrette

viola/voila

visa versa/vice versa

visable/visible

vitae/vita

vocal chords/vocal cords

volumptuous/voluptuous

vunerable/vulnerable

warrantee/warranty

wary/weary/leery

Wensday/Wednesday

were/where

wet your appetite/
   whet your appetite

whimp/wimp

whisky/whiskey

who's/whose

a whole 'nother/
   a completely different

wholely/wholly

wholistic/holistic

wile away/while away

women/woman

wont/won't

world-renown/
   world-renowned

wreckless/reckless

writting/writing

ya'll/y'all

yea/yeah/yay

your/you're

And be careful with these . . . your spelling checker won't catch them.

accept/except

angel/angle

marital/martial

quiet/quite

sacred/scared

though/thought/
   through

were/where

Mangled Expressions

These entries cover words and phrases that are prone to getting mangled.

access/get access to

actual fact/actually

agreeance/agreement

ahold/hold

ain't/am not/isn't/aren't

all goes well/augurs well

all of the sudden/all of a sudden

all the farther/as far as

alot/a lot

anchors away/anchors aweigh

anytime/any time

anyways/anyway

assumably/presumably

awhile/a while

baited breath/bated breath

beckon call/beck and call

beyond the pail/beyond the pale

born out of/born of

boughten/bought

bran new/brand new

brang/brung/brought

build off of/build on

butt naked/buck naked

buttload/boatload

card shark/cardsharp

calm, cool, and collective/
   calm, cool, and collected

carrot on a stick/
   the carrot or the stick

center around/center on/
   revolve around

center of attraction/
   center of attention

cheap at half the price/
   cheap at twice the price

chomp at the bit/champ at the bit

could care less/could not care less

cut the muster/cut the mustard

dialogue/discuss

down the pipe/down the pike

drug/dragged

due to the fact that/because

endquote/unquote

extracting revenge/
   exacting revenge

far and few between/
   few and far between

foul swoop/fowl swoop/fell swoop

in another words/
   in other words

in lieu of/in light of

in the fact that/in that

Islams/Muslims

nip it in the butt/nip it in the bud

no sooner when/no sooner than

old-timer's disease/
   Alzheimer's disease

on accident/by accident

once and a while/once in a while

one in the same/one and the same

one of the only/one of the few

perse/per se

proof is in the pudding/proof of the
   pudding is in the eating

reeking havoc/wreaking havoc

right of passage/rite of passage

road to hoe/row to hoe

rot iron/wrought iron

slight of hand/sleight of hand

sluff off/slough off

soup du jour of the day/
   soup of the day

spit and image/spitting image

taken back/taken aback

tender hooks/tenterhooks

tie me over/tide me over

tongue and cheek/tongue in cheek

tow the line/toe the line

track home/tract home

veil of tears/vale of tears

vicious/viscous circle/cycle

wet your appetite/
   whet your appetite

a whole 'nother/
   a completely different

wile away/while away

without further adieu/
   without further ado

worse comes to worse/
   worst comes to worst

you've got another thing coming/
   you've got another think coming

Inexact Words & Phrases

These entries cover words and phrases that are used imprecisely.

about	hero/protagonist
all	highly looked upon/highly regarded
almost	holocaust
blatant	home page
brand names	hypocritical
celibate/chaste	-ic
cement/concrete	ignorant/stupid
chemicals	immaculate conception/virgin birth
Chicano/Latino/Hispanic	impact
crescendo/climax	incredible
criticism	individual/person
decimate/annihilate,	infinite
slaughter, etc.	intensifiers
Democrat Party/Democratic Party	issues/problems
differ/vary	kick-start/jump-start
disinterested/uninterested	koala bear/koala
dolly/handcart	large/important
electrocute/shock	late/former
empathy/sympathy	legend/myth
envious/jealous	literally
ethnic	mediocre
exponential	motion/move
floppy disk/hard disk	music/singing
footnotes/endnotes	only
for sale/on sale	orders of magnitude
Frankenstein	organic
frankly	Oriental/Asian
from the beginning of time	percent decrease
ground zero	personality
grow	podium/lectern
hardly	pretty/somewhat
hearing-impaired/deaf	prioritize
help the problem/	priority
help solve the problem	quantum leap

real/really
religion
religion believes/religion teaches
satellite
schizophrenic
select/selected
self-worth/self-esteem
simplistic
so/very
sort of
stereo

substance-free
substitute with/substitute for
surfing the Internet
times smaller
today's modern society/today
UFO
unrest
vague reference
wheat/whole wheat
-wise
ye/the

Pronunciation

These entries cover words and phrases prone to pronunciation problems.

absorbtion/absorption
accede/exceed
accessory
acrosst/accrossed/across
anticlimatic/anticlimactic
artic/arctic
asterick/asterisk
athlete
ax/ask
barb wire/bob wire/barbed wire
bourgeois
bouyant/buoyant
Celtic
chaise longue
click/clique
comptroller
coupe de gras/coup de grace
dialate/dilate
doctorial/doctoral
drownding/drowning

ecstatic
ect./etc.
-ed/-t
electorial college/electoral college
elicit/illicit
emigrate/immigrate
eminent/imminent/immanent
envelop/envelope
enviroment/environment
epitomy/epitome
excape/escape
exceptional/exceptionable
expecially/especially
expresso/espresso
Febuary/February
fiscal/physical
genre
government
grievious/grievous
harbinger/harbinger

heighth/height

an historic/a historic

hone in/home in

Illinois

integral

interesting

interment/internment

interpretate /interpret

jewelry

laissez-faire

lamblast/lambaste

larnyx/larynx

laxidaisical/lackadaisical

library

lived

lose/loose

mauve

minature/miniature

mischievious/mischievous

Nevada

nuclear

offense/offence

Oregon

perogative/prerogative

perscription/prescription

picture

practicle/practical

preemptory/peremptory

preferably

primer

probably

prophecy/prophesy

racism

realtor

recent/resent

recognize

Rio Grande River/Rio Grande

safety deposit box/

   safe-deposit box

specific/Pacific

tentative

valuble/valuable

volumptuous/voluptuous

vunerable/vulnerable

wash

Wensday/Wednesday

Problem Prepositions

These entries cover misused prepositions.

about

based around/based on

between

bored of/bored with

born out of/born of

build off of/build on

center around/center on/

   revolve around

close proximity/close/

   in proximity to

compare to/compare with

contrasts/contrasts with

couple/couple of

depends/depends on

different than/different from/

   different to

emphasize on/emphasize

ending a sentence with a preposition

evidence to/evidence of

for free/free

graduate/graduate from

like for/like

myriad of/myriad

of

of/'s

off of

on accident/by accident

onto/on to

over/more than

possessed of/possessed by/
    possessed with

prepositions (repeated)

prepositions (wrong)

substitute with/
    substitute for

suffer with/suffer from

that kind/that kind of

think on/think about

to home/at home

try and/try to

Redundancies

These entries cover questions of redundancy.

access/get access to

actual fact/actually

added bonus

and also/and, also

and plus

as of yet/yet

ATM machine/ATM

CD-ROM disc/CD-ROM disk/
    CD-ROM

cents

chai tea/chai

close proximity/close/
    in proximity to

compare and contrast/compare

ect./etc.

end result/end

French dip with au jus/French dip

heading/bound

HIV virus

irregardless/regardless

medieval ages/Middle Ages

Mount Fujiyama/Fujiyama

of/'s

off of

organic

over-exaggerated/exaggerated

PIN number/PIN

please RSVP/
    please reply

point being is that

point in time/point, time

prepositions (repeated)

reason because

redundancies

return back/return

Rio Grande River/
    Rio Grande

salsa sauce/salsa

Sierra Nevada Mountains/
    Sierra Nevadas

soup du jour of the day/
   soup of the day

time period

today's modern society/today

where it's at

you've got mail/you have mail

❦

Commonly Misused Expressions

These entries cover words and phrases that are susceptible to being used in the wrong situations, for one reason or another.

abject

about

alleged

almost

alternate/alternative

alumnus/alumni

American

amongst/among

as far as/as far as . . . is concerned

as follow/as follows

as of yet/yet

as per/in accordance with

begs the question

behaviors/behavior

bias/biased

Bible

blatant

borrow/loan

both/each

caring

catch-22/catch

chemicals

Chicano/Latino/Hispanic

concerted effort

conflicted/conflicting feelings

criticism

critique/criticize

decimate/annihilate, slaughter, etc.

Democrat Party/Democratic Party

depends/depends on

disrespect

documentated/documented

doubt that/doubt whether/
   doubt if

doubtlessly/doubtless

drastic

each

either

either are/either is

emphasize on/emphasize

enthuse

envious/jealous

ethnic

everyday

everytime/every time

evidence to/evidence of

exponential

expresses that/says that

factoid

finalize/finish, put into final form

first come, first serve/
   first come, first served

floppy disk/hard disk

foot/feet

footnotes/endnotes

frankly

fulsome

goes

gone/went

good/well

got/gotten

graduate/graduate from

ground zero

grow

had ought/ought

hairbrained/harebrained

hardly

hardly never/hardly ever

heared/heard

hearing-impaired/deaf

heart-rendering/heart-rending

hero/protagonist

hisself/himself

holocaust

home page

how come/why

howsomever/however

hypocritical

incent/incentivize

infamous

infinite

interface/interact

into/in to

intrigue

is, is

issues/problems

Jew/Jewish

last name/family name

late/former

light-year

like

like for/like

medal/metal/meddle/mettle

mediocre

misnomer

most always/almost always

motion/move

much differently/very differently

muchly/much

myriad of/myriad

nonplussed

notorious

one-dimensional/

    two-dimensional

one of the only/one of the few

orders of magnitude

parallel/symbol

parameters/perimeters

penultimate/next to last

per/according to

percent decrease

personality

peruse

plead innocent

point in time/point, time

quantum leap

quote

ratio

religion believes/

    religion teaches

satellite

schizophrenic

sci-fi/science fiction/SF

sea change

simplistic

sour grapes

try and/try to

unrest

❦

American English vs. British English

These entries cover differences between American and British English.

alternate/alternative

defence/defense

different than/different from/
   different to

-ed/-t

enquire/inquire

got/gotten

jewelry

judgement/judgment

off of

offense/offence

parallelled/
   paralleled

practice/practise

quotation marks

single quotes

supposably/supposingly/
   supposedly

they/their (singular)

toward/towards

❦

Misheard Expressions

These entries cover problems that arise when writers write what they heard; or rather, what they *think* they heard.

all goes well/augurs well

all of the sudden/all of a sudden

allude/elude

allusion/illusion

alterior/ulterior

anchors away/anchors aweigh

augur/auger

barb wire/bob wire/barbed wire

bazaar/bizarre

beckon call/beck and call

better

case and point/case in point

could of, should of, would of/could
   have, should have, would have

deep-seeded/deep-seated

do to/due to

doggy dog world/dog-eat-dog world

down the pipe/down the pike

duck tape/duct tape

ice tea/iced tea

in sink/in synch

intensive purposes/
   intents and purposes

low and behold/lo and behold

next store/next door

nip it in the butt/nip it in the bud

no sooner when/no sooner than

often

old-timer's disease/
   Alzheimer's disease

once and a while/once in a while

one in the same/one and the same

past time/pastime

pawn off/palm off

rapport

reeking havoc/wreaking havoc

right of passage/rite of passage

road to hoe/row to hoe

rot iron/wrought iron

safety deposit box/safe-deposit box

slight of hand/sleight of hand

sluff off/slough off

spit and image/spitting image

suppose to/supposed to

taken back/taken aback

tender hooks/tenterhooks

tie me over/tide me over

tongue and cheek/tongue in cheek

tow the line/toe the line

track home/tract home

use to/used to

veil of tears/vale of tears

Wensday/Wednesday

whim and a prayer/
    wing and a prayer

wile away/while away

worse comes to worse/
    worst comes to worst

you've got another thing coming/
    you've got another think coming

William, James & Co. invites you
to take advantage of a special offer

Paul Brians'
Common Errors in English Usage

A Great Book *and* a Great Gift Idea

Now available in volume discounts
on orders of five or more

10% off on orders of 5–9
20% off on orders of 10 or more

FREE SHIPPING AVAILABLE ON ORDERS
DELIVERED TO ONE ADDRESS

To order, call 1-800-322-2665
or visit us online at www.wmjasco.com/89-9.html

Soon available as a
2006 page-a-day calendar—
check www.wmjasco.com for details